BUNG KARNO'S INDONESIA

BUNG KARNO'S INDONESIA

by Willard A. Hanna

Revised Edition

A Collection of 25 Reports Written for the

American Universities Field Staff

AMERICAN UNIVERSITIES FIELD STAFF, INC.

366 Madison Avenue, New York 17, New York

1961

Purposes of the American Universities Field Staff

To develop, finance, and direct a corps of men to study mainly
at first hand the contemporaneous affairs of significant areas
of the world and, through reports and their personal services,
to make their knowledge available primarily to universities,
colleges, and other educational institutions with a view to aid-
ing the American educational system in the diffusion of knowledge necessary to a better understanding of world conditions;

To make the findings of members of the corps available also
through publication and otherwise, to the American people generally and to publish reports and render services in connection
with the purposes of the Corporation;

To encourage the members of the corps and others to develop
improved techniques for the study of significant areas of the
world and for the dissemination of knowledge with regard to
such areas.

Sponsoring Member Institutions

University of Alabama
Brown University
California Institute of Technology
Carleton College
Dartmouth College
Harvard Graduate School of Business Administration
University of Hawaii
Indiana University
University of Kansas
Michigan State University
Tulane University

Bung Karno's Indonesia, by Willard A. Hanna
Copyright © 1959, 1960, American Universities Field Staff, Inc.
Library of Congress Catalog Card Number: 60-10485

Bung Karno's Indonesia (Revised Edition), by Willard A. Hanna
Copyright © 1961, American Universities Field Staff, Inc.
Library of Congress Catalog Card Number: 61-8511

FOREWORD

Willard A. Hanna wrote <u>Bung Karno's Indonesia</u> after a data-gathering visit to that country in 1959. A trip to Indonesia in 1960 gave him an opportunity to review his earlier findings. As a result, this revised edition, published in response to a continuing demand for the book, has new material in the preface and postscript. The body of the text is unchanged from the first writing as a series of Reports for the American Universities Field Staff Reports Service.

Dr. Hanna brings to his evaluation of Indonesian affairs an intimate knowledge of that country equaled by few Americans. Prior to his 1959 visit he had lived and worked in Indonesia for a total of seven years, during which he saw Indonesia's successful fight for freedom from Dutch rule and its subsequent struggle with the internal and external problems of independence.

The 25 Reports included in this volume constitute only part of a continuing series on Southeast Asia distributed to member universities and colleges of the American Universities Field Staff, Inc., and to subscribers to the AUFS Reports Service. Along with favorable comment on the quality of Dr. Hanna's analysis of how Indonesia is faring under President Sukarno's program of guided democracy, came suggestions from many readers that a collection of the reports be given wide distribution exactly as they reached subscribers, but in a bound volume.

For those to whom this book is a first introduction to the American Universities Field Staff, a word about subscription arrangements may be in order. Written by Associates who comprise a full-time career staff, AUFS reports from Asia, Africa, Latin America, and (in limited volume) Europe are distributed to institutional subscribers under a scale of fees ranging from $100 to $1,000 yearly. The number of reports issued each year varies as Associates move to and from their overseas bases. In some years it has approximated 100, and it has always exceeded 50. Subscription fees below the actual pro rata costs of delivering the reports are possible through the financial support given the program by the eleven universities and colleges that comprise its corporate membership, by the Ford Foundation, and by other organizations and individuals that subscribe to the purposes of the AUFS.

Phillips Talbot
Executive Director

CONTENTS

Note: Pagination of the reports as separately issued has been retained. Each chapter may be easily located by reference to the listed code number.

ONE YEAR OF USDEK: MID-1959 TO MID-1960

How an Acronym and the Slogans Related to It
Affect Indonesia and Its People

"Like an angel's visitation from the skies," such is the quickening effect upon a desperately troubled nation of the newly-revitalized Indonesian Revolution. So declared President Sukarno on August 17, 1960, in his annual Independence Day oration. The solution to the ten-year-long national crisis, he announced, is his personal guidance in the renewal, indeed the perpetuation of revolutionary zeal.

"I tell you frankly," he declared, "I belong to that group of people who are bound in spiritual longing by the romanticism of revolution. I am inspired by it. I am fascinated by it. I am completely absorbed by it. I am crazed, I am obsessed by the romanticism of revolution . . . . That is why I, who have been given the topmost leadership in the struggle of the Indonesian nation never tire of appealing and exhorting: solve our national problems in a revolutionary way, make the revolutionary spirit surge on, see to it that the fire of our revolution does not die or grow dim, not even for a single moment. Come, then, keep fanning the flames of the leaping fire of revolution! Brothers and sisters, let us become logs to feed the flames of revolution!"

"Is it necessary for everything to be done in a revolutionary way? Could it not be done more patiently?" Only the timid, the discouraged, the defeated, the traitorous, Bung Karno declared, are asking these questions. His reply was categorical: "Let there be none among us who seek to amend or to modulate the revolutionary spirit." The "enemies" of the Indonesian Revolution, those who suggest, perhaps, that ten years after actual achievement of independence from the Dutch the revolution might well simmer down, will be relentlessly pursued and punished. So, too, will all those who seek to preserve Western rather than distinctively Indonesian values. Most particularly, "free-fight private enterprise" and "liberal Western democracy," the latter both "the child and the mother of bourgeois capitalism," are finished in Indonesia. Their demise is mourned only by "the reactionaries, the cynics, the hyper-intellectuals, those whose wealth is 'made,' those of 'vested interests,' those who squeal and whose eyes roll in convulsions because every stronghold of their interest . . . is crumbling and falling," and along with their interests those of the foreign "profiteers," "exploiters," and "counterrevolutionary plotters."

Bung Karno on August 17, 1960, soared to his most emotional, most self-hypnotic pitch of revolutionary eloquence since December 27, 1949. The Indonesian people, perhaps not uncoincidentally, had reached their lowest ebb to date of well-being and morale. The decade had been distinguished, to be sure, by noteworthy advances in education and health, in national self-consciousness, and in international influence; it had been distinguished also by internecine political feuding, by nationwide armed disorders, both large and small, by reckless economic manipulation, and by questionable international dealings. It had been distinguished most of all, so far as the vast majority of the people of Indonesia were concerned, by disappointed expectations of achieving exactly what revolution was supposed to bring--more or better food, clothing shelter, and miscellaneous consumer goods. The last year had been by far the worst. The last year, from mid-1959 to mid-1960, might be designated the Year One of USDEK.

USDEK is a 1960 Bung Karno coinage from the initial letters of five slogans by means of which he seeks far more to agitate and to divert than to develop the nation. The five components warrant itemization and comment: (1) Undang-undang Dasar '45 (Return to the 1945 Constitution), meaning concentration of power in the hands of the President; (2) Socialisme à la Indonesia (Indonesian Socialism), meaning division and redistribution of wealth; (3) Demokrasi Terpimpin (Guided Democracy), meaning substitution of numerous unwieldy, nonvoting, appointive, consultative bodies for the former elective bodies of state, and of Bung Karno's intuitive "guidance" for majority decision; (4) Ekonomi Terpimpin (Guided Economy), meaning substitution of state ownership and operation for free, private, and capitalistic enterprise; (5) Kepribadian Indonesia (Indonesian Identity), meaning ultranationalistic revolutionary ardor.

USDEK, according to Bung Karno's critics and opponents, who include now not only the larger part of the Indonesian intellectual elite (the "hyperintellectuals"), rapidly increasing numbers of the middle class (the "reactionaries"), and even large numbers of the ordinary people (the "discouraged"), means an attempt at conversion of the Republic of Indonesia into an USDEKistan à la Tovarich Sukarno. As yet, however, like democracy à la Indonesia before it, USDEK-style socialism à la Indonesia isn't working out very well. Most of the potential USDEKistani, while they do not exactly reject USDEKadence, do not acclaim it either. The weak de facto Sukarno dictatorship, which virtually all thinking Indonesians deplore, either because it exists or because of its ineffectualness, means less the concentration of power in the hands of Bung Karno than the denial of it to anyone else.

"I can't and I won't," said Bung Karno three years ago, "ride a three-legged horse." He proposed, therefore, to prop up his wobbly coalition Government, which depended upon ministers affiliated variously with the Nationalists, the conservative Muslim and the liberal Muslim political parties, by assigning to the fourth major political faction, the Communists, their "due share" of office. This 1957 konsepsi of Sukarno's--that he could unite all feuding factions into one happy family, of which the Communists would be loyal and accepted members--shook the nation and all but shook it apart. It led directly to the 1957 regional insurrections, to the costly 1958 military suppression of those insurrections, to Bung Karno's own open assumption of open power, and to his attempt to disguise responsibility by appointing vast and numerous "consultative" and "advisory" bodies. It led also to USDEK, for Bung Karno proceeded by backtracking, switchbacking, and sidetracking onward toward his objective, until today he has a united national façade, USDEKorated with revolutionary slogans.

All political factions, meanwhile, continue their feuds, while being subjected simultaneously to manifestations of Bung Karno's favor and disfavor, and in turn bringing pressure to bear on Bung Karno himself. Under the USDEKified regime, factional members submissive to Bung Karno are rewarded with mutually overlapping and offsetting privileges, recalcitrant members are played off against each other, uncommitted members are wooed by explanations that USDEK means all things to all people. Sukarno himself, meanwhile, is a dictator as frequently dictated to as dictating. In his relations with the military and the Communists, his two chosen but only semicommitted and mutually-distrustful allies, he must practice highly skilled political acrobatics while at the same time keeping his eyes and his hands on a dozen other factions, each with schemes and demands of their own. Bung Karno, who in 1957 declined to mount a three-legged horse, now finds himself, as a result of his experiment in crossbreeding of dissident and unstable political species, mounted precariously astride a skittish hybrid of hydra, centipede, chameleon, and chimera.

The record of the Year One of USDEK requires brief review, with the preliminary notation that despite any appearances, the emerging USDEKistan is as yet no more a monolithic state than USDEK is a four-legged equine yearling. Bung Karno on July 5, 1959, dismissed the elected Constituent Assembly and reverted by unconstitutional decree to the 1945 Constitution. On March 5, 1960, he "deactivated" the elected Parliament; on June 27 he appointed a new "Gotong-Rojong" (Mutual Aid) Parliament of 283 hand-picked members; on August 15 he expanded this Parliament into a monster 609-member People's Consultative Congress. On August 17 he ordered the dissolution of the Masjumi (Liberal Muslim) and the Socialist parties, the sources of the most outspoken anti-USDEK criticism. On September 13 he suspended overt public activities of all other parties, but only after various regional military commanders had already banned Communist Party activities, in part at least as an independent countermeasure to Sukarno's moves against the Masjumi and the Socialists. On September 24 he suppressed the opposition press and confiscated its properties, but two weeks later, after signing statements pledging support of USDEK, some of the papers resumed publication. Throughout the year, individual critics of the Bung Karno regime have been subjected increasingly to its vigilance. High-ranking military officers, for instance, have found themselves suddenly relieved of their posts, although at times they have been assigned on face-saving missions abroad.

Opposition to USDEK, however, has persisted and even increased. In March 1960 prominent political and intellectual leaders organized the Democratic League to support "liberal Western democracy" in preference to "Guided Democracy." Bung Karno has not as yet dared to disband them. Top-ranking military officers have repeatedly resisted Bung Karno's manipulations. They have not amassed an impressive record of successes, but neither have all of them as yet been purged. Within the Communist Party, which has gained enhanced prestige and increased following in recent years, partly as a result of Bung Karno's favor, a strong faction keeps advocating a break with him before the party is inextricably implicated in an USDEK debacle. In early July 1960 the Communists published an outspoken indictment of 1959-60 government failures, a document soon suppressed and retracted, but indicative, despite later parade of amity, of a deep party disaffection with the regime.

In economic affairs, Bung Karno experimented first (August 24, 1959) with overnight devaluation by 90% of approximately one half of the nation's currency and the devaluation and freezing of large bank accounts. This "financial reform" was carried out for the announced purpose of soaking up the "hot," "black market" money of the "corruptors," of checking inflation, and of reducing prices. It was to be followed up, it was announced, by thoroughgoing reorganization of the nation's whole financial and economic system. By January 1, 1960, the amount of money in circulation had exceeded the predevaluation total, deficit financing was proceeding at an even faster pace than before, inflation was continuing its upward spiral--the black market rate for a time going as high as 500 rupiahs to the United States dollar--and no follow-up economic measures conceivably conducive to improvement were yet in sight. As of mid and even late 1960, inflation was still unchecked, economic recovery and development were still stalled. To be sure, a grandiose 5100-page, Rp. 240 billion, eight-year "blueprint" of economic and social development has been compiled under the direction of one Mohammad Yamin, no economist or sociologist but rather a lawyer, antiquarian, politician, and poet. The plan took one year to contrive, and when it emerged, just before the anniversary of National Independence Day (August 17, 1945), Bung Karno paid special tribute to the "richness of symbolical fantasy" which had prompted its designer to divide it into 8 volumes, 17 chapters, and 1,945 items. It was then consigned to the monster People's Consultative Congress from which it seems unlikely soon to re-emerge as any realistic working plan appropriate to the nation's requirements or its resources.

The Sukarno regime had already in 1957 and 1958 adopted the politically and economically vindictive policies of nationalizing the properties of the Dutch and of the Kuo Min Tang Chinese, with the result that production for export had speeded up its long-term decline and local business had stagnated. The Government proceeded late in 1959 with a program of expelling from the rural areas those Chinese businessmen who had not opted for Indonesian citizenship, most of them Communists of convenience hoping for Peking's protection which was not effectively forthcoming. As of January 1, 1960, most of the Chinese merchants who had formerly "monopolized" the rural trade were put out of business. Other Chinese and alien businessmen not as yet directly affected were anticipating drastic new antiforeign measures and were adopting drastic devices of self-protection--such as, for instance, the export of capital at any rate the rising black market might set.

The Government met the emergency by coining a new slogan: "Sandang-pangan," signifying abundant food and clothing at low subsidized prices. It set up co-operatively-run Sandang-pangan shops to replace the dismantled Chinese collection-distribution system and to handle the supplies which had not been either produced or imported. Sandang-pangan, according to Bung Karno's own admission in his August 17, 1960, oration, has to date been a failure. Even rice and textiles, the two indispensable commodities for the ordinary citizen, have often been in critically short supply at unprecedentedly high prices. The ordinary worker can now no more manage to support a family on the standard daily wage of Rp. 5-10 (US$0.10-.20 at the new, but still unrealistically low official exchange rate) than can the high government official on a monthly salary of Rp. 2,500 (US$50). Readjustment of the wage-salary system, like readjustment of the price system, also years overdue, seems not even to be contemplated by the USDEK- and revolution-obsessed Sukarno.

On the international front, Sukarno has stepped up both the frequency and the extravagance of his international junkets, as well as the intensity of his drive, first, to force the Dutch to concede to Indonesia the possession of stone-age Irian Barat (Netherlands New Guinea), and second, to establish Indonesian leadership of an Afro-Asian bloc of nations. His latest foray into international travels and affairs occurred when he turned up at the United Nations General Assembly meeting last September. He traveled by Pan-American jet plane--chartered at an undetermined cost--and arrived with an entourage of 51 persons, including such ill-assorted fellow travelers as Indonesian Communist Party Chairman Aidit and Army Chief of Staff Nasution, altogether an astounding troupe of politicians, assembled and transported, conceivably, to keep them from conspiring against him in his absence. Bung Karno publicly supported the Khrushchev position on modification of the United Nations Secretariat, added his own proposal for transfer of the United Nations headquarters away from the United States, and lobbied privately on the Irian Barat question and on assignment to Indonesia of a Security Council seat. He then hustled off to Europe, first to Paris whose pleasures had been denied him on his previous round-the-world junkets by French obstinacy in refusing to invite him either as an official or unofficial visitor.

Bung Karno remains today as for the last 30 years the key figure about whom Indonesian events continue to revolve, or as now seems more commonly the case, to whirl. He has now become a figure of Greek tragedy proportions, combining the role of hero, victim, and villain of the Indonesian nationalist revolution, trapped in his own legend as the ideological father of his country, interested primarily in escapist diversions from the dilemmas revolution has induced, betrayed as much by fate as by folly.

The nation of Indonesia, like Bung Karno, seems almost inevitably to arouse in the observer the extreme reactions of enthusiasm or of despair, or of fluctuations between the two. Indonesia is breathtakingly beautiful, immeasurably rich in both natural and human resources, altogether exhilarating in its potentialities as by far the biggest, most populous, most richly endowed, most strategically located nation of Southeast Asia. Nevertheless, the task of organizing, disciplining, and developing the nation has defeated to date the best efforts of everyone who has attempted it. Ex-Vice President Hatta, for instance, has retired in defeat and dismay, as did ex-Prime Minister Sjahrir before him. Ex-Prime Minister Natsir joined an insurrection that failed, as did ex-Minister of Economic Affairs Sumitro and ex-Governor of the Bank of Indonesia Sjafruddin. The present Sukarno clique opportunistically exacts its rewards while it prepares to escape retribution. Bung Karno himself, "crazed" with nonstop revolution, seeks personal diversion wherever he may find it. Resourceful, reliable, even hopeful men and women remain, but those who are identifiable invite discrimination or frustration, and those who have still to be identified remain, of course, unknown quantities so far as truly effective and constructive leadership is concerned.

The how and the why of Indonesian national deterioration was the subject of a series of 25 American Universities Field Staff reports on Indonesia a year ago, reports which comprise the chapters which follow. The answers to the whether and the whither--whether national disaster can much longer be postponed, whither the yet unidentified new leaders will take the nation--remain as obscure as before.

Belief that in the near future, by reliance upon USDEK under Bung Karno's leadership, the nation can be healthfully regenerated, seems in view of all the evidence to date to be quite without foundation. Fear that in the near future the nation will pass behind the totalitarian curtain or else fragment itself beyond the fact or fiction of national unity seems, unfortunately, rather better founded. Foregoing, however, the temptations of enthusiasm and of despair, it seems prudent to anticipate two contingencies: first, the collapse within a very few years, perhaps even within months, of the disastrous Bung Karno regime; second, the emergence of some new leaders not now closely associated with Bung Karno's failures. The new leaders, whoever they may be, probably will be unable completely to ward off violence, regional defection, or further deterioration. On the other hand, they need not necessarily be either totalitarian or Communist, and, over the long haul, the problems with which they will be confronted are not irresolvable.

In Indonesia the stakes are big, the gamble is desperate, and the show-down is approaching. The consequences are predictable only in that they will be dramatic, and that at some crucial point not just the wrong men but the right men may have a chance to take over.

W. A. H.

November 28, 1960

SOUTHEAST ASIA SERIES
Vol. VII   No. 16

American Universities Field Staff

REPORTS SERVICE

<u>INDONESIA:</u>

BUNG KARNO'S INDONESIA

Part I: Backtracking a Revolution

by Willard A. Hanna

September 7, 1959

This publication is one of a continuing series on current developments in world affairs written by associates of the American Universities Field Staff. It is distributed by the AUFS as a useful addition to the American fund of information on foreign affairs.

AUFS Associates have been chosen for their skill in collecting, reporting, and evaluating data. Each has combined long personal observation and experience in his foreign area with advanced studies relating to it.

WILLARD A. HANNA, the author of this report, is based in Kuala Lumpur to write about Southeast Asian affairs. Before joining the AUFS in 1954, Dr. Hanna had spent a total of more than ten years in East and Southeast Asia as a teacher, administrator, and writer.

Publications under the imprint of the American Universities Field Staff are not selected to accord with an editorial policy and do not represent the views of its membership. Responsibility for accuracy of facts and for opinions expressed in the letters and reports rests solely with the individual writers.

"We went astray," declares President Sukarno. "We went astray in all fields." "The democracy we have applied up to now is Western democracy--call it parliamentary democracy, if you like. Because it is not in harmony with the Indonesian atmosphere, excesses are bound to occur..., excesses such as misuse of the idea of 'opposition' in the political field; violation of discipline and hierarchy in the military field; corruption and other such like offenses in the socio-economic field."

"Excesses" and "errors," "deterioration" and "disintegration," "deviations, deviations, deviations" from the "sacred principles" of the Pantjasila: this is what Bung Karno sees wherever he looks in Indonesia today. He sees a nation which is suffering "all kinds of tortures from all kinds of devils," a nation which is now "in Purgatory," and "going through the process of purification in all matters, so that when we have been purified, after we have been cleansed, we can enter the happiness...of a just and prosperous society." "At the right moment," says Bung Karno, " we were startled into consciousness." But it was only after "voices were heard--at first as whispers, but gradually gaining strength and ultimately assuming the force of a hurricane," voices calling

[WAH-12-'59]

Banking district in Djakarta.

Two Views
of Indonesia

Rice terraces on Bali.

"a halt to the process of leading our Country toward the abyss of annihilation." [Emphasis mine.] These voices, asserts Bung Karno, declared that the solution to the nation's problems could be found only by "Return to the 1945 Constitution" which "harmonizes best with the Indonesian atmosphere" and provides for "Guided Democracy," that is, "Democracy led by wise guidance in consultation with representatives."

"Back to the Spirit of '45," "Back to the Group of '45," "Back to the Constitution of '45," back to his konsepsi[1] of 1957, with "guided democracy" and now, as a later extrapolation, "guided economy" as the formula for national regeneration: this is Bung Karno's current "revolutionary" message. "Correct" the nation's "errors," halt the "sliding-down process," "hurl as far away from us as possible liberalism and capitalism," reject the "free-for-all" "free enterprise economy" of "vulture capitalists" "subservient to foreign masters"; only thus, he announces, can Indonesia "retool" to achieve "its own identity," its own "pure soul and spirit." "Let the imperialists abroad be in an uproar," he orates. "Yes, let the imperialists be in an uproar! We will march on. Let the dogs bark, our caravan will go passing by."

In speeches totalling hundreds of thousands of words, delivered during scores of hours over thousands of miles of travel, Bung Karno has sounded the tocsin for "a thoroughgoing and revolutionary overhaul of our State and social system." "The cant of communism," say his critics, who are multiplying in numbers and volume, both at home and abroad. "The admission of failure," "the same old resort to slogans and nostrums and posturings." "The prelude to military dictatorship" --"or to a 'people's democracy.'" In sum, the substitution of the backward for the forward look.

There can be no dispute with Bung Karno on two points: first, that the Indonesian crisis is

---

1 See Bung Karno's "Conception" (WAH-3-'57), Southeast Asia Series, Vol. V, No. 3, an AUFS publication.

"hair-raising"; second, that "drastic
action is imperative." There can be and
there is dispute as to whether his proposals are genuinely revolutionary, as he
claims, or in fact reactionary, whether
they place greater stress on accusing
the West and soaking the prosperous, or
upon identifying with the East and succor-
ing the poor. In 1945 the Indonesian
Revolution promised an impoverished and
oppressed people freedom, plenty, and
progress, by expelling colonialism and
establishing democracy. In 1959, by
Sukarno's own admission, it has brought
them indiscipline, scarcity, and retrogression. In 1959-64, if it fulfills Bung
Karno's new promises, it will bring them
at last "adequate food and clothing"--
an astonishingly modest goal for a "revolutionary overhaul."

President Sukarno

The "Back to '45" movement seems to many persons in Indonesia and
abroad to signify not an advance but retrenchment, not the satisfaction but the
curtailment of the nation's expectations, not freedom and progress, but a new
regimentation, deprivation, and stagnation. It seems to involve sudden, rash
measures, enforceable, if at all, only by rigid military authority, leading, if
enforced, to suppression of freedom and initiative. These newly evolving
policies may well prove even more disastrous to the nation than has the
accustomed incoherence of policy and action. In all fairness, however, it
must be conceded that the new government (sworn in on July 10) has only
just begun to translate promises into programs, that it operates under intense
pressure to give evidence of actually implementing reforms, and that in Indonesia drastic efforts have a way of dissipating themselves so that they seem
at first to be much more drastic than they really turn out to be in the end.
Furthermore, government action, almost any action, may help to relieve one
major ill: the stifling sense of stalemate which has long afflicted the nation.

I have recently returned from a five-week visit to Indonesia, after an
absence of two years. Perhaps I made my visit at the worst possible time--
just after the last government had conclusively failed and just before the new
cabinet had had a chance to show what it could do. Perhaps I should, therefore, accept the advice of many of my friends, that I refrain from report or
speculation but merely wait and see--for six months at least, perhaps a year.
But I do not refrain, for to me it seems important to give a forthright account
of the situation at the critical mid-1959 period, if only as a basis for assess-
ment later, say in mid-1960, either of credit for national resuscitation or
blame for national collapse. I admit at the outset, at the risk of seeming

unsympathetic and anti-Indonesian to my Indonesian friends, and destructively rather than constructively critical to other readers, that my own attitude is pessimistic. In brief, I was appalled at the further deterioration I observed in a political, economic, military, and social situation which was already alarmingly bad in 1957. I see little reason as yet to believe that on the over-all it will grow better and not worse in 1960 or 1961 or 1962, or that the clear trend is not toward totalitarianism--and ineffectual totalitarianism at that. But if the situation itself is grim, the attitude of many Indonesians seemed to me to be heroic. "Any country except Indonesia would have collapsed long ago," they kept telling me. "We Indonesians can take it indefinitely."

Practically no Indonesian I talked with really expected to do anything else for quite some time to come except to keep right on taking it. A great many of them were urbane in their acceptance--but they displayed less good humor and more acerbity than used to characterize the Indonesian even in the periods of his greatest adversity. In conversations on every side I heard three new catchwords which provide a capsulized commentary upon much that is going on in Indonesia today: "pampasan," "rampasan," and "paspasan."

"Pampasan" means "reparations." The reference is to Japanese repa-rations goods, much touted by the government as the answer to the poor man's needs for food, clothing, and building materials. Like other panaceas, pampasan has come to signify scandal and muddle. The first big consignment of repara-tions consumer goods--textiles advertised to give each Indonesian the tradi-tional new clothing for Lebaran[2] this past spring--arrived too late, turned out to be of shoddy quality, proved totally inadequate to the need, and became the object of political manipulation to divert them from the general public to the privileged classes. Pampasan, say the wags, may filter down to them even-tually--after the next war, for instance.

"Rampasan" means "robbery by violence." Practically every Indone-sian can provide from his own experience and that of his friends numerous instances in which food, clothing, homes, and other valuable properties have either been seized, stolen, confiscated, or destroyed. It makes little difference whether the outrage was committed by guerrillas or rebel bands, by the mili-tary or persons masquerading in uniform, or by authorized, unauthorized, or semiauthorized agents of government. Rampasan has become so standard a feature of life in Indonesia today that a foreign diplomat--not the first to encounter the phenomenon--need not have been surprised at what happened to him recently. While week-ending at his mountain bungalow in a heavily guarded area, he was visited by armed callers who stripped him of watch, wallet, and other valuables, and then went right on stripping until he was left only with his undershorts. Then, too, no one need have been surprised lately when all Rp. 500 and Rp. 1,000 notes were arbitrarily reduced to Rp. 50 and Rp. 100 in value and all large bank accounts frozen.

---

2 The end of the month of fasting for Muslims and an occasion for much festivity.

"Paspasan" means "getting by." It signifies the subsistence standard of living which, by a combination of ingenuity and miracle, most Indonesians still manage to maintain and, what is more, for the most part to enjoy. "Paspasan," says the Indonesian, as his clothes wear out and sugar disappears from the market, the military requisitions a large part of his house and his month's wages are spent long before he actually receives them.

"Pampasan," "rampasan," and "paspasan" come more frequently to the lips of many Indonesians these days than do the carefully rehearsed slogans of Bung Karno. The "Return to the Spirit of '45" strikes the more cynical as a return to the earlier, rather than the later months of the year in question. In early 1945, under Japanese military occupation, the people were on the verge of destitution, while a few of the revolutionary leaders, including Sukarno, were feted and flattered. Or it strikes them at times as being more like a return to the spirit of '35, save that now a new Indonesian privileged class occupies the homes, enjoys the revenues, and exercises the prerogatives of the onetime Dutch colonial masters. The opprobrium which once attached to the Dutch and to the Japanese is now attaching to some of the Indonesian elite, including a "palace guard" of military men and politicians. It is attaching most of all to Bung Karno himself, who hails the members of this "palace guard" as the "true sons of the Revolution" and sets them his own example of high and extravagant living.

It is endlessly debated in Indonesia today whether Bung Karno or the "palace guard" or the military or the Communists or anyone at all is actually or potentially in command of the situation. What is commonly accepted without debate is that the new government--basically only an expansion and reshuffle of the old--represents one last chance for Indonesia to pull itself together. Privately and contradictorily, however, a great many knowledgeable Indonesians will say, "But these same leaders have failed us already. How can they succeed now when the problems are infinitely worse? And who else is there to turn to?"

This acceptance of apparent incompatibles is what makes the situation peculiarly baffling. But bafflement and frustration are the norm in Indonesia and have been for years. For the foreigner, they make Indonesia half irresistible, half intolerable; for the Indonesian they make Indonesia as inscrutable to himself as to an outsider. For both, they make Indonesia endlessly engrossing. Southeast Asia's biggest, its most populous, potentially its most prosperous and powerful, and certainly its most beautiful and culturally endowed nation has persistently and perversely refused to develop its vast human and natural resources. And there seems to be very little that any right-thinking Indonesian or foreigner can do about it--unless, of course, this new government should indeed prove to be a new deal.

The background factors are a matter of historical record. Indonesia achieved independence from the Dutch with far too little preparation for self-government, too few trained leaders in any field, too lopsided an economy, and too much bitterness generated during a prolonged armed struggle accompanied by widespread suffering and destruction. Its revolutionary struggle, however, was magnificent. Its leaders, although few and inexperienced in running a nation, were gifted with extraordinary brilliance of intellect and personality. Its people were endowed with irrepressible high spirits. There was reason to hope that intelligence and courage would prevail over immense obstacles.

Today, many of the Indonesian leaders have become cynical and opportunistic. Large segments of the population seem discouraged and apathetic. The political, economic, and social system could scarcely be worse disrupted. The military and the Communists seem at times on the point of a showdown for seizure of power, at times on the point of mutual infiltration. The nation, which has seemed close to collapse for a period of years, is now undergoing at the hands of the new government a treatment which some Indonesians designate as "shock therapy," scientifically calculated to work a cure. Others describe it as "quackery," irresponsibly compounded to maintain in power a clique of charlatans. Still others shrug it off as beyond their comprehension and even, such is their fatigue with interminable crisis, almost beyond their caring. This development is not unique in the history of modern nationalist revolution, and it is not irreversible. But in Indonesia it seems particularly pronounced and, in view of the immense potential of the land and the people, particularly tragic.

In the series of reports to follow, I shall attempt to give candid snapshots of Indonesia today. I shall not attempt any comprehensive survey, for any such effort would be outdated long before it could be completed. I shall not offer any extended diagnosis of Indonesia's ills or their cure, for that is far beyond my intention or competence. I shall have to rely upon general personal impressions, reinforced for illustrative purposes by specific facts and observations, with more of the former in the earlier sections of the series, more of the latter in the subsequent ones. My thesis, such as it is, and it will remain hereafter more in the background than in the foreground, can be summarized in the following broad, brash generalizations:

(1) The basic responsibility for the long-continued Indonesian crisis attaches to those at the top of the government, primarily to President Sukarno and his immediate associates, including the military command, and on a diminishing scale on down the line. The basic factors stalling Indonesian progress are these: first, the contagious autointoxication of the nation's top leaders with ultranationalistic agitation; second, their propensity for personal intrigue and extralegal maneuver; third, their conviction that all can be accomplished by devising new regulations, that if only they can regulate advantages away from the haves (excluding themselves) they will automatically create a sufficiency for the have-nots. Expenditure of time, energy, and ingenuity upon international recrimination, personal maneuvering, and the devising and evading

of bureaucratic controls leaves little opportunity for co-operative and constructive effort. Indonesian politicians being as reluctant as any others to
forego the easy devices of personal publicity and personal advantage, it is
unrealistic to expect their sudden transformation. The politicians may soon
be displaced by the military, but such a change would not in itself be much of
an improvement. The military may ultimately be displaced by the Communists,
but that does not seem to be an immediate prospect. The most likely prospect
for the near future is an unstable compromise among politicians, military,
and Communists--which is precisely what exists now.

(2) The Indonesian people, as a whole, when compared with those of
the same social and educational level in many other countries, are surpass-
ingly able, eager, and alert. Like people everywhere, they are both proud
and sensitive and are disposed to regard either unsolicited assistance or
advice--including, of course, any comment of mine--as both presumptuousness
and interference. They are possessed, nevertheless, of a rather remarkable
degree of detachment which makes them inclined at present to play the role of
spectators at their own national collapse rather than that of participants in
their national regeneration. With the exception of the minority which partici-
pates in "mass action groups," they are prone to be more politically skeptical
than impassioned, to endure rather than to rebel, and if called upon for a show
of public enthusiasm, to oblige and then forget. They tolerate and can even
enjoy a mere subsistence level of living, and are most resourceful in com-
pensating for what might seem to be intolerable shortages. The typical Indonesian, in other words, might be described as a spirited fatalist. His breaking
point is well beyond the international norm; but when he does break, he is
likely to do so in the manner of the amok (now disclaimed, incidentally, by
Indonesians themselves as an Indonesian phenomonon), that is, suddenly, vio-
lently, and more or less deliberately. That the Indonesian government or
people may eventually go amok must be considered as a possibility.

(3) Indonesia, as Bung Karno and his associates reiterate, must work
out its own destiny in its own way. Bung Karno's way of revolutionary nationalism has turned out, however, to be a blind alley. His revamped revolutionary-
nationalistic formula of "Guided Democracy" and "Guided Economy" provides
for guidance which, from the present evidence at least, seems likely to lead
the nation back past its original starting point on the road to freedom. Nevertheless, it would be rash to assume, first, that the Indonesian leaders, like
Bung Karno, do not after all know best what is best for Indonesia, or at least
what will work; second, that they are not now resolute in their promise, after
many admitted failures, this time to make a success of government; or third,
that the underlying rationality of the Indonesian people will not of itself com-
pensate for the irrationality--if such it is--of their leaders. The last is perhaps the most reassuring factor in the whole situation; that, plus the historically demonstrated fact that the situation in Indonesia is chronically subject
to sudden change without notice and even without apparent reason.

The sum total of my reports, I hope, will lend some support to the thesis that the Indonesian situation may yet improve as a result of forces not at the moment readily apparent; it may improve merely because Indonesia exhibits a built-in resistance to observable trends, most of which, over the 1955-59 period, were sharply downward. The cumulative effect will not, I fear, lend support to any thesis that the explosive situation in Indonesia today can be de-fused by adroit maneuver, either from within or from without, deliberately to bring healthful influences to bear upon the people now in key position. Bung Karno, who set the Indonesian Revolution moving in high gear toward the unattainable objective of "total independence," has now thrown it into reverse it seems, toward the more possibly attainable objective of total-itarian control. It will take Bung Karno or some other Indonesian, deciding on his own, either to make the totalitarian controls work--which would in itself be in many respects a change for the better, although an unlikely one-- or to select a new direction and a new speed. Bung Karno is what and where he is precisely because he typifies Indonesians both in their strengths and their weaknesses. He is a highly individualistic operator who is guided by his own inspiration. He is susceptible not to the planned focusing but to the random convergence of many influences such as make him at once, but to varying degree at different times, a Marxist, a socialist, a capitalist, a democrat, a dictator, a puppet, a playboy, a prophet, and more than a little of an intellectual anarchist.

Willard A. Hanna

SOUTHEAST ASIA SERIES
Vol. VII   No. 17
(Indonesia)

American Universities Field Staff

REPORTS SERVICE

BUNG KARNO'S INDONESIA

Part II: What Has Happened to Bung Karno?

by Willard A. Hanna

September 9, 1959

This publication is one of a continuing series on current developments in world affairs written by associates of the American Universities Field Staff. It is distributed by the AUFS as a useful addition to the American fund of information on foreign affairs.

AUFS Associates have been chosen for their skill in collecting, reporting, and evaluating data. Each has combined long personal observation and experience in his foreign area with advanced studies relating to it.

WILLARD A. HANNA, the author of this report, is based in Kuala Lumpur to write about Southeast Asian affairs. Before joining the AUFS in 1954, Dr. Hanna had spent a total of more than ten years in East and Southeast Asia as a teacher, administrator, and writer.

Publications under the imprint of the American Universities Field Staff are not selected to accord with an editorial policy and do not represent the views of its membership. Responsibility for accuracy of facts and for opinions expressed in the letters and reports rests solely with the individual writers.

"I think Sukarno has been President for too long. I think he is no longer the Bung Karno we used to admire. But we can't reject him after all these years. And besides, there is no one to take his place. With him we may dissipate our strength, but without him we may disintegrate."

Approximately this judgment, stated with more or less reserve and with more or less lurid reference to the personal and public conduct of the "Big Bung" today, was a constantly recurring theme in conversations with the persons I encountered in Indonesia. The popular image of Bung Karno, the revolutionary hero[1], is rapidly being replaced by the image of Bung Karno, the postrevolutionary profligate. The real Bung Karno today is a composite of both. In achieving any balanced judgment regarding him one must be aware that one is dealing with an exceptionally gifted and troubled man, that consequently any attempted appraisal is both a delicate and a chancy business. During the last several years, the tendency both at home and abroad has been to judge him less generously for his genius than harshly for his failings, a tendency which, if he carries off his new program for Indonesia, might swiftly be reversed.

---

1 See Bung Karno, Parts I and II (WAH-7-'56 and WAH-8-'56), AUFS publications.

[WAH-13-'59]

Bung Karno's genius, to get that on the record first, where it belongs chronologically, is a composite of personal charm, cosmopolitan breadth of intellectual attainment, inspired if bombastic oratory, intuitive rapport with his people's aspirations, an almost uncanny perceptiveness regarding supporters and opponents alike, and a mystical sense that he is the chosen instrument of destiny in leading his people in their revolutionary struggle. By the emotional resonance of his voice, the flash of his smile, the apparently effortless recall of the exact word or allusion, the focusing of his whole personality upon his audience, he can achieve astounding theatrical effects, whether upon one person or one hundred thousand. He can persuade a shrewd American journalist, for instance, that declarations of undying affection for the USSR do not spell sell-out. He can persuade a Russian or Chinese state guest that all those Americans he sees about Djakarta imply no commitment to the West. He can persuade a mob of hostile demonstrators, as he did during the October 17, 1952 Incident, that they are not against but with him.

Bung Karno's genius, many think, is becoming a bit threadbare these days. Beneath the fraying, the failings are becoming more evident. His weaknesses, none of them of recent origin, include vanity, escapism, egocentricity, demagoguery, and, to be as delicate about it as possible, women.

"The presidential palace," said one informant, who has every reason to know, "is worse than the Court of the Susuhunan of Surakarta ever was. Sycophants, rogues, and houris seal Bung Karno off from the Indonesia he used to know and which used to know him."

To many Indonesians, Bung Karno has become the "Big Bung," either ignorant of or oblivious to the privations of the people, bedazzled by his own ostentation. He can no longer pose as a simple man of the people, they say, not when he is preoccupied with palaces and villas (currently four, soon perhaps six), planes (one Russian Ilyushin and a helicopter, as well as requisition and charter jobs), cars (many, including a new gift Karmann-Ghia), an art col-

The Presidential Palace

lection (Indonesia's biggest and best), uniforms (expensively simple), entou-
rages (motorcycle, jeep, and limousine processions), investitures and state
ceremonials, levees and soirees. Bung Karno, some say, has reverted to the
type of the Oriental potentate, brought up to date. He is a dictator, say others,
or an artfully disguised Communist.

"My friends and my children," says Bung Karno to the thousands who
turn out in rain or sun to hear his two-hour orations, "I am no Communist.
But I am open minded. I am not prejudiced." "I am no dictator." "I am no
holy man or reincarnation of God. I am just an ordinary human being like you
and you and you. . . .Why is it that people ask me to give a speech to them,
even when the sun is at its hottest? The answer is this: What Bung Karno says
is actually already written in the hearts of the Indonesian people. The people
want to hear their own voice but. . .they cannot speak eloquently for themselves
. . . .When I die. . .do not write on the tombstone: 'Here rests His Most Exalted
Excellency Dr. Ir. Raden Sukarno, the first President of the Republic of Indonesia'. . .write. . .'Here rests Bung Karno, the Tongue of the Indonesian
People.'"

Bung Karno's insistent identification of his own message with the aspirations of the people has been, in the past at least, no mere symptom of mono-
mania but a correct reading of history. His revolutionary philosophy became
the philosophy also of the nation. It may perhaps best be defined as a combination of Marxism, perfectionism, and opportunism, all imperfectly blended
into revolutionary nationalism, each element of which is bound to conflict with
the others.

Bung Karno's Marxism is typified by his theory of the "Marhaen"[2]--
the Indonesian masses, whose unspoken, unthought aspirations for freedom from
exploitation by alien colonialists, capitalists, and imperialists, he, Bung Karno,
both articulates and achieves. Bung Karno's Marhaenism has led to what
many Indonesians, including now apparently Bung Karno himself, recognize
today as an extremely dangerous commitment to fellow-traveling doctrines
and companions. The threat is now apparent that the Communists may snatch
the revolutionary torch from Bung Karno's own hands as he merely flourishes
it without advancing it.

Bung Karno's perfectionism is apparent in his formulation of the Pantjasila, or Five Principles of the Indonesian State (Belief in God, Humanitarianism, Nationalism, Democracy, and Social Justice). The emphasis is upon
swift achievement of total rectitude, as is, of course, standard with state
ideologies. But the obvious incompatibility of many of the policies and actions
of the Indonesian leaders with the principles of democracy and social justice,
for instance, has led to recrimination as to who is and who is not genuinely

---

2 See Indonesia's Political Parties, I (WAH-24-'56), an AUFS publication.

(Above) At Petrodvorets, near Leningrad, Bung Karno joins a group of school children welcoming him with songs and dances.

(Top Left) Bung Karno at Ann Arbor, Michigan, in 1956. At right, President Hatcher of the University of Michigan.

(Bottom Left) Bung Karno steals the show from Mao Tse-tung and Chou En-lai.

(Bottom) President Sukarno in a Central Asian beanie at a football match in Leningrad between the All-Indonesia and the local teams. He is rarely photographed without his black velvet pitji.

devoted to the Pantjasila. It has led to even greater dispute as to who is and who is not dedicated to that other perfectionist extension of the Pantjasila, "total independence."

Bung Karno's opportunism is evident in his employment of that most tested of nationalistic and revolutionary devices, the incessant reiteration of an uncompromising national claim. The campaign for the "liberation" of West New Guinea, although Bung Karno savagely refutes the "imputation" and brands it as "reactionary" and "imperialist," has served again and again to distract both attention and effort from Indonesia's urgent domestic problems and to justify Indonesia's unilateral renunciation of international agreements. But there has come a point when even within Indonesia itself some people are beginning to wonder whether greater attention to progress and order within the nation as it is currently constituted--implementation of the Pantjasila for the benefit of the Marhaen, so to speak--is not preferable to mounting a campaign to expand into an unknown area.

The disappointment of Indonesia's revolutionary hopes, the growing realization that the disappointment will continue and perhaps grow worse, and the parallel realization that the key responsibility rests with him, has turned Bung Karno into a troubled and restless man. All the contrived glitter of giant rallies, of state visits abroad, of entertainment of state guests in Indonesia, always accompanied by public display of affection for Bung Karno, apparently have become indispensable to his personal gratification and reassurance. Between times, he buoys himself up with a formidable lot of medications, vitamins and injections--and the rumor persists that he is seriously ill. He consults again and again with the soothsayers--one of whom, it is rumored, went to jail shortly after making an unwelcome prediction. He welcomes all the diversions which the "palace guard" provides.

The tragedy of Bung Karno is the not unprecedented one of a truly great man who has been a vital national leader but has failed to provide new inspiration for new times. It is also the personal tragedy of a man of compelling drive and personality now dissipating his energies upon causes and persons unworthy of him. Of recent years, Bung Karno has developed a consistent behavior pattern in reaction to his own and his nation's troubles. He has attempted repeatedly to diagnose the illness and prescribe the cure. His prescription, invariably, has been more frequent and more powerful dosages of revolutionary nationalism. But the nation has built up a high level of immunity to the prescription. As each new treatment has failed to revitalize the patient, Bung Karno has sought to revitalize himself. He has sought escape in triumphal progresses, both foreign and domestic, and in the trappings of presidential majesty which make the past pretentions of the sultans look almost proletarian by comparison.

The cycle of effort, frustration, and escape becomes clear in a brief recapitulation of Sukarno's actions during the major national crises of 1957,

1958, and 1959. Each crisis came as a result of the long-familiar maladies of the Indonesian nation: Djakartan bureaucratic arrogance and muddle, regional and military insubordination, nation-wide economic maladjustment, public privation and discontent, and recurrent scandal over official incompetence and corruption, all exacerbated by nationalist, militarist, Communist, and for that matter anti-Communist machinations.

Bung Karno on February 21, 1957, after a long preliminary build-up, came forward with his famed konsepsi for national reconstruction. "Minimize" the political parties, invite the Communists into a "gotong-rojong (mutual aid) cabinet" and a "musjawarah (consultative compromise) council," substitute "guided democracy" for "Western democratic liberalism," and step up the campaign for "liberation" of West New Guinea: such was the gist of his proposal as it continued to develop. The konsepsi ran into stubborn opposition, mainly on the grounds that it presaged Communist or dictatorial control. Ultimately, Bung Karno had to settle for a new Government that was little different from the old, save that it provided for a "Musjawarah Council" and "preparation for Guided Democracy." Bung Karno's konsepsi miscarried; the regional and military insurrection movement gathered momentum; the new Government proved as incompetent as the old; the economic situation rapidly worsened; the West Irian campaign fizzled out in the United Nations but was stepped up again in December 1957, by adopting Bung Karno's threatened "other way"--expulsion of the Dutch and seizure of Dutch property, a move which made for neither political nor economic stability; Bung Karno was himself made the object of an assassination attempt (Nov. 30, 1957); and all the counsel of the Musjawarah Council couldn't provide a "way-out" from the **national dilemma.**

Bung Karno with members of the Takarazuka Girls Revue during his 1958 visit to Tokyo.

On January 5, 1958, Bung Karno departed on a rest, recuperation, and propaganda mission abroad. He visited and consulted with Nehru, Nasser, and Tito, among others, all to the accompaniment of as much fanfare and as many joint communiques as possible. He ended up on holiday in Japan. While still in Japan, on February 10 he received an ultimatum from the regional and military insurgents in Sumatra and Celebes, demanding that he break with the Communists, appoint a new Cabinet with certain designated members, and set seriously about the task of cleaning up the administration and rationalizing the economy. Bung Karno rejected the ultimatum in toto. Insurrectionist terms were promptly expanded to include a demand that Sukarno must go; the rebels declared their independence of Djakarta, named a Cabinet of their own, and announced their readiness to resist armed attack. Bung Karno returned to Djakarta, called for united national effort to destroy the "traitors" and their "foreign imperialist" allies, and ordered military action which, to the surprise of local and outside observers, proved to be both swift and effective. But defeat of the main rebel forces did not mean an end to rebel guerrilla operations, which drag on interminably and threaten to bankrupt the nation. Indonesian operation of seized Dutch enterprises, rather than enriching the nation as had been promised, still further dislocated the badly deteriorated economy. Government policies proved as vacillating as before, notwithstanding a mid-1958 Cabinet reshuffle, and achievement of the "liberation" of West New Guinea seemed even more distant. Both the military and the Communists increased in power, and each threatened to clash with the other. The over-all Indonesian situation was very much worse in mid-1958 than in mid-1957.

Bung Karno then embarked on a series of triumphal tours of the nation. Most triumphal of all was a visit to the remote eastern islands adjacent to West New Guinea, in company with a dozen ambassadors and members of the local and foreign press. He orated for hours to big crowds on the triple thesis that the nation had once again demonstrated its solidarity in the revolutionary cause and its affection for him as a revolutionary hero; that the rebellions were crushed and the "foreign interventionists" foiled; that West Irian would inevitably be free. During his public addresses he called for mass demonstrations of enthusiasm, leading the crowds at Dobo for instance in shouting "Merdeka" (freedom) in unison, long and loud, so that "the Dutch might hear it on West Irian." After fiery platform performances of one or two hours in length, he exhibited superhuman stamina by feasting and dancing from early evening until early morning.

The twelve ambassadors, a startling and startled mélange representing the United States, the USSR, Communist China, the Philippines, Japan, Pakistan, Malaya, Turkey, the United Arab Republic, Canada, Hungary, and Iraq, witnessed and swelled this Bung Karno progress. As they sat behind him on the platform, they would at times suddenly and individually be brought into the act--although the Chinese Ambassador was occasionally detected slipping off to build his own political fences. It was on their program, too, to feast and dance until late at night, to sleep two to a stiflingly hot Navy ship cabin until six, and then to arise and prepare themselves for the next day's equally strenuous schedule. The Ambassadors returned to Djakarta by plane exhausted, while Bung Karno, refreshed and exhilarated, stopped off in Bali. There, in a recently completed and expensive hilltop vacation palace, he frequently enjoys the beauty and relaxation of the island, together with his "palace guard" and his guests.

Early in 1959 Bung Karno publicly announced that the nation was close to "the abyss of annihilation," and the 1959 crisis was thereby made official.

People of South Sulawesi (Celebes) in their traditional dress say farewell to Bung Karno.

The Presidential party aboard the Indonesian Navy ship "Patimura" off Wakiki beach, Saparua.

Bung Karno and members of his party at Makam Pahlawan, Maluku, in the autumn of 1958. (United States Ambassador Howard Jones at the far right.)

"Misuse" of political opposition to "obstruct" all orderly government; "indiscipline and warlordism" on the part of the military; "grabbing for fortune and wealth" on the part of the "new bourgeoisie" and the "national capitalists": all this had led to "a process of pauperization" which must be arrested at once. "Return to the Constitution of 1945," he demanded of the Constitutent Assembly which had been rather aimlessly debating a new constitution ever since 1956; do so without delay, without debate, and without modification. The 1945 Constitution, he declared, was a "'magically-sentimentally-nationally' loaded" document enshrining the "genuinely Indonesian" principles of "Guided Democracy" which he had put forward earlier. Under it, the nation would have a President endowed with strong powers, a nonpolitical Presidential Cabinet assured of a five-year term (contrasting with 17 previous Cabinets in 14 years); a partially appointive Parliament "truly representative" of the interests of "regional" and "functional" groups, and no longer disposed or empowered to topple governments; a system of appointive national councils to "consult" and "guide" the Government on the basis not of vote-counting but of implied and understood consensus. From the moment Bung Karno first hinted at the Return to the 1945 Constitution, it was evident that there would be powerful opposition to the scheme. When he demanded on April 22 that the Constituent Assembly promptly

adopt the Constitution and then dissolve itself, it was fairly clear that it would do no such thing.

The next day Sukarno departed on a 68-day round-the-world junket, billed as a state visit to Latin America but including a holiday stop-over in the Crimea, also visits in Ankara, Copenhagen, Rome, Moscow, Budapest, Mexico City, Hollywood, Tokyo and Hanoi. He had, incidentally, just concluded a round of lavish entertainments for state visitors to Indonesia, notably for President Prasad, Marshal Tito, and Ho Chi-minh. During the period of his local entertainments and his foreign travels, the developing situation in Indonesia gave indisputable support to his own appraisal: "The economic situation of the State is deteriorating, the financial situation of the State is deteriorating, the social condition of society is deteriorating--in all fields we are deteriorating and. . .deteriorating continuously."

Such being the case, a great many people began to ask: how could one explain Bung Karno's own action in chartering, at a reported cost of about US$250,000, a special Pan-American plane, loading it with an easy-spending entourage of 35 prominent people, including Ministers of State, and absenting himself for a prolonged period to pay unnecessary state visits to "unimportant" nations--the Latin American nations, that is--which had been rather less than lukewarm in their invitations? And what was he going to do on his return to set things right--or was he going to be met with another ultimatum, this time not from rebel but loyalist military commanders?

As usual in Indonesia, much speculation and excitement about the unpredictable was prelude to the retrospectively predictable. On July 5 Bung Karno decreed the Return to the 1945 Constitution and the dissolution of the Constituent Assembly (which had failed three times to pass the demanded resolution). He then formed the new Cabinet and consultative bodies. Save that he himself for the first time took the portfolio of Prime Minister, the new Government, about which there had been so much stir, looked almost indistinguishable from the old.

The new Government has begun, however, to adopt vigorous policies and to take strong action, whether for the better or for the worse, whether resolutely or not, whether sustained or sporadic, whether under Bung Karno's personal guidance or that of some new clique--presumably military--only the next few months will show. At any rate, for the time being, Bung Karno is in both senses of the term on the spot--or will be, once he returns from a current two-week tour of Sumatra and Borneo, again with an entourage of diplomats and newspapermen. Once again he is making the effort to deal with a situation which many informed persons believed almost impossible to deal with, this time openly gambling his personal reputation on the outcome.

The year 1957 Bung Karno designated, rather incongruously it seems in retrospect, "Indonesia's Year of Decision." The year 1958 he designated, with much more of his accustomed perspicacity, "Indonesia's Year of Challenge." The year 1959 he has just designated "The Year of the Rediscovery of the Revolution." It might be even more appropriate to name it "The Year of the Rediscovery of Bung Karno." That rediscovery is almost certain to involve reassessment of Bung Karno's strength and will to devote himself to the rigorous tasks of rehabilitating a nation. That the nation has already been brought close to ruin is the consequence in large part of his own past predilection for demagoguery rather than statesmanship. Should he indeed have hit upon a constructive new formula and should he indeed make it work, that will constitute something of a political miracle, one almost without historic precedent. But Bung Karno has worked miracles before, and may do so again.

Willard A. Hanna

[All photographs courtesy Ministry of Information, Djakarta.]

SOUTHEAST ASIA SERIES
Vol. VII   No. 18
(Indonesia)

American Universities Field Staff   REPORTS SERVICE

BUNG KARNO'S INDONESIA

Part III: The Politics of Mystification

by Willard A. Hanna

September 12, 1959

This publication is one of a continuing series on current developments in world affairs written by associates of the American Universities Field Staff. It is distributed by the AUFS as a useful addition to the American fund of information on foreign affairs.

AUFS Associates have been chosen for their skill in collecting, reporting, and evaluating data. Each has combined long personal observation and experience in his foreign area with advanced studies relating to it.

WILLARD A. HANNA, the author of this report, is based in Kuala Lumpur to write about Southeast Asian affairs. Before joining the AUFS in 1954, Dr. Hanna had spent a total of more than ten years in East and Southeast Asia as a teacher, administrator, and writer.

Publications under the imprint of the American Universities Field Staff are not selected to accord with an editorial policy and do not represent the views of its membership. Responsibility for accuracy of facts and for opinions expressed in the letters and reports rests solely with the individual writers.

"If you think you understand the political situation in Indonesia today, then you're just badly informed." This epigram perennially makes the rounds of the Djakarta diplomatic cocktail circuit and is widely attributed to whatever Foreign Minister happens to be in office. Its period of currency may well prove to be as extended as that of a bon mot coined years ago, allegedly by the Chief of Police. The Communists were just then staging their spectacular come back and come on, with profuse displays of what he dubbed "that extinct and prehistoric fowl, the dove of peace." Today, that extinct and prehistoric fowl flutters across a darkling political plain swept with confused alarms, as partially dismantled political parties clash with a partly mutinous, partly overbearing, partly crusading military establishment. A partly discredited Bung Karno, meanwhile, leads the charge of nobody is sure quite what or whose forces in quite which direction, and councils of elder statesmen, many of them in their thirties, meet during engagements to compound unformulated guidance. The political situation, like the economic, the military, and the social, seems to have achieved what even for Indonesia is a new high in mystification.

"If you think the situation can't get still more confused, remember that's what people said two years ago," declared one newspaper editor who

[WAH-14-'59]

has given up writing analytical editorials. "We Indonesians may not be systematic," he said, "but you must admit, we're rarely dull." It is still possible, however, for an outsider to attempt to be analytical and therefore, no doubt, dull in appraising at least the long-range political trends in Indonesia. Some of the most significant of them are as follows--or, more accurately, they seem to be as follows: (1) Increased acceptance by President Sukarno of acknowledged official responsibility; (2) Increased participation of the military in all aspects of government; (3) Increased volubility of the Communists in constituting themselves Bung Karno's most loyal supporters; (4) Decreased activities of the other political parties; (5) Increased reliance of the nation's leaders upon revolutionary mass action movements; and (6) Increased disposition on the part of the top leaders to bypass parliamentary procedures, to govern by special decree, and to turn ostensibly for guidance to vague, cumbersome, reduplicative national councils.

If one is particularly optimistic, he may include also on the list of long-term trends these three others: (7) Increased realization on many sides that the situation is desperate and that something not merely drastic but constructive must be done about it; (8) Increased determination to contain the forces of disintegration, or, more specifically, those of Communist integration, even at the risk of military dictatorship; and (9) Increased disposition on the part of Indonesian leaders and people to busy themselves less with international and more with domestic problems, less with nationalistic agitation, and more with achievement of food, clothing, and basic essentials. If one is particularly pessimistic, he may include: (10) Increased drift toward the Left and toward association with Communist bloc nations, policies, and methods; (11) Increased drift toward national disintegration. Whether one is optimistic or pessimistic, one is likely to predict the emergence in Indonesia of increasingly rigid authoritarianism. Forecasts differ mainly as to whether it will be more militarist or Communist in application, more or less successful than previous Indonesian Governments in solving the nation's critical problems.

President Sukarno addressing
a mass meeting in Semarang,
Central Java.

The developments in the next few months under the new Government which has already begun to take vigorous if not necessarily constructive action, will probably serve to show whether the more optimistic or the more pessimistic interpretation applies. Meanwhile, working on the basis of developments over the last several years, all of which add up to greatly increased if muddled authoritarianism, I shall concern myself with the first six trends listed above.

1. <u>Bung Karno's increased powers</u>. In the past, Bung Karno has exhibited a marked preference for the perquisites rather than the responsibilities of the Presidential office, for the behind-the-scenes or under-the-floodlights political maneuver rather than behind-the-desk official responsibility. Now, as his own Prime Minister, he has accepted open responsibility for the administration--and therefore, as his critics point out, for its failures. He has undertaken to devote himself for extremely long hours not just to the showmanship, public and private, of the Presidential office, but to the harassment and tedium of the Prime Minister's.

This state of affairs grew out of his <u>konsepsi</u> of 1957[1] and his continuing but unsuccessful effort to find an ally or a group of allies to whom he could safely assign most of the responsibility and, if things went wrong, most of the blame. He has turned to three groups which, even though there is overlap in membership and common profession of loyalty to Bung Karno, exhibit nevertheless such rivalries among themselves as to make effective co-ordination virtually impossible, and such ambitions as to constitute a potential threat to Bung Karno's own position. The three are the Communists, the military, and the "Group of '45."

Bung Karno's 1957 <u>konsepsi</u>, had it been adopted, would have brought the Communists into strong position in Government and made them perhaps his primary ally. Had the new Government itself proved stable and effectual --as Bung Karno declared with apparent conviction that it would be--he would have earned the gratitude of the nation. Had it proved weak and unstable, then the blame could be attached again to feuding politicians, Communists among others. But the <u>konsepsi</u> was in large part rejected; and while Bung Karno was able to attribute the blame for failure of the Djuanda ("Karya") Government to the politicians who had blocked his plan, he had also put himself in the position of accepting increased personal responsibility. He had constituted himself the emergency "formateur" of the Djuanda Cabinet; he had all but openly dictated its program; and he himself became the personal object of much of the attack--including an assassination attempt and regional insurrections--which the program precipitated.

In early 1958, Bung Karno was confronted with the alternatives of either capitulating to the demands of insurrectionists or, as Commander in Chief, of

---

1 See <u>Bung Karno's Indonesia, Part II: What Has Happened to Bung Karno?</u> (WAH-13-'59), an AUFS publication, page 6.

assuming emergency powers and giving the command and the powers to the
military forces to put down the insurrections. He chose, of course, to start
military action and to confer, therefore, more and more power upon the military which had already, as a matter of chronological fact, largely succeeded
the Communists as his ally. Military action, although on the whole successful,
worsened the over-all problems of the nation, and by late 1958 Bung Karno
found himself still possessed of strong emergency powers, still allied with an
increasingly powerful military, still at the head of a weak and unstable government. It must have occurred to him, as it occurred to virtually every other
informed person inside or out of Indonesia, that there were strong elements
within the military which were giving thought to deposing him. It must have
occurred to him also that his previous quasi-allies, the Communists, had
increased greatly in strength, partly because of his patronage, and were also
giving thought to renouncing him.

Bung Karno turned next to the "Group of '45." From the time of the
announcement of the konsepsi, some of the leaders of the newly-emerging
Group of '45 had been among Sukarno's prime supporters in organizing "spontaneous" demonstrations. They had continued and increased their activities
in the interim, especially during the course of the West Irian agitation and the
subsequent seizure of Dutch-owned properties. The Group of '45 had the advantage that it was an amorphous body which could be interpreted to include the
most reputable of the revolutionary leaders, and that it actually included a
group of young activists, a good many of them Communists sympathizers and
others of them Army officers. In fact, it could include almost anybody and it
cut across party, regional, and "functional" group lines in precisely the manner
than Bung Karno had proposed in his konsepsi. By early 1958 Bung Karno had
already adopted as one of his prime oratorical themes the necessity to return
to the revolutionary spirit of '45, under the leadership, naturally, of the Group
of '45. By logical extension, he came to the conclusion that it was essential
to return to the Constitution of '45, involving as it does concentration of powers
in the hands of the President himself.

Bung Karno, therefore, according to this admittedly oversimplified and
partly theoretical reconstruction of confused recent events, is now possessed
not only of emergency powers but also of regular statutory powers far in
excess of anything he deliberately chose either to acquire or to exercise in
the past. He is busily sharing his authority with the Group of '45 and with the
military, members of both of which feature prominently in the new Government.
But Bung Karno does not at the moment have any one paramount ally--unless
it is the military, an hypothesis which is open to question since the military
seems now more of an agent than a prime-mover. He does not, therefore,
have any one scapegoat. He is at last in a position of both real and acknowledged authority. He seems determined to exercise that authority both openly
and vigorously. Whether he succeeds or fails in reforming the nation, the
judgment must be: the responsibility is Bung Karno's.

2. <u>Increase in military powers.</u> In the course of the last several years, Indonesia has been gradually converting into a semimilitary police state. To the Army has accrued not only direct administrative authority over the newly "liberated" areas in Sumatra and Sulawesi (Celebes) but also, as a result of the prolonged State of War and Siege (declared early in 1957), discretionary control over virtually the whole apparatus of administration. To the civil police--in effect, a fourth branch of the military establishment, and in some respects better organized, better disciplined, and better armed than the Army itself--has been delegated increased responsibility that over- laps that of the Army. The military in general, whether Army or police or in some instances Navy and Air Force, exercises overriding authority in such diverse matters as immigration, customs, export-import activities, movement of aliens, distribution of goods, operation of communications, operation of many commercial enterprises, censorship of the press, super- vision over political activities, public meetings and even social gatherings, plus dozens of other matters, including investigation of suspected corruption. Military liaison officers swell the already congested ministries and add new and even more labyrinthine channels through which official papers must pass with decreased expectation of ever emerging. Military personnel are stra- tegically placed, therefore, either to expedite or to obstruct the conduct of a vast variety of government activities. Under the circumstances, a military <u>coup</u> would seem to require little more than the announcement that it had occurred. But it hasn't yet occurred, or hasn't yet been announced, and speculation has veered in recent months from the question of when it will come, to whether it will come, to why it doesn't come.

One possible explanation of the failure of the long-expected military <u>coup</u> to materialize is that the military, like Bung Karno, seems to prefer the potentiality and actuality of power to the open acceptance and acknowledg- ment of responsibility. In any event, rather than consistently exercising clear-cut powers under martial law, the military exercises the prerogative of intervention, and even that inconsistently. For instance, the military does not actually regulate the import of automobiles, but it requisitions for its own use a large percentage of the new cars that actually come in. It does not actually run the transportation system, but it appropriates ships, planes, and trains to its own use and sees that favored users get priority on what- ever transportation is available. It does not actually control housing, but it requisitions for its own use, with or without consultation with the housing authorities, the buildings it wants. It does not actually control factory pro- duction, but it assists operators, if it wishes, to acquire raw materials that are in short supply, and it prevents operators, if it wishes, from closing down and laying off labor when supplies are not available. It does not actually man- age the distribution of gasoline, but it gets all it requires for its own purposes and considerably more besides, with the result that during periods of shortage --which are increasingly frequent--military personnel do a brisk if incon- spicuous business in marketing their excess at a 100 to 700 per cent mark-up.

Another possible explanation is that the Indonesian military shares a weakness--or perhaps it is a strength--which is by no means exclusively Indonesian or exclusively military, that is, a versatility which makes for diffusion rather than concentration of effort. Just as other Indonesians tend, by reason of personal preference, shortage of trained personnel, and the necessity to have several different sources of income, to be at one and the same time, say, a government official, a medical or legal practitioner, a teacher, a businessman, and a patron of the arts, so it is not uncommon for the military officer to practice many occupations and no one of them, not even that of military officer, exclusively or predominantly. And just as in an Indonesian Government or private office, everyone in sight tends to have a hand in whatever business is under way at the moment, while no one accepts the responsibility to co-ordinate or complete the job, so too the military seems to prefer a combination of administrative meddlesomeness and dilettantism to routine, systematic control. Appearances may be deceptive, and in the new Government, in which 12 out of some 38 senior, deputy, and ex-officio Ministers are military men, the military may indeed supply the drive and the direction. For the moment, at least, it looks as though they are content merely to play an increasingly prominent but by no means predominant, and hence perhaps an inconclusive role, in a new Government which few outsiders expect to be really successful or to reflect credit upon its military participants.

3. The PKI as the loyal support. Of all Indonesian political parties, the PKI has been the most consistent and vocal in its support for President Sukarno's successive proposals, from the konsepsi through the "Return to the '45 Constitution." PKI support, naturally, has not been 100 per cent-- that would be too much to expect, if only because the party itself experiences internal friction; and it has at times been retroactive rather than concurrent in its support, as with regard to the Return to the '45 Constitution which it approved unequivocally only after some little confusion and delay. Furthermore, PKI support has been accompanied by various quite audible asides about certain consequences of the Bung Karno program, always with loud acclaim for Bung Karno himself, however, while condemning some of the policies adopted with his consent if not on his demand--the postponement of the 1959 elections, for instance, in which the PKI would undoubtedly have made great gains.

Of all the PKI critical asides, the most significant relates to the increase in power of the military. Not too deeply buried away in the PKI documents for its Sixth National Congress this month is an itemization, for instance, of the "negative aspects" of the military exercise of authority: "the restriction of democratic rights for the people, such as bans on holding meetings convened by parties, including parties that oppose the counter-revolutionary rebellion, strike prohibitions, including prohibitions of strikes in enterprises that side with the counter-revolutionary rebels, and other prohibitions which impose serious limitations on the development of the democratic and progressive movement."[2]

Regardless of objection to some parts of Bung Karno's program, regardless also of the sharp clash between the PKI and the military which many observers see shaping up, the PKI has regularly and vigorously promoted such basic Bung Karno slogans, which the military also supports, as: "Liberate West Irian," "Crush the Rebels," "Adopt Guided Democracy" (and "Guided Economy"), "Drive out the Imperialists, the Colonialists, and the Capitalists," "Reject Dutch Thinking," "Simplify the Party System," and "Return to the Spirit of '45." It produces a vast literature of polemic which seems at times to echo, at times to anticipate Sukarno's own speeches. Parallel extracts from PKI documents and Sukarno speeches would baffle any student as to exact origin if it were not for the give-away clues of Sukarno's highly emotional oratorical style and the PKI's more pedestrian prose. For purely illustrative purposes, the following two extracts regarding the rebel movement may repay comparative reading:

"This is a national crime! . . .Indonesians who call themselves patriots have invited foreigners to stab their brothers in the back. . . .But what, in fact, was the consequence of the [rebels'] alliance with the foreign imperialists? . . .The whole nation loathes [the rebels]. . . .The Government had no choice but to take firm action. . . .The alternative would have been everything which is not in accordance with the Pantja Sila. . . .There would have been the complete failure of the realization of the principle of democracy of our Pantja Sila and the complete destruction of any hope for a just and prosperous society, because we would have become a satellite of imperialism and capitalism. . . .These rebellions are basically the emergence of reactionary and counter-revolutionary forces which are waging a life-and-death struggle against the continuation of our Revolution. . . ." (Sukarno, Aug. 17, 1958)[3]

"Ahmad Husein's ultimatum was issued after he had obtained guarantees from SEATO that the government he would proclaim would speedily be recognized and that it would be given armed assistance to fight the Central Government. . . .This makes it clear that the desperate actions of the counter-revolutionaries are. . .based. . .in the first place upon assistance from abroad . . . .These actions of the rebels were on the one hand enthusiastically welcomed by the American, Dutch, British and other imperialists. The imperialists thought that these actions would hold back the upsurge of the national independence movement which is now in progress in Indonesia, that it would smash the Republic of Indonesia. . . .On the other hand, the rebels' proclamation of their 'central government' aroused the widespread anger of the masses of the people. With this supreme act of treason, the Husein-Sjafruddin clique have completely

---

2 Material for the Sixth National Congress of the Communist Party of Indonesia, page 33. (Published by Agitation and Propaganda Department of the C.C. of the C.P.I. No other imprint. Preface dated Djakarta, December 8, 1958. 137 pp.)

3 A Year of Challenge. Speech by H.E. the President of the Republic of Indonesia in commemoration of Independence Day, 17th August 1958. Ministry of Information, Republic of Indonesia. Special issue 18. 39 pp.

exposed themselves. . . .As long as the Government remains firm and realistic
. . .it will be able to prevent the disintegration of the Republic, and this is the
basic prerequisite for shutting the door tight to intervention." (PKI documents
of the 6th Plenum)[4]

These citations, and hundreds more which could be made, are not evidence that the PKI is irrevocably committed to Sukarno or that Bung Karno is
irrevocably committed to the PKI. They are evidence only that congruity of
policies, pronouncements, and thought processes are sufficient to make for
compatibility.

The PKI in recent years has profited vastly from being on Bung Karno's
side and enjoying Bung Karno's favor. It has gained increased respectability,
influence, and following. Although it has not gained Cabinet posts--and as a
result has not shared in responsibility for repeated Cabinet failures--it has
gained representation in the various national councils and it has infiltrated
more and more PKI members and sympathizers into significant positions in
government agencies and the armed services. It has grown so powerful, in
fact, that Bung Karno, the Cabinet, the military, and various important individuals and agencies have apparently become increasingly uneasy regarding
the real intentions underlying its manifestations of support. The PKI itself,
according to informed rumor, has given serious consideration to the question
whether, in view of its own increased power and of the danger that someone--
the military?--will attempt seriously to curtail it, the policy of nearly total
support for the Bung Karno regime is any longer opportune.

So far as present evidence goes, the PKI seems resolved to continue,
publicly at least, in its pious role as the loyal support. There seems to be
one compelling reason that it should. The PKI, it may reasonably be conjec-
tured, is placing its bets on the proposition that the Bung Karno regime is
traveling in its direction but is itself a losing show; if such is the case, the
regime deserves all PKI support, short of direct and extensive participation--
which it publicly demands and privately evades. The worse the Indonesian
economic situation becomes, and the more Bung Karno, the other political
factions, and the military are implicated in the process, the better will be the
prospects for the PKI. It will remain the one organized, disciplined, active
political force to which direct responsibility for maladministration cannot be
attached. When and if the PKI shifts to the opposition, that will be one of the
best indicators that the over-all situation in Indonesia is beginning perceptibly
to improve.

4. Decline of the other political parties. While PKI strength and

---

4 Documents of the 6th Plenum of the Central Committee of the Communist
Party of Indonesia. March 31st - April 3rd, 1958. Jajasan "Pembaruan."
Jakarta 1958. 123 pp.

activity has been on the increase, the strength and activities of the three other major political parties[5] have been sharply on the decline. The Masjumi (Muslim) Party, once the most powerful, had already slipped badly by 1957. Since then, as a result of defection to the rebel cause of some of its top leaders (including its Chairman, Natsir), and of the well-known anti-Sukarno, anti-Communist stand on the part of many others (Dr. Hatta, for instance), it has become identified as a party of the Opposition, and a weak Opposition at that. It is an Opposition which now seems at a loss for new leaders, policies, and programs. The N.U. (Muslim Scholars) has shown itself highly inconsistent, unreliable, and opportunistic. It has made deals now with the Masjumi to form a religious bloc, now with the PNI (Nationalists) to form a nationalist coalition, ending up, at the moment, more closely, albeit ineffectually, associated with the Masjumi than with the Government. The PNI has tended to discredit itself as a result of incompetence, corruption, and maladroit deals with the Communists on the part of the last PNI Cabinets. Even the long-time patron of the PNI, Bung Karno, seems now to have disowned the party. Bung Karno, who stirred up nation-wide protest in late 1956 by his sudden proposal to "bury the parties," need only, it seems, have been a bit more patient. The major parties, other than the Communists, of course, seem in effect almost to have buried themselves.

Many of the minor parties, of which there are 30 or more, have also had rough going these last several years, witness, for instance, the dilemma of Sjahrir's Socialists. This little group of "unemployed brain-trusters" has for years constituted an Opposition of the intellectual elite. Like the Communists, they have deliberately held themselves aloof from responsibility for deterioration in national affairs. Indeliberately, and quite unlike the Communists, they have remained aloof also from the millions of ordinary people whose dissatisfaction with the present state of society might be converted into political advantage. The prominent Socialists, since they are critical, articulate, and often courageous, have met with increased official suspicion. In certain cases they have met with hindrance and even arrest on the supposition that since they oppose many central Government policies, it follows that they probably support the rebels to whose side at least one top Socialist leader (Dr. Sumitro) defected, and to whose support others (including Sjahrir, according to Communist charges) were thought to contribute. The Socialists, who had proposed after their crushing defeat in the 1955 elections to train an elite corps of workers who would in turn elicit popular support, have instead been thrust back upon themselves. They appear to be considerably weaker and more dispirited today than they were two years ago. And meanwhile, various Left-wing groups, both old and new, both closely and loosely affiliated with the PKI, have increased in numerical strength and popular appeal.

The Government has just recently delivered a new blow to the major

---

5 See Indonesia's Political Parties, I & II (WAH-24 & 25-'56), AUFS publications.

political parties most conspicuously entrenched in government by putting out a regulation requiring the higher echelon government employees--the 5,000 or so in the Rp. 1,000-2,000 per month salary range--either to resign from their parties or from their jobs. Practically all of them have chosen to resign from their parties. Since high government officials are likely also to be important party officials and members, this mass resignation would seem to leave much of the key party machinery unmanned, including, ironically, that of the PNI, which for a long time controlled the Government and rewarded its members with government posts.

That the new regulation will lead to further decrease of party activity as such--save that of the Communists--seems altogether likely. But that it will lead to a decrease in internecine feuding among the politicians themselves seems much less probable. Indonesian party politics in the recent past have consisted of about 50 per cent effort to win the popular vote--now no longer an urgent consideration, since elections are postponed indefinitely--and 50 per cent personal maneuver on the part of individual politicians and cliques to gain position and privilege for themselves and to deny it to others. Indonesian politicians being no more selfless or enlightened than those of other nations, the question quite naturally arises: now that they are freed of the tedious business of appeal to the voter, are they more likely to devote their energies to co-operating with each other in rebuilding the nation, or to intensifying old feuds?

So far as party and personal politics are concerned, as in other matters as well, the Indonesian Revolution seems to have made almost a 360-degree swing since 1945. The new Republic started off with a single party in which all leaders of all political hues were thrown together to devise revolutionary strategy. These were for the most part the top leaders of the minute Indonesian intelligentsia, men and women who had gone to school together, intermarried into each other's families, been in and out of political troubles or prison together during the Dutch and Japanese periods, and developed deep personal friendships --and animosities. In a matter of months they had broken up into bitterly feuding political cliques which soon headed diverging political parties. They periodically patched up their differences sufficiently to fight the Revolution against the Dutch, then fell out more bitterly than before, once independence had been achieved. The postindependence period has been one of unremitting and unrestrained political quarreling, not always so much over basic principles as over personal prerogative, often conducted with an urbane show of personal compatibility, most of it intensified by intimate knowledge of each other's personalities and proclivities. Bung Karno's long-standing plan to dissolve the parties and to bring the politicians together into one happy, co-operating, nonpartisan family--excluding, of course, the many who have fallen completely into disfavor--seems to leave out of account at least one crucial factor, namely, that the Indonesian politician who is still active often tends to be a little Bung Karno, much less interested in national development than in political manipulation.

5. <u>Mass action movements</u>. The intention of Bung Karno, which was becoming apparent even before the announced <u>konsepsi</u> of 1957, is to substitute for numerous, feuding political parties a national revolutionary mass action movement, nonpartisan--or rather suprapartisan--in sponsorship, ultranationalistic in objective, authoritarian in leadership. Mass movements, of course, are no new thing to Indonesia, but the recurring celebrations, parades, demonstrations, and conferences of recent years had been, on the whole, uncoordinated, or co-ordinated largely under Left-wing or Communist leaders, among whom, of course, were members of the Group of '45. Bung Karno's recent intention has been to mobilize this vast but scattered potential for government purposes, including that of overawing the recalcitrant political parties.

The attempt to create a new revolutionary mass action movement has passed through various overlapping phases in the last several years. While the developments discussed below were not strictly distinct or consecutive, the main phases may be distinguished as follows:

First was the phase of "simultaneous" demonstrations at the time of Bung Karno's <u>konsepsi</u>. This was a continuation of the well-established tradition of "spontaneous" demonstrations to "fight for peace," to demand the "return" of West Irian, to denounce "Dutch conspiracy," British-French intervention in Egypt, and Western military pacts. All these motifs, incidentally, got into the pro-<u>konsepsi</u> show. The prime mover behind many of these 1957 demonstrations was Chairul Saleh,[6] youth leader and Sukarno kidnapper in 1945, Left-wing conspirator, prisoner and exile for some years thereafter, newly returned to Indonesia in late 1956 to become leader of the Group of '45 and Sukarno's confidant. The main participants were labor, youth and veterans' groups.

Second was the phase of openly government-sponsored mass action. Such action got well under way in early 1957 when Chairul Saleh became Minister for Veterans' Affairs and a Left-wing journalist, Hanafi, became Minister for Mobilization of the People's Potential. Saleh and Hanafi became constant companions of Sukarno, and wherever the three of them showed up, there one could confidently predict mass demonstrations in support of Sukarno and in opposition to all "reactionary" elements such as the provincial rebels and their "imperialist supporters," including, naturally, the Dutch in New Guinea.

Third was the phase of wavering government support for mass movements, in the face of the obvious threat that the demonstrators might get completely out of hand. Chairul Saleh and Hanafi had already run into strong criticism by late 1957 for permitting Left-wing and Communist infiltration

---

6 See pages 7 and 8 <u>Bung Karno's Konsepsi</u> (WAH-3-'57), an AUFS publication.

and manipulation of the mass movement. In mid-1958 the Ministry of Veterans' Affairs was to be reorganized; the Ministry for the Mobilization of the People's Potential then was to be abolished, and Hanafi assigned primarily to the job of organizing receptions for state guests. But meanwhile the West Irian campaign had been stepped up greatly. When the United Nations declined to act on the case and the Dutch refused to yield, Sukarno resorted to the "other way" he had earlier threatened: he called for expulsion of Dutch residents and the nationalization of Dutch enterprises in Indonesia. The revolutionary mass action groups responded so swiftly and enthusiastically that the military had to move fast to establish a semblance of order and legality in the "spontaneous" take-over by labor, youth, and veterans groups of Dutch properties.

Fourth (1958 to the present) was the phase of greatly increased military control and sponsorship of mass action movements. By early 1958 the Government had two separate mass action programs on its hands, each commanding the presumed adherence of a bewildering lot of formal, informal, and semi-formal organizations which tended to overlap and compete in leadership, membership, and goals, and, in any event, to be dominated by the Left Wing. First was the New Life Movement, launched August 17, 1957, by unco-ordinated government agencies with rather vague objectives of national regeneration. Second was the "National Front for Recovery of West Irian," formally inaugurated by the military on February 13, 1958, to develop still another " new approach" to the same old objective.

The New Life Movement had involved such basically unpopular features as community work projects to build roads, bridges, and administrative centers. Despite the example set by Bung Karno and other notables in performing an hour or two of voluntary manual labor repairing the roads and sweeping out the markets, the movement failed to catch on, "chiefly," according to official report, "due to the cynicism of some parties and the intellectuals." The New Life Movement also involved such rather more popular efforts as crusades to ban rock 'n' roll, Western-style dancing, cowboy films, and the hoola hoop, with varying degrees of success. Even these, however, were not sufficient to keep the movement from almost fizzling out. Meanwhile, the West Irian drive had both failed and all but got out of hand. The Government proposed, therefore, to graft the moral uplift of the New Life Movement to the emotional intensity of the West Irian drive, to put the new movement under direct military supervision, and to rally mass enthusiasm for national reconstruction as the new method of asserting Indonesia's "national claim."

The local leaders of the new National Front for Recovery of West Irian --in each instance the regional military commander and his deputies--are more or less busily at work, therefore, promoting and co-ordinating more and bigger organizations of youth, labor, peasants, veterans, women, intellectuals, artists, soldiers, and other "regional" and "functional" groups. They are encountering some serious problems of organization and co-ordination, since such groups tend by nature in Indonesia to be amorphous, transitory, and

susceptible to the blandishments of the Left--including military officers of
Leftist sympathies. The leaders are also discovering that it is rather difficult to maintain revolutionary ardor for liberation of New Guinea when they
let it be almost explicitly understood that they do not propose to launch expedi-
tionary forces of heroic youth but instead, perhaps, to organize "voluntary"
labor batallions. They are discovering that the still vaguely-defined and all-
inclusive objectives of the National Front for Recovery of West Irian seem
little different from the proposed objectives of a new and distinct "National
Front" which Bung Karno proposes to set up to support his "Guided Democracy"
and "Guided Economy." They are discovering, further, that Bung Karno himself advises against the diversion of effort on the part of the National Front
for the Liberation of West Irian to general reconstruction programs. "Do not
let it deal with other things which do not directly concern the struggle for
West Irian, for instance shipbuilding and shipping concerns. . .," he said in
his Merdeka Day address last month. "The National Front for the Liberation
of West Irian must concentrate its effort upon arousing and stirring the
masses for the struggle for West Irian!"

Whatever the confusion as to organization, objectives, and leadership of
mass movements in Indonesia today, the mass movement psychology has certainly taken a new hold and the number of individuals and groups experienced
in the techniques of manipulating mass action have certainly increased. The
official objectives of national regeneration and acquisition of West Irian
remain vague in definition and remote in achievement, but specific grievances
are at hand, individual leaders are ready, and action groups might unexpectedly
be mobilized not to support government demands but to make demands upon the
government. In the city of Djakarta, for instance, there are approximately
100,000 trishaw riders, most of them young, tough, and impoverished, also
excitable and mobile; and if once rallied and aroused, extremely difficult to
cope with.

6. The national councils. Since early 1957, opposition to his konsepsi
notwithstanding, Bung Karno has made repeated moves to implement one of its
major provisions--the formation of an appointive supreme state council. On
July 12, 1957, accordingly, he swore in the 41 members of a National Council
to which Parliament later, with some little prompting, gave de facto constitu-
tional status by the not atypical parliamentary device of refraining from
recognition of the Council itself but accepting its budget. The Council was
made up of representatives of "functional groups," i.e. trade unions, youth
movements, intelligentsia, religious leaders, peasants, journalists, women's
organizations, artists, veterans, businessmen, and foreign-born citizens.
The representation was so arranged as to give regional as well as "functional
group" distribution.

The members of the Council met repeatedly in the course of the next
year and, according to its official report, "deliberated and advised" upon such
matters as: the New Life Movement, Questions of National Security and

Alertness, Culture, the Chinese Minority Problem, Current and Foreign Affairs, and the Asian Games. Meanwhile, to supplement the deliberations of the National Council, Bung Karno convoked also a "National Conference," a "National Construction Conference," also military conferences between the General Staff and the regional commanders, and various other conferences --regional, military, civil, and all combined.

Despite the formation of the National Council and quite a few others besides, and despite the total amount of guidance received, the national situation continued to deteriorate dangerously. A prime provision of Bung Karno's 1959 formula is the reconstitution, expansion, and reduplication of the council system. As a result of his "Return to the Constitution of 1945" program, Bung Karno has now not just one National Council but two, with the national Parliament in a fair way of being transformed into a third by reason of addition of "regional and functional groups." The new Provisional Advisory Supreme Council has 44 members; the new National Planning Council has 74; and the new Council of People's Representatives (Parliament) will have a yet undisclosed number of new appointive members. The new Supreme Council is constituted along exactly the same lines as the earlier National Council, with most of the same members; it is chairmanned by Bung Karno himself; it considers only such topics as the Chairman places before it; its guidance is not formalized by summarized consensus or by vote, and is not binding upon the President or the Cabinet. The members of the Councils are on notice that just as they are appointed by the President, they are subject to removal at his discretion.

Since the technique and the philosophy of these Councils is a bit difficult for the Westerner to grasp, they are perhaps best described by Bung Karno himself, who explains how all is in conformity with the "true, original Indonesian democracy":

"How was democracy of former times in Indonesia? It still is practiced in the villages in Java, Minangkabau, Sulawesi, Lombok, Bali, and other places, namely in their laws and system of 'Musjawarah' and 'Mufakat' ['discussion' and 'agreement']. Every village, dusun, and nagari practices democracy. But do they in these village meetings apply the practice of voting? Of free-fight liberalism where half plus one always is right? No, my friends, the musjawarah is held under the guidance of the Lurah, the Chief of the Elders, or Nini Mamak, the guidance of whoever is leader. Everybody says something different until at one time a compromise is achieved out of all these different opinions, without voting. . . .There is no dictatorship in Musjawarah and Mufakat. That is why democracy with leadership is a true, original Indonesian democracy. This is one of the most important sources for us from where we can draw material to find a new, clear democracy, not American democracy, Dutch, French, British, German, or Soviet or anybody else's democracy. Let us find a democracy which is suitable for our own identity. And use sources and material which are to be found in our own country."[7]

Few will dispute Bung Karno's thesis that Indonesian democracy should be distinctively Indonesian, or that the <u>musjawarah</u> and <u>mufakat</u> principles have indeed prevailed in traditional Indonesian councils. A very great many, however, including Indonesians, will dispute his apparent conviction that the answer to Indonesia's national problems today is to be found in more and bigger councils of less and less clear-cut authority. What worked in small village councils in the old, leisurely days, when problems were local ones and delay was of relatively little importance, will not necessarily work for a huge nation whose backlog of unresolved problems is already critical, and whose prospect of mere survival as a unified nation is not reassuring. Bung Karno may indeed be on the right track in attempting to adapt democracy to Indonesian tradition; but in cases of national emergency such as this, there are worse things, perhaps, than Western-style vote-counting. Two of them, it seems even to some Indonesians, may be Eastern-style indecision and obfuscation. A third may be swift, rash, "positive" actions taken in desperation under the alleged mandate of councils which have agreed unanimously that something must be done, but haven't considered what.

*   *   *   *   *

The Indonesian political situation seems to be clarifying in two respects only, now that Bung Karno's new Government has come into office under the Constitution of '45, with promises to build a "guided democracy" and a "guided economy." For the time being at least, President Sukarno is determined upon dramatic action, and he is determined that the "exploiters" and "corruptors" shall bear the burden and the "Marhaen" receive the advantages.

Dramatic action does not necessarily mean consecutive, co-ordinated, or constructive actions, of course, and discrimination as between "exploiters" and "Marhaen" may not be easy to apply--witness the first dramatic action, on August 24, the 90 per cent devaluation of large denomination bills, which constitute approximately 47 per cent of the money in circulation and the freezing of bank accounts. The move served virtually to confiscate a good half of the cash money wealth of the nation, most of it, to be sure, inflationary, and much of it in the hands of Chinese "exploiters." The move served also virtually to wipe out the small savings of many laborers and peasants who consider, with reason, that they belong to the "Marhaen," and to confiscate a good part of the recently-acquired wealth of the "true sons of the Indonesian Revolution." It has served to bring the total value of money in circulation back to approximately the 1957 figure, but it has also almost paralyzed the business activity of the nation, for how long, remains to be seen. A series of sudden dramatic actions can spell disaster, not salvation, for the nation, unless they are carried out according to a well-considered plan and policy,

---

7 Lecture by President Soekarno before Students of the Hasanuddin University, Makasar, October 31, 1958. Min. of Information, President's Lectures Series - 1959. Special Issue 20. p. 34.

and even then they are vulnerable to sabotage from many directions. A well-considered plan and policy is exactly what the Indonesian Government has lacked for the last ten years. To patch one together in ten days or ten weeks seems a superhuman task, especially when many of the "true sons of the Revolution," who are consulting on follow-up policies, are among those hard hit by the devaluation and eager to retrieve their losses.

The fact remains, of course, that the over-all Indonesian situation has deteriorated so desperately in the last few years that any new Government, even one with a presumably assured five-year tenure, must produce quick results. Otherwise, it seems certain to encounter such a combination of resistance and apathy as will make either outright disintegration or outright totalitarianism inescapable. Results which are both quick and favorable, as Bung Karno knows from his own experience, are all but impossible to achieve in Indonesia. The credit is all the greater, therefore, if he succeeds.

Willard A. Hanna

SOUTHEAST ASIA SERIES
Vol. VII   No. 19
(Indonesia)

American Universities Field Staff   REPORTS SERVICE

BUNG KARNO'S INDONESIA

Part IV: The Economics of Incongruity

by Willard A. Hanna

September 15, 1959

This publication is one of a continuing series on current developments in world affairs written by associates of the American Universities Field Staff. It is distributed by the AUFS as a useful addition to the American fund of information on foreign affairs.

AUFS Associates have been chosen for their skill in collecting, reporting, and evaluating data. Each has combined long personal observation and experience in his foreign area with advanced studies relating to it.

WILLARD A. HANNA, the author of this report, is based in Kuala Lumpur to write about Southeast Asian affairs. Before joining the AUFS in 1954, Dr. Hanna had spent a total of more than ten years in East and Southeast Asia as a teacher, administrator, and writer.

Publications under the imprint of the American Universities Field Staff are not selected to accord with an editorial policy and do not represent the views of its membership. Responsibility for accuracy of facts and for opinions expressed in the letters and reports rests solely with the individual writers.

One gallon of gasoline, worth about US$0.15 on the international market, costs Rp. 4.24 at Djakarta filling stations, provided, that is, you can find it. Government controls have held the official retail price of gasoline, locally produced by foreign companies, at such a fantastically low level that the companies are selling at confiscatory prices, consumption is outdistancing supply, and black marketeers are making a killing at the expense not only of the foreign companies but of the Government and of the consumer.

NOTE: As this report was being prepared, there came the news that once again Indonesia's monetary and economic system is being subjected to drastic overhaul. The Indonesian Government announced on August 24 the devaluation of all Rp. 500 and Rp. 1,000 notes by 90 per cent, and the freezing of 90 per cent of all bank accounts over Rp. 25,000, thus withdrawing about 47 per cent of the currency in circulation. It has also scrapped (for the nth time) existing export-import regulations, and fixed the official exchange rate at Rp. 45. to US$1.00. Whether or not the overhaul will put the system in order--as past overhauls have not--it will at any rate introduce new variables. Price, wage, and salary figures assembled in July and quoted in this report, for instance, may no longer obtain. While some of the old incongruities may be wiped out, the immediate effect has been business paralysis.

[WAH-15-'59]

One tin of condensed milk, worth about US$0.15 on the international market, costs Rp. 45 in Djakarta. Condensed milk is a standard import item indispensible to the millions of Indonesians to whom sweet, milky coffee constitutes a social if not a dietary necessity. Indonesian government regulation of the minute local dairy industry has resulted in curtailment, not increase of production, recently estimated by the Bogor Agricultural Experiment Station as sufficient for one tablespoon per Indonesian per day. Government control over imports has run up the price of tinned milk approximately 400 per cent in the last two years, and one tin of condensed milk now costs 10 per cent of the monthly take-home pay of the average government employee, or ten days' cash wages of an estate worker. Consequently, a tin of condensed milk is a luxury item on the Indonesian market to compare, say, with a case of whiskey on the American.

The price equation that ten gallons of gasoline equals one tin of condensed milk equals ten days' cash wages of a rubber tapper typifies the upside down, inside out economy of present-day Indonesia. It may help to explain, perhaps, why Indonesia's wobbly rupiah has ricocheted lately between 100 and 150 on the black market, while the Government has maintained until very recently the fiction of a basic 11.40 to 1 exchange rate. It may help also to explain why government statistics indicate each year a favorable balance of trade, even though gold reserves have dropped farther and farther below the statutory minimum, money in circulation has skyrocketed, government budgets have plummeted deeper and deeper into the red, production has stagnated, exports and imports have got wildly out of phase, and wages and salaries have borne only the remotest relationship to actual cost of living. Or, if the equation does not exactly help to explain all that, it does help to illustrate how close

The gasoline pump itself costs about as much as 50,000 liters of gasoline at the current fixed price (about Rp. 50,000). The car is worth about 800,000 liters, and the house beyond about 1,500,000 liters.

the Indonesian economy comes today to the point of total incoherence. The real explanation, to be brief, categorical, and controversial about it, is that an economically reckless Government tinkers erratically with production, distribution, and wage and price controls as though kaleidoscopic change of regulations could produce a vibrant and viable economy.

One liter of gasoline (1/4 gallon)--the usual unit of measure--is being sold today to the privileged automobile-driving class in Indonesia for the same price as one large banana, one box of matches, one copy of a four-page newspaper, or one car-guarding-cum-parking fee to insure that your windshield wipers, hub caps, and taillights are still in place when you drive away. The black market operators, naturally, were not slow to cut themselves in on the deal. In many provincial cities and sometimes in Djakarta itself, unless you are willing to send your driver to queue up in the early morning hours or even the night before, you will have to pay at least two to three times the fixed price, and in some areas as high as 600 per cent markup. You won't, however, if by discreet exercise of influence or distribution of favors you arrange it so that you are not subject to queuing up or to rationing, or, should there still be some slip-up, to a Rp. 1,000-5,000 fine for patronizing the black market. You will then have the full-time use of your Rp. 1,200,000 Chevrolet Impala, provided, of course, you have taken the precaution of having all your papers in order, which may cost you well over half a million in various formal and informal customs arrangements.

One other bit of economic trivia. You can see the latest American film from a first-class seat in a first-class (but not air-conditioned) Djakarta theatre by purchasing a ticket for Rp. 6.50. It is generally prudent, however, to send a proxy well in advance. He should be patient enough to stand in the ticket line for one or two hours, and rugged enough to fend off strong-arm squads of black market operators. These "cross-boy" scalpers prefer to purchase blocks of tickets for themselves at the fixed price, then sell them to you outside the theatre at prices ranging from Rp. 50 to 100 for a good show on a Saturday night. Or, if you prefer food to entertainment, you can use your Rp. 6.50 to purchase one liter of medium-high quality rice, comforting yourself that although the price has risen over 200 per cent in the last two years, it is still, relatively speaking, a bargain; and your one liter, with very slight supplementation of meat, fish, and vegetables, constitutes the standard diet for two for one day. Should your larder already be well stocked but your supply of tobacco low, you have only to add one rupiah to your movie ticket money in order to buy a pack of locally manufactured Escort cigarettes. A pack of American or British cigarettes would set you back Rp. 35, but if you are really hospitable, that is what you will offer your guests. To be sure, you may not always be able to find Escorts on the market, but there seems to be no shortage of the imported brands.

The Indonesian Government, by sheer genius of mismanagement, has effectively prevented the development of the nation's vast natural resources

You can travel from
Djakarta to Bandung by
Garuda Airways for
Rp. 120, that is, if you
can get a ticket at the
official price.

and has ensnarled the nation's patient, industrious, and intelligent citizens in
a welter of bureaucratic controls or, more commonly, evasion of controls.
In all fairness, of course, the exonerating factors should be stated. The Indonesian Republic inherited an exploitative colonial system, administered by an
intricate and by no means incorruptible bureaucracy; it drifted almost inevitably toward a new variety of indigenous exploitation, rather than toward anything resembling free enterprise or, for that matter, welfare statism. The
central Government, furthermore, has been attempting to find a new economic
modus vivendi in a very short time during a very disturbed period of world
and regional history. It has suffered from an acute shortage of experienced,
competent personnel, and an equally acute shortage of basic physical facilities
--telephones, for instance, and office space. It has experienced internal unrest
that has flared at times to insurrectionist proportions and also--but to nothing
like the extent it claims--from foreign interference. Finally, the peculiar form
of the Indonesian economy is such that the frightening economic dislocations
which show up in the metropolitan centers and on the statistical reports are
not automatically indicative of imminent national collapse. The Indonesian
economy is a dual economy of a modern Westernized system superimposed
upon a subsistence agricultural system, and of delayed interaction between
them. High Indonesian Government officials--including, by reliable report,
President Sukarno, First Minister (and concurrently Finance Minister)
Djuanda, and Foreign Minister Subandrio--are of the opinion that Indonesia's
economic crisis can continue for another five to ten years without the nation

You can travel from the
airport to the downtown
area in a taxi for about
Rp. 120. Or you can
hire a trishaw for two
days for that amount,
or, if you prefer, a
horse carriage.

cracking up for economic reasons. If only the masses of the people can be provided with minimal quantities of food and clothing, which in Indonesia are indeed minimal, then the nation, they believe, will have time to pull itself together. Almost enough food is grown locally, almost enough textiles can be procured through Japanese reparations, and with a little extra increment-- say, from eagerly offered United States, USSR, and China aid--presto chango! the basic problem is solved, and the long-range problems of economic development can be undertaken at leisure.

The counter-case should be stated in no less categorical terms. The present economic chaos in Indonesia has enriched a clique of political and economic opportunists, many of them heroes of the Revolution, who are rapidly attracting to themselves as much public hatred, as "brown Dutchmen," as the worst of the colonialist Dutch ever engendered. Their leadership in Bung Karno's still extremely vague new proposals of "guided economy" are not likely to create either a healthful economy or to inspire public confidence. The central Government has profited as well as suffered from the regional and world disturbances of the last few years. Its spokesmen like to overlook the fact that the Korean War, which they condemned with much wrath, added hundreds of millions of dollars in rubber profits to the national treasury--profits which were quickly dissipated by reckless policies of importing luxury goods and subsidizing get-rich-quick local operators. The central Government has greatly intensified Indonesia's shortage of trained and competent manpower by expelling the Dutch residents and by handicapping the local Chinese, both of whom were ready and willing--at a profit, to be sure--to supply necessary know-how. It has accelerated the drop in national production by seizing Dutch- and Nationalist Chinese-owned enterprises and turning them over to inexperienced new Indonesian management. It has shown itself extremely reluctant to accept advice or assistance from the Western world--or, for that matter, the Eastern--on any scale commensurate with the need, and on any terms other than unrealistic "no-strings" cash grants and loans.

The central Government has by its own incoherent, Java-centric economic policies induced the regional opposition which led to the most serious of the regional insurrections--insisting, for instance, upon the central Government's right to the major proportion of the profits from regional exports. The central Government has exhibited a distinct preference for the easy and delusive nostrum, like confiscation of Dutch and Chinese properties, rather than for policies of new development. It may be deluding itself now with the theory that just enough food and textiles is really all that is necessary to stave off disaster. The Indonesian people, as past experience has shown, can indeed subsist on less than almost anyone else, except the Indian peasants, and remain relatively healthy and happy while doing so. For the past 15 years, however, they have been promised a better life, and for the past ten they have seen many of their own leaders conspicuously enjoying it. At present, the real question about the Indonesians' capacity to endure the unendurable seems to be not can they, but will they?

If you can get one of these houses assigned to you by the Government, your monthly rental comes to about Rp. 100.

If you can't get a government housing priority, then you will have to pay about Rp. 100 per month for a very small room in a house like this.

If you are a high official, you may live here in the formerly Dutch-owned Hotel des Indes (now Hotel Duta Indonesia) for a year or two while waiting for a house. The cost for one room for one family per day, three meals included, is about Rp. 50 per day out of your pay check, a good deal more for the government. The cost is Rp. 500 per day for a tourist couple, provided one of the dozen transient rooms is available.

Two brief case histories--neither of them, admittedly, related to "the masses"-- may help set the mood of present-day Indonesia. Case History Number One is that of Sutomo, a medium-upper level government official drawing approximately Rp. 2,000 per month in salary and allowances, after taxes and pension deductions. At the 30-1 "tourist" rate of exchange, this is about US$66, between US$15 and $25 at the fluctuating black market rate. Sutomo and his wife and two children live in one room of a government-run hostel, so his office withholds Rp. 1,400 of this sum for room and board. The accommodations, incidentally, are not merely crowded but dilapidated, the food is bad, and even at that the Rp. 1,400 falls far short of paying the real cost to the Government. Sutumo's take-home pay is Rp. 600 per month; but since he has certain privileges, such as cost-free use of a government car, Rp. 600 goes a bit farther than might be expected. It is less than half enough, however, for him to purchase a new Arrow shirt, and a good white shirt is virtually obligatory at the diplomatic receptions which he is invited to attend. It is a bit more than enough to buy his wife one medium-quality batik sarong, but not half enough for one of the handsome hand-processed batiks which the ladies all prefer. It is sufficient for one pack of locally manufactured cigarettes per day (Rp. 225), plus a couple of small bananas per person each day (Rp. 100) to supplement the dreary hostel diet, plus, by careful selection, one meal for four at an inexpensive Chinese restaurant to reciprocate hospitality. Sutomo, it happens, has served abroad, and has developed an extravagant and unorthodox taste for an occasional Scotch and soda. Unless he depends exclusively upon the cocktail circuit supply, he will only briefly consider buying a bottle--at Rp. 650. He has brought home from abroad a record player. Now he has the choice of buying one new LP recording at Rp. 600, or selling off the record player and record library for something like Rp. 10,000. Since costs of tuition and clothing for the children must be paid, his choice is clear. But next time it will not be so easy, for it is his watch and camera that will have to go.

Case History Number Two is that of Mohammad, the driver for one of Indonesia's new "national capitalists." His employer, operating on purely political security, has floated a series of government loans totalling quite a few millions of rupiahs and has acquired, in addition to a house and a car, a small textile factory which is now virtually closed down for lack of imported yarns to manufacture into undershirts. Mohammad earns Rp. 450 per month as a driver, working from about 7:00 a.m. to 2:00 p.m. He has a wife and three children, and his basic outlay for rice each month is Rp. 450. Therefore, Mohammad has taken a second job and now earns an additional Rp. 250 per month as night watchman at the home of a wealthy Chinese. The Rp. 250 is a little more than sufficient to keep him in cigarettes. It allows also for an occasional glass of iced cocoa-nut milk when the heat of the day is particularly oppressive, as he waits in the car outside the government buildings while his employer makes the rounds each day seeking new allocations of yarn to reopen his factory. Mohammad worries that he may sleep too soundly at night and waken to find not only that his Chinese employer has been robbed but that his own irreplaceable clothing has been stealthily removed without rousing him. He worries also that he may drop off to sleep at the wheel and smash up his Indonesian employer's Mercedes--second-hand resale value: Rp. 1,000,000.

These boys sell local cigarettes at Rp. 7.50 per pack. It costs each boy Rp. 7.50 per day to meet his mini-mal living expenses.

"Don't ask me how we get by!" Indonesian after Indonesian replied, when I expressed bewilderment at the economics of present-day family budgeting in Indonesia. "We do, that's all. Maybe we sell something we managed to get hold of at a cheap official price a few years ago and don't absolutely need right now. Maybe we have generous relatives or friends who are in solid enough with the Government that they can make a quick million or two by getting and selling an import license. Maybe we turn a little corrupt and pick up extra money where we can get it."

Defying the laws of economic gravity is the practiced accomplishment not only of the individual Indonesian but of any business concern that remains in business, and, for that matter, of the Government as well. The cases of rubber export and of the national trade and budget figures are both illustrative and interrelated.

Rubber is Indonesia's most important export. It accounts for approximately 35 per cent by value of all of Indonesia's export products. (Oil stands now at about 33 per cent; tin ranks third, at 6 per cent.) It accounts also, as will presently appear, for an extremely important segment of government revenue. Indonesia's officially controlled and reported export of natural rubber, which constitutes about one third of the world's total, used to approximate 700,000 tons annually. The officially reported export value over the last few years has been in the neighborhood of Rp. 4 billion.

But the real picture of the Indonesian rubber industry is more accurately presented by moving from officially reported statistics to unofficially admitted facts. Fact A: Indonesia's 700,000 tons of officially exported rubber has been worth at least three to four times the official Rp. 4 billion figure, and the Indonesian Government, not the producer, has pocketed most of the difference in good hard foreign currency. Fact B: Indonesia's 700,000 annual tons of rubber export does not include an estimated average of at least 150,000 tons smuggled to Singapore or Malaya, often with the connivance of local officials, the motivation for the brisk smuggling trade being apparent in Fact A. Fact C: Indonesia's rubber production is falling off (down 7.5 to 15 per cent since the peak Korean War boom year of 1951) at a time when world production, demand, and prices are rising, and energetic Malaya next door has now displaced Indonesia as the world's biggest producer. Fact D: Both the big rubber estates and the small-holders, producing about 40 per cent and 60 per cent respectively of the Indonesian total, are increasingly frustrated as a result of bad management, superannuated plantings, and Government bungle in making available essential materials and equipment, also in maintaining communications and security.

The situation of a typical Sumatran small-holder is educational. He is industriously overtapping overage trees and home-processing the latex by antiquated methods with insufficient chemicals and inadequate equipment. Every kilogram of rubber which he manages to produce will bring something between Rp. 20 and 30 on the local government-controlled market--just barely enough to repay his effort. On the Singapore market, it will bring about M$2.00 which is easily convertible, with a little know-how, into Rp. 75 to 100 or better. A good fast boat can make the journey to Singapore in one night, and there are Indonesian military personnel, loyalist or rebel, who are willing to share the risk for a share in the profits. Consequently, the Sumatran small-holder, if he can manage it, does just what almost anyone else would do too.

The situation of the big estate operator is equally educational. The big estates in the Medan area, those of American Goodyear included, find rubber production these days yielding not the 25 per cent annual profit which is standard in Malaya but financial loss, plus occupational hazard and frustration. They cannot replant their old low-yield estates with new, high-yield stock, for any land which is cleared for replanting is likely to be occupied overnight by squatters and there is no way to get squatters off except to buy them out at

greatly inflated prices. They cannot tap all sections of the estate each morning, because terrorist activities close off first one area, then another, and that
unpredictably. They cannot count upon getting their produce regularly to
market, because illegal tapping, theft of rubber in process of curing, and
hijacking of shipments all interfere with systematic scheduling. The neighbor-
ing Dutch estates have been taken over by the Government for operation by
relatively inexperienced Indonesian managers. Various other European
estates have been seriously interfered with. Furthermore, loyalist and rebel
troops are fighting a little hit-and-run war in the area, and estate personnel
get hit and put on the run in consequence.

          The miracle is that rubber production holds up as well as it does.
Another miracle is that the Government still manages to get hold of the major
share of the foreign exchange profit from rubber and other exports. Still
another is that the Government continues to turn in a virtuoso display of financial sleight-of-hand. It would take a team of international accountants, experienced in all known techniques of bookkeeping, accurately to analyze the Indonesian economic situation today. Has Indonesia long since passed the point
of irretrievable bankruptcy, as is likely to be the snap judgment of a Western
visitor? Or is it the still basically healthy victim of an attempt to apply
inappropriate Western concepts to a non-Western system, as is the opinion of
a good many Indonesian observers, some of them well acquainted both with
the highly theoretical European economics, and with the deeply involved
extralegal maneuvering that actually keeps Indonesia's own economy running?
The Rp. 4 billion rubber statistic, when placed in juxtaposition to certain other
key figures, may serve, with a little explanation, not so much to clarify the
situation as to indicate why clarification is virtually impossible.

          The Rp. 4 billion in rubber exports is counterbalanced, for bookkeeping
purposes, by an average annual import of consumer goods valued at about the
same amount. Of these consumer goods, about half by value are rated as
"absolutely essential" commodities, mostly rice, wheat flour, and textiles.
Just as the value of the rubber exports is calculated at a completely artificial
exchange rate, so the value of "absolutely essential" imports is calculated at
the same exchange rate--or one not very much higher. The correlation up to
this point, therefore, is real and accurate. The rubber producer is paid an
artifically low official price for his product; the licensed importer is permitted to buy foreign exchange for "essential commodities" at an artificially low
rate in rupiahs; and the commodities themselves, once they come on the
market, are retailed at artificially low prices--that is, if price controls
actually work, as frequently they don't.

          The value of the other half of the consumer goods imports, however,
especially those items classified as "luxuries," is calculated according to a
highly variable exchange rate that goes up to 175 per cent of the official rate.
Furthermore, for the necessary licenses the importer must pay another
100-300 per cent in various complicated surcharges. The correlation between

PRICE INDEX FIGURES FOR A NUMBER OF ARTICLES
IN THE RETAIL TRADE

DECEMBER 1958
1953 = 100
APRIL 1959
(FIRST WEEK)

CIGARETTES   208 286
MATCHES   364 436

SUNLIGHT SOAP 239
              285
MACARONI   203
              258
SALT   164
              167
EGGS   218
              357
SUGAR   190
              237
RICE   288
              393

TEA   620
                    624
CONDENSED MILK   441
                    595
TINNED MEAT/
FISH ETC.   153
                    291
RED PEPPER   192
                    351
RAZOR BLADES   512
                    549
BEER   324
                    338

POTATOES   200 278
PEANUTS   264 282
FLOUR   385 572

ECON/2P/59
13-4-1959

Djakarta housewives who patronize basic supplies stalls such as this have
to adjust their budgets to the constantly rising price indexes alongside.

most export-import values, therefore, becomes a job for UNIVAC, and inter-
pretive reading of Indonesian balance of trade figures calls for application of
equal parts of skepticism, intuition, and astrology.

What seems to happen is that for about one half the foreign exchange
proceeds of rubber the Government can import and distribute at controlled
low prices the nation's minimum requirements in food and clothing. This
seems to be the underlying reason for Indonesian official sanguineness that
the national economic crisis is in fact a tempest in an imported teapot (price,
Rp. 250), and that the ordinary Indonesian can go on happily drinking his home-
grown tea (about Rp. 20 per pound for poor quality), sipped from a locally
manufactured drinking glass (Rp. 2), confident that he can afford his other
basic necessities of half a liter of rice per day (Rp. 3.25) and a few yards of
textiles per year (about Rp. 500-1,000). What also seems to happen is that
with the other half of the foreign exchange proceeds from rubber, plus foreign
exchange proceeds from other exports, plus rupiah revenues from local taxa-
tion, plus quite a lot of foreign aid, the Government can somehow manage to
keep the Westernized and governmental sector of the economy stumbling along.

In the process of keeping the modernized section of the economy functioning, the Government relies, of course, to a very great extent upon a handsome and well-equipped engraving plant. It managed in 1957 to increase the
currency supply from Rp. 9 to 14 billion, in 1958 from Rp. 14 to 20 billion.
In 1959, just in case the presses slow down for shortage of paper, ink, or electricity, and the recent devaluation of some Rp. 8 billion or more, plus the
freezing of huge sums in bank accounts does not check inflation, the plant is
prepared to issue beautifully designed new Rp. 5,000 notes to supplement the
Rp. 1,000 denomination which has until now been the largest. The Government
has managed also to run up a budget deficit of Rp. 2.2 billion in 1956, Rp. 5.8
billion in 1957, and Rp. 12 billion in 1958. The estimated total budget for 1959
is Rp. 30 billion; the estimated deficit is Rp. 12 billion. Each figure seems
likely to turn out to be an underestimate. A deficit of Rp. 18 million was
widely anticipated before the recent economic "reforms" which may or may
not improve matters. Rp. 18 billion, to backtrack, is a rough approximation
of the actual value in rupiahs of Indonesia's exports at 1959 prices. Furthermore, Rp. 18 billion is just one billion more than the latest revised estimate
(17 billion) of 1958 defense expenditures, which were earlier reported at
approximately Rp. 4 billion. Either way, the value of rubber exports seems
almost exactly to offset the expenses involved in trying to achieve internal
security.

The fundamental economic problem in Indonesia is not one of shortage
of resources or even over-all excess of population, as tends to be the case in
other areas of acute economic maladjustment. Rather, it is the refusal to date
of the Government not merely to encourage but even to permit new economic
development on any truly significant scale, and its obsession with imposing
new controls on top of the old. It is understandable, therefore, that the rupiah

is one of the world's spectacularly soft currencies, and that the correlation between values, prices, wages, and government expenditures is one of economic madness. New Government measures, under the yet undefined "guided economy" program, but starting with 90 per cent devaluation of that half of the nation's currency which is in large notes, seems symptomatic once again of a fixation with confiscation and control rather than development, and of a new rash of economic incongruities. So long as for the cost of one automobile you can buy enough gasoline to drive it four to six million miles, and so long as for little more than the proceeds from the sale of one to two kilograms of rubber on the international market you can supply the basic one-month pay of a new Army recruit (Rp. 139, plus up to 100 per cent in allowances), Indonesia's economic snarl-up seems unlikely to unsnarl itself.

Willard A. Hanna

[Photographs on page 4, courtesy of Ministry of Information, Djakarta.]

SOUTHEAST ASIA SERIES
Vol. VII   No. 20
(Indonesia)

American Universities Field Staff   REPORTS SERVICE

BUNG KARNO'S INDONESIA

Part V: The Indecision of the Military

by Willard A. Hanna

September 25, 1959

This publication is one of a continuing series on current developments in world affairs written by associates of the American Universities Field Staff. It is distributed by the AUFS as a useful addition to the American fund of information on foreign affairs.

AUFS Associates have been chosen for their skill in collecting, reporting, and evaluating data. Each has combined long personal observation and experience in his foreign area with advanced studies relating to it.

WILLARD A. HANNA, the author of this report, is based in Kuala Lumpur to write about Southeast Asian affairs. Before joining the AUFS in 1954, Dr. Hanna had spent a total of more than ten years in East and Southeast Asia as a teacher, administrator, and writer.

Publications under the imprint of the American Universities Field Staff are not selected to accord with an editorial policy and do not represent the views of its membership. Responsibility for accuracy of facts and for opinions expressed in the letters and reports rests solely with the individual writers.

The military, or at any rate the Army, represents Indonesia's best hope for putting its disorderly house in order. Such is the opinion of many observers, Indonesian and foreign alike. The Army, they argue, is moving in, not as swiftly or as openly as in Burma or Pakistan, but just as surely. It is officered by vigorous young men of the type the nation requires for effective national leadership; it is both ready and able to establish firm over-all control; it is determined to clean up the mess created by incompetent, corrupt, and feuding politicians; it is equally determined to muzzle the Communists; it is merely waiting its time to impose much needed discipline upon an indisciplinary nation. The upshot may one day very soon be a military dictatorship, with or without Sukarno as a figurehead President, but at any rate with a form of government that will be relatively efficient and benign as compared with any of the apparent alternatives. The military, they conclude, whatever its shortcomings and whatever the long-term incompatibility between a military regime and a free society, deserves the moral support of the Indonesian people and the material support of nations interested in promoting regional stability.

This line of reasoning--which, it should be pointed out, its adherents advocate more commonly in part than in toto--is especially attractive since

[WAH-16-'59]

it is one of the very few which holds out much hope for improvement in the desperately deteriorating Indonesian situation. There are many evidences that can be brought forward to support it. To offset almost every favorable factor, however, there is counterbalancing evidence against it. The military services, it can be equally well argued, are divided, indecisive, corrupt, Communist-infiltrated, and mutinous.

The ultimate evaluation, obviously, will be made by future historians. Meanwhile, a truly informed forecast would require thorough familiarity with Indonesia's Army (200,000 men), its Navy (10,000), its Air Force (10,000), and its Police Force (100,000); with all of the top officers, all of the top defectors, the history of the military establishment and its obscure and controversial role in all of the recent crises that have rocked the nation--a familiarity which no foreigner I know of possesses and which I for my part can make only the slightest claim to.

My intention in this brief report is to offer some evidence, of both a specific and general nature, with reference primarily to the Army which is by far the largest and most important service, in support of my own admittedly rash conclusions. In my personal opinion, the Indonesian military, most specifically the Army as presently constituted, represents no more hopeful a factor for national stability than do the politicians. It has already, indeed, proved responsible for far more than its share of disappointed expectations, and it has already passed up what would seem like the best possible opportunity for effective reform, namely, the late 1958 period when the rebel insurrections were apparently smashed, the nation was awaiting and even inviting a dramatic new departure, and the political leaders, including Bung Karno, were foundering.

The quality and unity of military leadership. Any military regime to prove effective obviously requires high-caliber officers who are capable of co-operative effort. The Indonesian Army, in recent years, has produced a clique of young officers who are extremely impressive as individuals but who have wasted themselves in a series of personal feuds and failures. To this statement it is necessary to add one important qualification: operations against the rebels were well conceived, well conducted and well co-ordinated. The fact remains, however, that the over-all Army performance--which helped to precipitate the insurrections in the first place--has not been one to inspire confidence in the effectiveness and unity of military leadership: witness, the situation within both rebel and loyalist officer ranks.

Of the rebel military leaders, the most important have been Colonel Simbolon, Colonel Kawilarang, Colonel Warouw, Lt. Colonel Hussein, and Colonel Sumual, with Colonel Zulkifli Lubis hovering in the wings.[1] Each of

---

1 See Coups, "Smuggles," Demonstrations, and Korupsi (WAH-1-'57) and Challenges to Central Government in Indonesia (WAH-2-'57), AUFS publications.

the six is undoubtedly a man of extraordinary personal competence and attainment. It should be noted that each of them organized effective guerrilla resistance to the Dutch with so little in the way of supplies, equipment, or logistical support that resistance might have appeared impossible; that each of them has doubled or tripled as troops commander, regional administrator, and public speaker and organizer; and further, a point particularly impressive to Americans, that each of them speaks at least three languages fluently (Indonesian, Dutch, and English), and generally a couple more, that they are widely read in the international literature of politics, economics, world affairs, and military science, and that far from being narrowly military-minded, they are highly sophisticated and cosmopolitan in their interests. Of the six, Colonel Lubis generally impressed foreign observers as being brilliant but fanatical; Colonels Simbolon and Kawilarang they regarded as being among the half dozen or so most energetic and competent of the nation's top leaders; Colonels Warouw, Sumual, and Hussein, less well known, were believed to be definitely on their way to the top. Nevertheless, all six of them became involved in an intricate series of plays for power; then in open insurrections against the Djakarta Command; then in the dismal military show of rebel resistance to loyalist operations; and, both then and now, if rumor is to be credited, in considerable bickering among themselves. Five years ago, if anyone had asked who was the most probable candidate for heading an Indonesian military regime, assuming one is ever to be established, the most common answers would have been either Colonel Simbolon or Colonel Kawilarang, each of whom today seems not only to have disqualified himself from the running but to have announced his opposition to any military regime at all.

The most frequently named candidate today is Lt. General Abdul Haris Nasution, Minister of Defense, Chief of Staff, and reputedly the "strong man" of the nation. The question whether General Nasution, a man of drive and personality comparable to that of Simbolon or Kawilarang, can provide a leadership which, in the context of loyalty rather than rebellion, is any more likely to succeed, can best be approached perhaps by a brief résumé of his career to date.

General Nasution is a Sumatran from Tapanuli, aged forty-one, trained as a military officer in prewar years by the Dutch and during World War II by the Japanese. He was one of the early heroes of the Indonesian revolutionary fighting and then became especially famous for his leadership in putting down the Madiun Communist Rebellion of 1948. He emerged in 1949 as the first Army Chief of Staff of the newly-recognized Republic. He became identified at that point with an unpopular Dutch-advised movement to enforce training, discipline, and loyalty upon the hodgepodge of jungle guerrillas, youthful volunteers, and ex-colonial troops who constituted the new Republican Army. He became identified also with the "Right-wing" movement to limit the powers of the feuding Members of Parliament and to strengthen the central Government. Subsequent to the October 17, 1952 Incident, in which an Army clique, with the support of mass demonstrators, attempted to dissolve Parliament and to force Bung Karno to call for new elections, Nasution resigned as Chief of Staff. He returned to that post in October 1955, a Masjumi-backed appointee. He was assigned the priority task of bringing order and discipline into an Army Headquarters that had just been badly torn by a sort of passive preliminary preview of the 1957-58 regional insurrections, on the part of anti-Communist officers: namely, the June 27, 1955 Incident when Headquarters officers, led by Colonel Lubis, then Acting Deputy Chief of Staff, boycotted the installation as Chief of Staff of a Left-wing political appointee. Nasution succeeded in establishing a tenuous balance of power in the Headquarters, while he himself moved closer and closer to Bung Karno. He advocated Bung Karno's acceptance of greater responsibility in government; also, apparently, he accepted Bung Karno's thesis that the Communists must be given their proportionate share of Cabinet portfolios. Nasution seemed rather uncertainly poised between Right and Left.

In late 1956 and throughout 1957, Nasution encountered increasingly powerful opposition within the military establishment itself. He was accused of aggrandizing his personal position, of identifying himself uncritically with Bung Karno's causes, of reducing the influence within the Army of the Masjumi and the Socialist parties, of enhancing that of the Nationalists, and of at least tolerating the growing influence of the PKI. Insubordination smouldered for months and then flared. Deputy Chief of Staff Colonel Lubis, in mid-November 1956, with the promised but not forthcoming support of many other officers, attempted to depose Nasution. The coup failed, Colonel Lubis vanished, and dozens of high Army officers were placed under arrest, where many of them still remain, if they have not been relegated to inconsequential duties or encouraged to resign. Then came the series of 1956-57 insurrections when virtually every regional military commander outside of Java renounced Nasution's authority and demanded thorough-going reforms within the central Government. During the period March-June 1958, however, General Nasution and the central Government successfully reasserted their authority and reoccupied most of the rebel strongholds.

General Nasution's position, it seems, should be stronger today than a year or two years ago. Nevertheless, the fact is that guerrilla warfare continues, Headquarters intrigue continues, and regional commands continue to claim semiautonomous powers. Recent efforts on the part of General Nasution greatly to reinforce the concentration of military forces in the Djakarta area for a show of force during the continuing political and economic crisis have been met, according to informed report, with effective obstruction both in central and regional headquarters. General Nasution seems at times less to command or consult than to negotiate with his subordinates.

As a person, General Nasution is youthful and vigorous, handsome, animated, and proud. Extremely photogenic, he is always smartly uniformed, even his favorite green fatigues featuring fit, press, and style. He is endlessly energetic, whether in traveling about among his troubled commands, or in

holding innumerable conferences, or in playing tennis--his one relaxation.
He creates at first the impression of being both unassuming and retiring, for
he is particularly adroit at dodging Djakarta's onorous social life and at keeping to a minimum such other troublesome chores as press conferences and
nonmilitary ceremonies. Nevertheless, he is proud to the point of arrogance,
demanding and exacting almost subservient agreement from those who surround him, resenting any reminders of the reversals and insubordinations
that have marked his own past career and the past careers of many of his
staff. He is possessed of many of the personal attributes of Sukarno, and
seems in the numerous military ceremonials at which he officiates to be deliberately cultivating Bung Karno's oratorical fluency and fervor, and Bung
Karno's appetite for applause and adulation. He exhibits also Bung Karno's
flair for leaving crucial problems permanently unresolved, one of the most
crucial being whether he does or does not exercise paramount control within
his own Headquarters, which has been repeatedly aroused to rebellion and then
purged. Now, to all outward appearances, it is no more solid a monolith than
in the past.

        The degree and effect of military participation in civil administration.
The Indonesian military force is now possessed of nation-wide powers which
come close to being totalitarian. As yet, however, it does not exercise these
powers either fully or consistently. It has acquired its special powers, first,
by gradual increment over the last few years, as a result largely of default
on the part of other agencies, and arrogation to themselves of new authority on
the part of the regional military commanders; second, by the declaration of a
State of War in early 1957 and consequent promulgation of martial law; and
third, by assignment to the military of special emergency powers necessary
to conduct operations against the insurrectionists and then to administer the
"liberated areas." Succession of the military to a position of potential over-
all control in civil administration has thus been in part deliberate, in part
accidental, and in all cases inconclusive. Just as the insurrectionists in
Sumatra and elsewhere preferred to share authority and responsibility--each
of the groups setting up joint military-civilian councils as the presumed
governing bodies--so the Djakarta Headquarters prefers, apparently, the
present system of a Presidential Cabinet on which the military is conspicuously
but not exclusively represented. The fact that the military has for several
years been able in theory at least to do practically anything it liked, but has
either restrained itself or has been restrained, may not indicate that outright
military dictatorship is now unlikely. It does seem to indicate, however, that
the military itself is dubious as to either the possibility or the desirability
of assuming outright control.

        The emerging pattern of administration in Indonesia is an extremely
curious one, with parallel civil and military regimes often overlapping each
other's authority, often conflicting, seldom co-ordinating, and each apparently
content to let the situation continue that way. President Sukarno has reiterated
again and again in his recent speeches that Indonesia is afflicted by an excess

of "dualisms"--"between the government and the leadership of the Revolution," between "a just and prosperous society or a capitalist society," ". . .of 'the Revolution is over' or 'the Revolution is not yet completed,'" "in. . .democracy for the People, or the People for democracy." He refers at times also to the dualism between central and regional administrations, but he does not even mention two dualisms which seem most conspicuous of all: a dualism of central administration, whereby the military headquarters governs by decree at the same time that the President and the Prime Minister do so too, occasionally, it seems, without advance notification to each other; and dualism of regional administration, in which the military commander quite commonly usurps functions which the central and the regional administrators are either ignoring or disputing, and then, as often as not, gives a part of them up again.

These dualisms, which apparently escape Bung Karno's attention but not that of the general public, show up in Djakarta, for instance, when it is the President who decrees that Rp. 1,000 and Rp. 500 notes are devaluated by 90 per cent, but the military which decrees that speculative trading in such notes is illegal. They show up when the military decrees that foreigners need police passes in order to travel about Indonesia, but civilian officials and even some police officials apparently know nothing more about it than what they read in the papers. They show up when the Ministry of Communications presumably controls all shipping, but the military decides where the ships will go, what cargo they will carry, and what passengers will be accepted. They show up also when the military arrests the Acting Attorney General, as it did on September 10 last. In this instance, at least, the dualism did come to Bung Karno's attention, since the now ex-Acting Attorney General is a Bung Karno man.

Dualism shows up most vividly, however, in the remoter provinces, especially the small islands where life is simpler and contrast accordingly sharper, as, for instance, in the small islands of the Moluccas. The central Government is still presumably responsible for such essential matters as collection and shipment of copra, and import and distribution of rice, and it still maintains functionaries who go through many of the same old motions as before. It is the military command, however, which actually collects a large part of the copra for itself, markets the copra for its own profit, takes delivery on much of the rice which is actually imported, and distributes it at its own discretion. To be sure, the military virtually controls what shipping is available--and since there may not be a ship in port for months at a time, the military is therefore in a position to dictate import-export priorities. But it is not exclusively involved. Residual functions still attach to the civil administration, and major operational functions still attach exactly where they did before--to the local Chinese entrepreneurs who actually handle the copra and the rice, splitting the profits not only with the military but with civilian officials, and chartering space on military-controlled vessels to transport merchandise and passengers, for which they are obliged to pay perhaps a 100 to 200 per cent mark-up over the official tariff.

What is emerging in Indonesia may be a new form of government-military-private enterprise co-operation, half voluntary, half reluctant, but neither efficient nor clear-cut. The military equity in all aspects of administration has greatly increased and could, of course, predominate, but it still remains indecisive. The very composition of the new Cabinet, which many observers expected to indicate open military accession to paramount and acknowledged power, indicates instead a high degree of diffusion of authority such as could continue for a long time. Of 11 Ministers in the new "Inner Cabinet," only two are military officers. One is General Nasution, who was also for all practical purposes Minister of Defense in the previous Government. The other is Colonel Suprajogi, now Minister of Production, who carried virtually the same responsibilities in the previous Cabinet as Minister for Economic Reconstruction. It is quite possible that in the various new state councils of the new Government, the military will argue more convincingly or threaten more menacingly or even support more enthusiastically than in the past, but in the opening gambits at least it has turned in no performance that is significantly different from its role of a year ago.

The effect of the military clean-up drive. The military has repeatedly announced its intention to root out corruption and punish "corruptors." It has declared that it would put an end to the interminable series of scandals over misappropriation of government funds, buying and selling of housing permits and import-export licenses, bribery, smuggling, kickback, and similar abuses. It has decreed (1957) that everyone must hold himself ready to satisfy the military as to the "source of his wealth." It has just announced sweeping retrenchment and austerity measures, such as prohibition of use of official vehicles for other than official business purposes. It has arrested dozens of important persons, interrogated hundreds more, and investigated thousands of charges. So far as can be determined by the public, in the great majority of cases the arrested persons are either quietly released or are held indefinitely without definite charges being made, and in any event politics seems to be the determining factor. The investigations are permitted to peter out, and corruption and corruptors constitute as great a threat to the nation as before, perhaps much greater. The problem of stamping out corruption, of course, is not an easy one; but there is a considerable body of opinion in Indonesia that the military might make greater progress in its crusade if it started with itself.

One of the latest and biggest scandals regarding corruption within the military establishment has been the Tandjung Priok Barter Case. The full details have never been made public, but the essential fact is that high-ranking Djakarta Headquarters officers, charged with responsibility for supervising import-export trade in Indonesia's biggest port, went into business for themselves. They bypassed all of the official controls on big-scale export and import transactions which, since the Government did not receive its usual cut of up to 75 per cent of the value of the goods, resulted in big-scale profits. The Army investigated the case, announced that the officers had indeed been guilty, but took only mild disciplinary action against them in view of the "exonerating circumstances" that the profits were deemed to have been used for the benefit of the military establishment. There were certain aspects of the case, however, which have caused a degree of public incredulity about the findings. Certain of the officers, it was reported--those whose political tendencies were suspect--received much more severe disciplinary action than others; much of the money was still unaccounted for; and finally, as everybody knew, big-scale barter (smuggling) operations had been a primary and necessary source of revenue over the long term for a large group of military officers, including regional military commanders and their staffs, some of whom staged the 1956-58 rebellions, some of whom reversed or repressed them.

The Tandjung Priok Barter Case can be matched by others in which the military has featured with increasing conspicuousness as it has gained increased powers. Indonesian bureaucratic controls over commerce are so cumbersome that they constitute a challenge to human ingenuity--and avarice --to circumvent. The military has risen to the challenge with what might seem to the outsider at least like misdirected enthusiasm. It has exhibited little if any inclination to date to approach the national problem of corruption and corruptors by introducing simplified, workable regulations. It exhibits, rather, the same fixation as the civil authorities in devising more and more complicated schemes of control which not only challenge but necessitate circumvention--and pay-off for circumvention--if anything is ever to be accomplished.

One businessman who was interested in shipping a few cubic feet of merchandise from Java to Sumatra reported that in order to get an allocation of shipping space on one of the very few vessels available, he had to pay the military control officer for an authorization, then pay the company for the space, then pay an Army-sponsored veterans' association for a shipping permit, then pay another military officer not to requisition for himself the space in question, then pay still another military officer for permission to store his goods when the ship was indefinitely delayed--at which point he gave up the whole idea, abandoned his goods, and took his losses. The shipper may have exaggerated slightly, and the port of New York City, no doubt, can provide its own sad tales; but elimination of corruption in the port area of Tandjung Priok was to have been one of the high priority objectives of the military clean-up.

Just recently the Army has put out an order that Army personnel traveling abroad, on military procurement missions, for instance, may not accept gifts from foreign companies or individuals. The very announcement of the order has given rise to a spate of stories about military personnel returning from abroad with apparently unlimited funds for purchase of houses, automobiles, and luxury goods--the same sort of stories which circulate regarding civil government officials who have suddenly and mysteriously acquired business properties, mountain bungalows, and impressive bank accounts.

It may reasonably be argued that military personnel, like civil servants, must somehow manage to live. Life on a captain's salary plus allowances, a total of about Rp. 2,000 per month, is likely to be grim. The well-
dressed captain, furthermore, requires certain accoutrements--a pair of
German sun glasses at Rp. 1,500; a Rolex watch at Rp. 17,500; a British
Ronson lighter at Rp. 950-1,750, depending on whether he fancies the fluid or
the gas model; a Parker 61 fountain pen at Rp. 2,300.[2] These, or reasonable
facsimiles thereof, are status symbols. Even the cheapest facsimiles of some
items come to more than a month's salary. An army officer's pay anywhere,
it seems reasonable to assume, should provide for a pair of sun glasses, a
watch, a lighter, and a pen--not just instead of but in addition to mere necessities like civilian clothing, rice, and cigarettes. So long as the Army salary
scale--like that of the civil service--does not take into consideration such
basic realities as these, it seems unlikely that the Army will get very far in
its drive to eliminate corruption outside--or inside--the service.

The military policy vis-à-vis the PKI. Western commentators on the
situation in Indonesia are likely to label the Army and General Nasution as
anti-Communist, and as evidence, to point to General Nasution's role as an
officer in the crack Siliwangi Division in putting down the 1948 Madiun Communist uprising, and to recent military measures which restrict Communist
Party (PKI) activities in Djakarta and elsewhere. Nasution himself declares
that he is neither anti-Communist nor pro-Communist, that he and the Army
and Bung Karno and the Indonesian Government in general are merely non-
Communist. The General's noncommunism, like the "active independent,"
"non-Communist" but "pronationalist" policy of the Indonesian Government
manifests itself in a calculated balancing-off of forces--a rapprochement here
with the anti-Communist, there with the pro-Communist world; a restrain
here upon anti-Communist, there upon pro-Communist activities; a rebuke for
the Western bloc, a rebuke for the Communist; a kind word for the Western
world, a kind word for the Communist nations. All this is inherent in the
declared intent to pursue the best interests of the Indonesian nation, by the
promotion of trade and diplomatic and cultural relations with both sides.
Arms, therefore, can be purchased in London or Prague, aid can be solicited
in Moscow or Washington, cultural missions can be exchanged with Peking or
Paris, and United Nations votes favorable to Indonesia on the West Irian issue
can be elicited from Minsk, New Delhi, or Manila.

All this, of course, constitutes enlighted or at least expedient self-
interest, so long as the long-anticipated clash between the Indonesian military
and the PKI can be avoided, or, if it comes, can be expected to result in a
quick and easy victory for the military. But it does not constitute anticommunism in any widely accepted sense of the term. Furthermore, since Indonesia's
historical ties have been with the West, the balancing off of influences means
the weakening of ties with the Western bloc and the strengthening of those with

---

2 Standard prices in Pasar Baru, Djakarta, in July 1959.

the Communist nations. It means increasing commitment to the Communist world and increasing danger that the commitment may be greater and more difficult to control than General Nasution, for one, seems to think.

Some of the most advertised military measures to contain the increasing strength of the PKI appear, on close examination, to be measures designed primarily to control all political activity, not necessarily measures designed specifically to control the PKI. This is the result of Bung Karno's program, as first clearly enunciated in his 1957 konsepsi, to bury the political parties. Furthermore, vigorous military measures were taken a year ago to suppress the self-declared "anti-Communist" insurrectionist government in Sumatra and Sulawesi which had itself taken strong anti-Communist measures despite Djakarta's claim that their "anticommunism" was a ruse to gain Western support. To offset these anti-anti-Communist measures will require quite a program of anti-pro-Communist measures, and to date at least the balance has scarcely begun to swing.

The most recent example of an Army "anti-Communist" measure is one which introduces perhaps more than the usual quota of contradictions. On September 10 the Army arrested the Acting Attorney General Gatot Tarunamihardja. It was publicly declared that he had engaged in "attempts to defame the good name and to undermine the prestige of the leadership of the Army," that he "had created tension by undermining and destroying the hierarchy and discipline within the Armed Forces." The "real reason," however, according to informed Army sources, was that he was a dangerous Communist sympathizer. The "real reason," according to other sources, was that he had made accusations that high-ranking officers, already implicated in the Tandjung Priok affair, were still engaged in corrupt practices. In any event, the case either for or against the Acting Attorney General leaves a very great deal to be desired as a clear-cut case of anti- or procommunism.

The most conspicuous case of Army "anti-Communist" action just prior to the arrest of the Acting Attorney General, was General Nasution's ban on the PKI's Sixth National Congress. The ban was never formally announced, but it was rescinded on August 16, and the Congress, originally scheduled for August 22, convened between September 7 and 15. The party suffered no apparent hardship from fulfilling the current requirements that political meetings be held behind closed doors, such being the normal procedure in a PKI Congress anyhow, and that the agenda and minutes be submitted for Army inspection, since working papers had long since been published and a summary report was routinely scheduled. The reversible ban on the PKI Congress seems far less like repressive action against the PKI per se than like normal operating procedure regarding all political meetings, whose sponsors have to secure Army permission and are never really sure whether they do or do not have it--which seems to be exactly what the Army intends.

The most conspicuous "anti-Communist" <u>coup</u> of the military during the last several years has been the "recapturing" of certain youth, labor, veterans, and other "mass organizations" from Communist control and their reorganization under military auspices. Most important is the National Front for the Liberation of West Irian, which the Army organized out of a miscellany of mass movements which became particularly active at the time that youths, veterans, and laborers were seizing Dutch enterprises and the Army had to move fast to take over from them. By organizing the National Front for the Liberation of West Irian, declares Brigadier General Professor Doctor Mustopo, until recently the top organizer of the Front and its most voluble spokesman, the Army deprives the Communists of a vehicle and a cause. Furthermore, he states, in directing mass energies into constructive channels, the Army is succeeding in converting mere agitation for return of West Irian into collective effort to regenerate the Indonesian nation itself.

Yet a highlight of Brigadier General Professor Doctor Mustopo's address to 12,000 members of the "West Irian Pioneers" who answered a "roll call" in Djakarta's Ikada Square on April 17, 1959, was as follows, according to reliable press report: "that if in 1945 the people were ready to act like live-bullets with a spirit so high, now since we are not facing the risk of death the people should amplify that high spirit and enthusiasm for the benefit of the country's upbuilding." The flame which he seeks to rekindle, he declares elsewhere, "reached its climax at the end of 1957 when with the support of youths, workers, and other groups of the community a total action was undertaken to take-over Dutch enterprises in Indonesia. . . .We Indonesians are willing to die for the cause of returning West Irian to Indonesia's sovereignty and so long as this feat has not been accomplished, our spirit will never decline regardless of the psychological warfare which our enemy [the Dutch] tries to impose upon us." From all the available evidence, Brigadier General Professor Doctor Mustopo seems to have done very little to divert mass energy from rallies and demonstrations into constructive work projects; but even at that he seems to have done too much to please Bung Karno, for he was removed in August from the directorship of the National Front, just after Sukarno had criticised the National Front for dissipating its efforts on projects unrelated to Irian Barat. Spokesmen for the Front continue to sound, to many Western ears at least, as though they had no very clear idea what they intended, and were offering little that would offset the much more dynamic Communist message.

<u>The effectiveness of military discipline</u>. If the Army is to impose badly needed organization and discipline upon the nation--whether of a totalitarian or a more benevolent variety--then clearly it must be able to discipline itself. As to whether it can or will, the evidence, as usual, is conflicting. The Army as a whole has undoubtedly made major strides in achieving effective organization and discipline since it began to coalesce in 1950. But Army regiments and battalions and smaller units exhibit a pronounced tendency, in the case of higher-level disputes, to accept the views of their commanders in

preference to orders from higher authority. The commanders, in turn, exhibit a marked tendency, instead of accepting orders from their superiors, to ignore, to reject, or merely to debate in a manner which in most other countries would lead promptly to court martial but which in Indonesia seems to lead not infrequently either to promotion or to outright rebellion. It would appear then that military discipline is improving at the lower levels, and that at the higher levels it is deteriorating. It must be allowed, however, that at the lower levels there were instances of large-scale defections both to and from the rebel side during the recent insurrections and that at the higher levels there have been conducted such drastic purges of suspected malcontents that greater unanimity may now prevail than has ever been true in the past.

In various parts of Indonesia, I have observed detachments of troops which vary from clean, smart units to some of the most slovenly and surly specimens in all of Southeast Asia. The latter variety are those who have still been subjected only to a minimum of training, provided with a minimum of logistical support, including food, housed in wretched quarters, and called upon to do little more than mount sentry duty at some point--the waterfront in Macassar, for instance--where they can exact petty bribes for ignoring petty infractions of innumerable regulations governing movement of people and goods. On the other hand, in Bandung a few weeks ago I visited a non-commissioned officers' training school at which I saw as handsome, rugged, and competent an outfit as is to be found anywhere--trained to absolute precision, immaculately uniformed, well housed, well fed, and well disciplined, able to put on an exhibition-quality performance in marching, mock combat, athletics, and handling of equipment. The Indonesian Army, which started out as a raggle-taggle collection of Dutch-trained colonial troops, Japanese-trained youth corps, jungle guerrillas, and miscellaneous volunteers and hangers-on, is undoubtedly being shaped into a unified modern army. While the process still has a long distance to go, the achievement is already impressive and bespeaks an ability to impose and accept discipline which could be quickly transferrable from military to civilian context.

As already noted, the officers corps has been torn by feuds and has been more disposed to reject than to accept discipline. The typical Indonesian Army officer is a man of considerably more than ordinary education and intelligence, and his training has commonly been more along civilian than military lines. He tends, accordingly, to show more independence of judgment, to be rather more interested in politics than in military affairs, and to regard himself, quite properly, as belonging to the very minute group of the Indonesian elite and to carry a responsibility, therefore, not so much for carrying out orders but for arriving at value judgments regarding which instructions he will or will not obey. The history of the Indonesian officer corps, consequently, is a history of "incidents": the October 17, 1952 Incident, when an Army clique attempted to dissolve Parliament and call for new elections; the June 27, 1955 Incident, the boycotting of a new Chief of Staff; the November

1956 Incident, when Colonel Lubis attempted a <u>coup</u>; plus a whole succession of charters and oaths and pledges; plus, of course, the crowded series of insurrectionist incidents of 1956, 1957, and 1958. It seems unlikely that the score is now complete.

The record of individual officers is as instructive as the itemization of incidents. Take, for instance, the remarkable career of Colonel Warouw. He deposed his commanding officer in Macassar and himself assumed the command. He gained Djakarta's confirmation of his usurped position. He ignored frequent transfer orders. He finally consented to hand over his command in order to join Bung Karno on a trip around the world. He then accepted an assignment as Military Attaché in Peking. In 1958 he left Peking, threw in with the rebels, and became a leading propagandist in the campaign abroad to gain support for the rebel cause. Today, it is said, he commutes between the jungles of Sulawesi and such of the Southeast Asian capitals as will admit him; and there are those who think that tomorrow he could conceivably be back in Djakarta and in Bung Karno's favor.

Other branches of the Indonesian armed forces provide case histories which are equally illuminating--or bewildering. Take, for instance, the Navy, a chronically troubled service, a large percentage of whose officers found themselves either unwilling or unable to accept the authority of the ex-Chief of Staff, Vice Admiral Subijakto, a Sukarno favorite. The officers of certain naval patrol boats, for instance, refused to put into Tandjung Priok, the port of Djakarta, so long as Subijakto remained in office. They set their own courses, therefore, to shuttle between Surabaya and the Riouw Archipelago, bypassing Djakarta on each voyage. A group of naval air cadets--some 10 to 20 of them, according to various unpublished reports, but in any case the core of a newly-formed naval air wing--protested the appointment as their commanding officer of a relative of Subijakto who had himself washed out in flying school in the United States. The air cadets, who were undergoing training in England, were called home, placed under arrest on arrival, and detained in jail for four months. Vice Admiral Subijakto, meanwhile, departed for Europe on a holiday, and during his absence opposition to him grew so strong that when the new Government was formed in July, President Sukarno relieved him of his post as Navy Chief of Staff "in order to free him for ambassadorial appointment." Now that Subijakto is named Ambassador to Ankara, his successor as Navy Chief of Staff has released his air wing to complete its training in England, and will presumably welcome back to Djakarta the mutinous officers of the patrol boats.

The Air Force, like the Navy and the Army, has experienced sharp clashes between many of its officers and its Chief of Staff. The Air Force conflict has resulted in a couple instances of open insubordination but has resolved itself, in the main, by the departure of a considerable number of the unhappy officers, some of them to take well-paid jobs with Garuda Indonesian Airways. The Air Force and the Navy have found themselves at times in conflict with the Army. One recent incident involved a publicity release by the Air Force, declaring that it requested equal status with the Army. Upon publishing the release, three or four prominent Djakarta newspaper editors were haled in for Army interrogation. All this, it would seem, constitutes something rather more than SOP in interservice jealousy and intraservice rivalry. It seems, in fact, to constitute an intrinsic instability such as makes the establishment of an outright military regime in Indonesia in the immediate future on the whole unlikely, and the establishment of a firm military regime much more unlikely still.

*   *   *   *   *

The Indonesian military, it appears, lacks the nucleus of self-confident and decisive men which would be essential to the establishment of complete and overt military control over the nation. But in drawing any such conclusion, one must always allow for the fact that in Indonesia the unexpected is more likely to occur than the expected. Five years ago, or even two, few would have believed that Bung Karno would acquire or exercise clear-cut powers. As a matter of fact, few people believe even today that he really wanted these powers or that he wishes to retain them, preferring as he does the privileges to the responsibilities of the Presidency. The military, therefore, may one day soon find itself saddled with the responsibilities. If an outright military regime does come to Indonesia, it would be in keeping with the prevailing pattern of political, economic, and military developments that it should come, so far as the military itself is concerned, more accidentally than deliberately, and that it should quickly be denatured by renunciation on the part of some of the military leaders and defection on the part of others.

William A. Hanna

American Universities Field Staff

REPORTS SERVICE

BUNG KARNO'S INDONESIA

Part VI: The Enigma of the Communists

by Willard A. Hanna

September 28, 1959

This publication is one of a continuing series on current developments in world affairs written by associates of the American Universities Field Staff. It is distributed by the AUFS as a useful addition to the American fund of information on foreign affairs.

AUFS Associates have been chosen for their skill in collecting, reporting, and evaluating data. Each has combined long personal observation and experience in his foreign area with advanced studies relating to it.

WILLARD A. HANNA, the author of this report, is based in Kuala Lumpur to write about Southeast Asian affairs. Before joining the AUFS in 1954, Dr. Hanna had spent a total of more than ten years in East and Southeast Asia as a teacher, administrator, and writer.

Publications under the imprint of the American Universities Field Staff are not selected to accord with an editorial policy and do not represent the views of its membership. Responsibility for accuracy of facts and for opinions expressed in the letters and reports rests solely with the individual writers.

"Indonesia will be a Communist people's democracy within five years." This unequivocal prediction was made to me by at least a half-dozen Indonesians--and many more Chinese--who occupy positions which make their judgment meaningful. To be sure, a number of them two and a half years ago told me, in effect: "Indonesia will go Communist within the year."

"The Army has the Communists on the run." This flat statement was made to me by at least a dozen other informants, some Indonesian, some American, some of other nationalities, none, however, Chinese. To be sure, a number of the same people two and a half years ago told me, in effect: "The Communists have the Army on the run."

The Communists themselves are mostly inaccessible for comment, save for reiteration of the official Partai Komunis Indonesia line: The PKI does not propose to seize control of Indonesia but only, by working diligently with the growing number of Indonesians who prize the people's welfare and approve the correct national and international policies, to transform Indonesia from semicapitalism and semifeudalism into a socialist and then a Communist state.

That Communist effort to date has not been ineffectual is evident from even a brief survey of

[WAH-17-'59]

Communist strength. Party membership, according to PKI report, increased from 7,910 in 1951 to approximately 1,500,000--including members and candidates for membership--in 1958. There is no reason to think that the statistics are sheer fabrication or that the rate of growth has slowed down. The PKI commanded about 17 per cent of the total vote in the 1955 elections for the Parliament and the Constituent Assembly, seating 39 out of 257 members in the Parliament and 60 out of 514 in the Assembly. The PKI greatly increased its showing at the polls in subsequent regional and local elections, especially in Java, where it received 25.6 of the vote and now has either a very strong representation in or controls outright the municipal governments of the major cities, namely, Djakarta, Bandung, Semarang, Surabaya, Jogjakarta, and Surakarta (Solo). The party was fully prepared, according to both pro- and anti-PKI reports, to sweep into power in new national elections originally scheduled for 1959 but now indefinitely postponed by the Government--mainly, perhaps, to preclude any such eventuality. The PKI has not managed, despite Bung Karno's support, to get any Cabinet posts in the previous or the new Government, but it does have PKI sympathizers in important ministerial posts and it is represented by top party leaders on the Supreme State Council. The PKI has party members and sympathizers in the armed services, including, it is rumored, the headquarters staffs. It has long controlled both SOBSI, by far the most important Indonesian labor union, and LEKRA, the most influential organization of artists and writers. The party daily, Harian Rakjat, is at times the Indonesian-language daily of widest circulation, but yields at times-- at present, for instance--to the Socialist Party organ, Pedoman. Communist literature, some of it from Moscow, some from Peking, some published in Indonesia, pours into and out of the Indonesian book stores at give-away prices. Youth, labor, veterans, peasants, women's organizations and others are so heavily infiltrated by Communist influence that it now is less a question of Communists attempting to capture than of other groups attempting to recapture an important equity in control.

Most of this, of course, was equally true in 1957. It may be argued accordingly that the rate of acceleration has dropped off, or that new evidences of growth are hard to distinguish, or even that retrenchment has set in--indeed, that deliberate Government policy of curtailing Communist growth and influence has now at last been adopted and is showing effect.

Evidence that the Communists have perhaps already overreached themselves and have thus induced both a considerable degree of public reaction and official repressive action can readily be cited. It should be accompanied, however, by the caution that what may seem like a marked increase of outright anti-Communist sentiment often turns out on closer inspection to be a rather more complicated blend.

The most conspicuous and effective measures to contain Communist forces in Indonesia have been taken by the military. Stirred to action by the obvious danger that the PKI and its front organizations were likely to gain dangerous powers in troubled times, the military command began in early 1958 to adopt firm measures. It removed the "nationalized" Dutch enterprises, for instance, from the hands of the PKI-sponsored groups which had assumed responsibility for their seizure, and placed them under military control. It prohibited PKI-sponsored strikes, including those proposed against the "alien and imperialist" oil industry. It banned PKI-directed demonstrations, such as one in honor of a new Russian Ambassador and others directed against the United States. It banned explicit PKI emblems and slogans and cadres in "mass action" parades. It decreed that there was only one "authorized mass action movement"--the National Front, under the auspices of the Army. It prohibited one group of habitual trouble makers--the veterans, traditionally PKI-dominated--from engaging in any political activity. It even began openly to check up on the activities of the PKI itself.

These military measures against the PKI and PKI-front organizations must be placed in wider context. They were directed against the PKI, to be sure, but they were an outcome not just of anti-PKI sentiment but of the joint government-military program of clamping down on all political activity. The campaign is in line with Indonesia's domestic policy of weakening the political parties in general, and with its foreign policy of "independence" and "impartiality" vis-à-vis the Communist and anti-Communist world blocs. At the same time that it was applying checks to PKI activity, the military was also curtailing that of the anti-Communists. The openly anti-Communist groups were subject perhaps to even more suspicion than the Communists, and for two specific reasons relating to domestic developments. First, the 1957 assassination attempt upon Bung Karno, as it came out in the court trials, had been planned and engineered by a self-declared anti-Communist group, and all anti-Communist groups were suspected of being implicated. Second, the regional insurrection leaders had declared themselves anti-Communist in ideology--spuriously so, said the central Government, for purposes only of winning the sympathy and aid of the "Western imperialists." Spuriously or not, any one individual or group of openly declared anti-Communist tendencies became suspect of intended insurrection.

The "safe" position was the one declared by the Government, by the military, and by most leading individuals: not procommunism, not anticommunism, but noncommunism. Noncommunism involves, of course, neutrality, and hence the balancing off of restrictive actions against Communists by restrictive actions also against anti-Communists. So far as the Indonesian military was concerned, there was one additional and compelling reason to adhere to this sort of "positive neutrality." The Indonesian military was looking in 1958, as it is looking in 1959, for military assistance. It actually received such assistance, first from the Communist, then from the anti-Communist bloc. Assistance from either the USSR or the USA was and is more likely to be forthcoming for evidence of policies that can be interpreted as favorable to the USSR or the USA respectively, which means, in the end, two parallel sets of policies.

Additional evidences of sentiment or action against the Communists, each offset in part at least by evidences of favoritism toward the Communists, may be briefly summarized. The insurrectionist leaders in Sumatra denounced, arrested, and jailed Communists, banned the party, and even, according to PKI headquarters report, committed large scale "attrocities" of "persecution, murder, and execution." The Army, on retaking insurrectionist areas, adopted policies concerning which there is conflicting report. According to Masjumi and Socialist sources, the Army not only reinstated known Communists but gave them positions of greater importance than before. According to PKI reports, the "middle-of-the-road" group (presumably military) attempted to relegate the Communists to obscure jobs or to oust them altogether.

In either event, the example of strong and successful action to suppress the PKI and of inconclusive action either to keep it suppressed or to restore it have not failed to impress many Indonesians with the fact that the PKI will at least bear watching. The PNI, for instance, the Nationalist party which was long in control in Indonesia and which then exhibited pronounced tendencies to co-operate with the PKI, has in recent months exhibited a marked dichotomy on the subject. Prominent PNI leaders and branches, especially those in East Java, have condemned PKI policy and practices. The fact that the PNI has itself slipped from power at the same time that the PKI was improving its over-all position has no doubt helped to condition recent PNI reaction. In any event, PNI voices are now being added to Masjumi and Socialist voices in coun-selling alertness to the Communist danger.

One additional development, reflecting in part perhaps increased public and official suspicion of communism, is to be found in the series of restrictive measures against alien residents, mainly Chinese of course, and many of them Communists. After December 31, 1959, aliens will not be permitted to main-tain businesses or perhaps even residence outside the larger cities, and they are not permitted at present to circulate freely throughout the country without police permission. The regulations are aimed also, of course, at the Nation-alist Chinese who have already experienced special discriminatory regulations closing down their schools and confiscating their properties. But the new regulations hit the Communist Chinese as well, and what hits Communist Chi-nese also hits the PKI, even though by delayed and indirect action.

The Government has not as yet taken any such drastic action as the "intolerable provocation" under the "reactionary Hatta Masjumi" Government of mid-1951. At that time, several thousand Communists and Communist sympathizers were rounded up and jailed during nation-wide razzias which followed an attempt on the part of an armed force--"masquerading as Com-munists," says the PKI--to capture the police station at Tandjung Priok, Djakarta's port. It was the revival and growth of the party after its post-Madiun Rebellion period of near oblivion which touched off this 1951 action. The action led in turn to rethinking of the party line and redoubling of party activities, and this eventually to its dramatic post-1952 growth.

Thus the pendulum tends to swing in Indonesia, from Left to Right to Left again, each time perhaps a little farther, each time with considerably more danger to the national equilibrium. Measures taken against the PKI today may be expected, therefore, with historical precedent to reinforce the expectation, to generate an even stronger counterforce. Each cycle seems to leave the Communists stronger than before, and in a better position to assert their strength when and if they judge the time is right.

The PKI, in rethinking its strategy in the face of recent moves against it, has not as yet adopted any sharp change of policy line such as occurred in 1951 when it shifted from opposing the Government to promoting a United Front. The fact that it has not found it necessary to adopt a new policy may, as a matter of fact, be an important evidence both of party strength and of party confidence. The one most significant new trend, or rather strengthening of an earlier trend, is the PKI acclaim for Bung Karno and for most, but by no means all, of the actions and policies which have been proposed or adopted in the last several years under the Bung Karno aegis.

The definition by any outsider of PKI party position and policy is likely to be highly theoretical and subjective, so it seems well to turn from general attempts at interpretation to specific analysis of authoritative sources. The best source available is the voluminous PKI official documentation which, since it is prepared for the information and guidance of members and sympathizers, may be accepted on the whole as a faithful index to the party position rather than as fiction to delude the opposition. Two particular documents, representative of the party position as of 1954 and 1958-59, repay careful reading and analysis. One is The Road to the People's Democracy for Indonesia,[1] the general report by D. N. Aidit, General Secretary of the PKI, to the Fifth National Congress of the PKI in March 1954. The other is Material for the Sixth National Congress of the Communist Party of Indonesia,[2] prepared for presentation at the recently concluded 1959 meeting. For the sake of convenience the most essential points of the two documents are summarized below in parallel columns--this brief summary involving, of course, a degree of distortion inevitable in selection, rearrangement, paraphrasing and spot quotation:

---

[1] Jajasan Pembaruan, Jakarta 1955. 57 pp.

[2] Agitation and Propaganda Department of the C.C. of the C.P.I. Preface dated Jakarta, December 8, 1958. 137 pp.

1954	1958-59

The International Situation:

1. "People's democracies" are forging ahead; "imperialists" are troubled, hence aggressive.

"People's democracies" are inflicting sharp reverses on "imperialists" in Europe, Asia, Africa, and Latin America. Only Yugoslavia is backsliding.

2. "People's democracies" are encouraging free exchange of goods and cultures; "imperialists" are creating artificial barriers.

U.S. "economic crisis" is worsening, U.S. militarism is increasing; "peace-loving" countries are co-operating more and more closely.

3. Major enemy of Indonesia is Dutch imperialism.

American imperialism is replacing Dutch as major enemy to Indonesia.

The Domestic Situation:

1. Indonesia is still "semicapitalist, semifeudal" country, prevented by imperialists from achieving "true independence."

Indonesia is still "semicapitalist, semifeudal"; but it has now swung "to the Left." "Liberal Western democracy is discredited, being identical with corruption, bureaucracy, and inability to solve problems."

2. Indonesia is "in the grip of a perpetual economic crisis."

Indonesia's economic crisis has greatly worsened, and the sufferings of the people are becoming insupportable.

3. . . . .

Indonesian Revolution has suddenly speeded up with emphasis on 1945 spirit; PKI must not drop behind but must work systematically to stay in lead in solving every "mass problem."

4. . . . .

The Army is actually in control in Indonesia today; the "negative aspect" of Army control is its interference in political, economic, and social matters. The Army must not be permitted to "oppress" the people but must be the "servant" of the people.

Growth, Achievements, Weaknesses of the PKI:

1. Since "fascist" mass arrests of August 1951, PKI has grown from 7,910 to 126,671-plus members.

PKI has grown from 150,000 members in 1954 to 1,500,000 today. "People's Youth" number 800,000.

2. In 1952 PKI had branches only in Java and Sumatra; now it has branches throughout archipelago.

Java and Sumatra are now even more intensively organized; branches are now more evenly distributed throughout archipelago.

3. In 1952 PKI launched education program for cadres, members, masses.

New Three-Year Education Program has familiarized all members with Marxist-Leninist theories and trained cadres of "revolutionary fighters."

4. PKI has split bourgeosie into unreconstructable Right Wing and reconstructable but still unreliable Left Wing.

PKI has encountered new betrayal from "middle-of-the-road" group but has discredited the Right Wing (Hatta, etc.), reattracted many of the Left Wing, and checkmated the Center.

5. PKI has forced the overthrow of a "reactionary" Cabinet, the formation of the "fairly progressive" Ali Cabinet, which it supports in part.

PKI has failed to achieve position proposed in Sukarno's konsepsi; it gives staunch but critical support to Djuanda Cabinet.

6. PKI has consistently opposed all armed terrorist movements.

The 1957-58 rebel movements "raised the prestige of the PKI and the progressive forces in general." The PKI resisted the rebels from the first, suffered martyrdom in consequence. Then, when the "middle-of-the-road" forces attempted to deprive the PKI of its reward and indeed suppress it, the PKI gained public sympathy. The "middle-of-the-road" forces "discredited themselves" by thus "weakening the potentials of the Indonesian people in their effort to smash the counterrevolutionaries."

7. . . . .

PKI has played leading role in expelling the Dutch, renouncing treaties with Holland, confiscating Dutch property, asserting claim to Irian, fighting rebel movements, implementing Sukarno konsepsi, blocking foreign imperialists, and democratising the Government.

8. PKI has failed to build up essential "broad base" among peasants or to exploit its appeal to youth, intellectuals, etc.

Work among peasants is still unsatisfactory but peasants now constitute over 50 per cent membership; PKI work with youth, intellectuals, women is progressing, but "urban poor" are badly neglected.

9. PKI exhibits proneness to "dogmatic" "deviation of left," i.e. overstress on party; and "empirical" "deviation of right," i.e. overstress on united front.

Left and right deviations are still common, despite education program.

10. . . . .

Many "comrades" are devoting themselves to personal aggrandizement rather than party interests. They must be reorientated or expelled.

11. .... Most likely mistake of PKI at present would
                              be to push too soon for its total program
                              rather than working only for what is feasible
                              at the moment.

Foreign Policy:

1. PKI advocates a "Peace Policy" instead of the delusory "Neutral" or "Independent" policy.

Indonesian foreign policy in recent years has been orientating in fact toward Eastern bloc and the nation should now participate outright in "anticolonial and propeace" international front.

2. PKI advocates extension of "Good Neighbor" policy to China, North Korea, Vietminh, etc., and admission of China to UN.

Indonesia has made "some advance" in improving relations with Communist countries.

3. PKI advocates increased trade with Communist countries.

Indonesia has failed in critical matter of orientating her trade toward Communist countries. Indonesia should step up her drive for "no strings attached" loans.

4. PKI advocates support for "people's struggle" everywhere for "complete independence."

Indonesia has supported "independence struggles" in Africa, Asia, and must continue to adhere to and promote the Bandung Conference decisions and spirit.

5. PKI advocates abrogation of all treaties that "jeopardize Indonesia's independence" and "disturb the peaceful atmosphere."

Indonesia has abrogated agreements with Holland but must not permit Dutch imperialism to be replaced by American, or by bourgeoisie in league with Americans.

6. PKI opposes Holland's "shameless policy toward West Irian" which constitutes a "legal part" of the Indonesian nation.

Indonesia must "further intensify the struggle for the liberation of West Irian."

Domestic Policy:

1. PKI aims at formation of a "United National Front" of all Indonesians who wish "complete independence" and "peace."

PKI "aims at uniting the Indonesian people within a united front. . .to create a government of People's Democracy". . ."in conformity with the characteristics of the August 1945 Revolution." "The working class must lead the struggle."

2. PKI will co-operate with all who are willing to co-operate.

PKI demands 100 per cent implementation of Sukarno's konsepsi to replace "liberal" with "guided democracy."

3. PKI aims at an "antifeudal" agrarian system, confiscation of landlord property, and free distribution of land to "poor" peasants.

PKI still aims at "antifeudal" agrarian policy and stresses private peasant ownership of farmlands, state ownership of big estates; it demands cancelling out peasants' debts, development of transmigration program, distribution of arms so peasants can fight "against the terrorist groups."

4. PKI aims at replacing Indonesia's "colonial economic system" with a "national economic system," involving "liquidation" of Dutch interests.

PKI would complete "nationalization" process with reference to Dutch, also other foreign holdings; it would repeal the law on foreign investments, control the oil enterprises, revoke mining concessions, place the burden of Five-Year Plan on foreign capitalists and landowners; place prime emphasis on "State Sector" of economy but permit national capitalism.

5. . . . .

PKI demands fixed minimum wages for all laborers and office workers, such social benefits as paid vacations, medical care, control over employment of women and children, strict price controls, etc.

6. PKI aims to "raise the level of political activities among the people," promote study of communism, "hold high the standards of parliamentary democracy" against Masjumi and Socialist threat.

PKI demands "the broadest possible democratic freedoms," guarantee of "all rights and liberties to the workers," respect for the position of Parliament, "implementation of regional autonomy," the holding on schedule of 1959 national elections, the "democratization" of all public institutions.

7. . . . .

PKI demands development of a truly "national people's culture" with encouragements for science, arts, Indonesian language, free compulsory schooling, and establishing of community halls for youth and cultural groups.

8. PKI would crush all "terrorist gangs."

PKI would "completely crush" the various rebel movements, the terrorist gangs, "the Kuomintang subversives, and other imperialist agent gangs."

9. . . . .

PKI demands dismissal of all civil and military personnel who are "traitors to the nation, reactionaries, embezzlers, and corruptors."

10. . . . .

PKI demands "democratization" of the Army, and development of "close ties between the Army and the people."

Special PKI Priorities:

PKI should concentrate greatest effort on two tasks: 1) building up the "anti-imperialist united front"; and 2) "building up a bolshevised PKI. . .nation-wide in scope, with a broad mass character, and

PKI should continue its priority tasks as defined in 1954; "but the most important thing today is raising vigilance in opposing with all our strength modern revisionism both within and outside the Party. . . .Oppos-

fully consolidated ideologically, politically, and organizationally." This involves intensification of work among the peasants and of effort to unite workers and peasants in a common struggle in which the intellectuals, youth, women, the Left-wing bourgeoisie and others will share.

ing modern revisionism means opposing chauvinsim as the greatest enemy of the struggle of the proletariat to emancipate themselves, it means holding high the banners of proletarian internationalism and making it the possession not only of the proletariat but also a natural thing for the entire people engaged in the anti-imperialist struggle."[3]

Comparison of these two key documents seems to justify the following observations:

1) Parallel to PKI expressions of esteem and confidence as regards Bung Karno and his program, and reaffirmation of its policy of a United Front, run expressions of grave concern about four trends adverse to the PKI which it detects in national and party affairs. First is the increased power of the military and the utilization of that power to restrict Communist activities. Second is the "betrayal" of the Communist cause by various elements of the "middle-of-the-road" group, including, by inference, important elements of the military. Third is the "neglect" of the party cause by various of the PKI members themselves who seem interested primarily in personal, not party advantage. Fourth is the accelerated pace of the revolution, with the recent emphasis on the Spirit of '45, a pace with which the PKI feels it must make special efforts to keep up. It is evident that the PKI leaders see increased possibility of: a) outright clash with the military; b) mounting opposition from the "middle-of-the-road" group, that is, the "bourgeoisie" and the "petty bourgeoisie," including many high in the military command; c) internal PKI party purges; and d) serious challenge to the PKI (by inference, on the part of the military) in leadership of the revolutionary mass action movement.

2) The PKI today places less emphasis upon the peasant and more on the urban worker as the chief potential tool of revolution. It renounces the concept that the pattern of communism as applied in China is transferable to Indonesia--a proposition which it also denied, but not as vigorously, in 1954. Furthermore, it emphasizes Marxist-Leninist doctrines as the indispensable base of the Communist movement, making no mention in 1958-59 of Stalin's writings which were repeatedly referred to in 1954, and making much less frequent mention of Mao Tse-tung. The PKI, it seems, despite continuing

---

3 "Revisionism" certainly refers to the "betrayal" of the PKI by the left wing of the "middle-of-the-road" group, including segments of the military. "After the workers at great risk and in complete disregard of their own interests had taken over the Dutch enterprises," and after the PKI had consistently resisted the rebels, the middle-of-the-road group "tried to get these enterprises shifted over into their own individual hands". . .and tried also to build up an "anti-Communist movement." "But fortunately, it was possible to frustrate this policy. . .thanks to the strong resistance of the Indonesian people and President Sukarno."--Op. cit.

assertions of the necessity for a broad organizational base among the peasants and for "perfecting" the unity of peasants and workers, is tending sharply toward the point of view that the Indonesian Revolution is essentially an urban revolution, that for the time being at least it corresponds more closely to the Russian than to the Chinese. It depends for its vitality and for its leadership upon the urban proletariat--as contrasted, first, with the peasantry, and second, as is more significant for Indonesia, with the intellectuals, including the military.

3) PKI diatribes against Yugoslavia in its basic statement of 1958 would seem to be an attempt to refute the opinion, occasionally expressed, that Indonesian communism is more likely to resemble Titoism than Maoism. Furthermore, the constant reiteration of the importance of Marxist-Leninist studies seems to indicate a deliberate turning to the European fountainhead of Communist philosophy as the basis for the educational program which the party stresses, as the cure for its various manifestations of "subjectivism."

4) The new distinction between the party's "General Program" and its "Program of Demands," accompanied as it is by the declaration that the general program need not be advanced all at once but that the demands should be, proves, on close examination, to be quite misleading. The Program of Demands constitutes, in fact, a blueprint for specific steps which would lead automatically to conversion of Indonesia into the People's Democracy which the General Program specifies. It is by far the most detailed political, economic, and social program yet announced by the party. It is indicative of a new drive concentrating less upon conversion to Communist dogma and recruiting of party membership and more upon specific "reform" measures which non-Communists may support and which add up, one by one, to creation of a Communist state.

5) The 1958 document, like that of 1954, is the work of PKI General Secretary Aidit. The rumor persists that the top party leadership is far from being unanimous in approving it. Deputy Chairman Lukman, for instance, is widely believed to be arguing for a break with Sukarno, a closer affiliation with Peking than with Moscow, and a tougher party line regarding the military. For the time being, the views attributed to Aidit seem to prevail. There remains, however, the very real possibility that Lukman will gain supporters and that the PKI line may shift significantly.

6) The PKI in 1958, while still reiterating at times that the Dutch are Indonesia's Enemy Number One, tends more frequently and vigorously to declare that after all, it is not the Dutch but the United States.

7) In view of the close parallels between the ideology, objectives, and strategy of the PKI and of Bung Karno, the question naturally arises as to which dominates the other, whether between them they truly reflect and forecast, as Bung Karno himself so constantly claims that he does, the true aspi-

rations of the Indonesian people. The answer to the first question is probably that the alliance is one of expediency and that sudden ruptures are as possible at present as they have proven to be in the past. The answer to the second question is probably that Bung Karno, at least, has exhibited in the past an almost infallible instinct as to the lines which the Indonesian people would accept and follow, but that of late his intuition, like his reputation, has become somewhat clouded. The PKI may yet discover that the increasing identification of the PKI with the Bung Karno line may work not for the PKI's advantage but to its disadvantage, whether Bung Karno himself succeeds or fails. In the one case, Bung Karno may rid himself of a dangerous ally, and in the other he may implicate the PKI in his own debacle.

In talking with one shrewd Indonesian observer and participant in the recent national developments, I tried to sum it up this way: "What is not clear to me is who is leading whom where and how fast. What is clear is that forces build up counterforces, action builds up reaction, and confusion compounds confusion." He agreed with me. "Yes," he said, "And you know, we prefer it that way."

Willard A. Hanna

SOUTHEAST ASIA SERIES
Vol. VII   No. 22
(Indonesia)

American Universities Field Staff

REPORTS
SERVICE

BUNG KARNO'S INDONESIA

Part VII: The Rebel Cause

by Willard A. Hanna

October 9, 1959

In early 1958, the loosely co-ordinated insurrections in Sumatra and Sulawesi (Celebes) and their joint government, the Pemerintah Revolusioner Republik Indonesia (Revolutionary Government of the Republic of Indonesia), looked like potentially decisive factors in the interminable and inconclusive Indonesian national crisis. By mid-1958, they had begun to look more like decisively eliminated factors. By mid-1959, however, they had begun to look once again like potentially decisive factors, only not quite in the manner which the insurrectionists or many other originally anticipated.

In 1958 the rebel leaders challenged Bung Karno and his wobbly Djakarta Government to a showdown. They charged the central Government with incompetence, corruption, exploitation, and intent to lead the nation into the Communist bloc. They demanded efficiency, honesty, decentralization, and anti-Communist policies. The normally indecisive central Government, to almost everybody's amazement, pulled itself together to inflict upon the rebel forces a swift series of military defeats by land, sea, and air. Then, after a prolonged period of hesitation, Bung Karno went on to establish in mid-1959 what may yet, despite initial appearances of recklessness, prove to be a strong new regime. Nevertheless, although the rebel movement has seemed to be petering out with the decimation of its own forces and reconsolidation and reassertion of

[WAH-18-'59]

Djakarta's, it is producing a delayed effect which may yet be the cause of Djakarta's collapse, if not of rebel renascence. The fact is that the insurrectionist movement has placed a virtually intolerable strain upon the nation's already chaotic economy.

The regional insurrections have been mainly responsible for forcing the central Government in 1958 to devote an estimated 48 per cent of its budget and 45 per cent of its foreign exchange either directly or indirectly to military campaigns. The insurrectionist forces, further, have been responsible for diverting substantial quantities of Indonesia's export products into the illicit barter trade and thus have deprived Djakarta of at least 10 to 20 per cent of its anticipated revenue. The net effect has been a runaway inflation which the central Government abetted by printing and spending vast quantities of new banknotes, and which it has attempted recently to halt by arbitrarily devaluating by 90 per cent nearly one half of the currency in circulation and freezing all bank deposits over Rp. 25,000 (US$555, at the official exchange rate). The inflation badly demoralized the nation; for the time being at least, the attempted deflation has nearly paralyzed it. The rebel leaders are now saying that they had predicted something like this. But they don't seem really to have believed their own predictions. They didn't think Djakarta would actually risk destroying itself in order to destroy them.

Although the Indonesian insurrectionists themselves are not actually destroyed, their top leaders are fugitives, finding shelter in the jungles of Sumatra and Sulawesi, or in Singapore, Hong Kong, and Geneva. Their fighting forces now number no more than a few thousand scattered guerrillas--ten to fifteen thousand at most, a good half of them youthful volunteers rather than trained troops. Their funds and their military supplies are dwindling. Their sympathizers within Indonesia are discouraged and disillusioned. Their sympathizers abroad find it difficult to tune in on their low-powered radio transmissions from Sumatra or Sulawesi, or to get hold of their infrequent propaganda handouts, or to persuade themselves that much is to be accomplished by adhering to a forlorn cause. Nevertheless, the regional insurrections and their leaders warrant another look and perhaps a reappraisal.

In 1957 and early 1958 the tendency, on the part of many Western observers at least, was to take the insurrectionist leaders at very much their own appraisal--as a group of competent and dedicated patriots determined to force Bung Karno to forego his forensics for a while and to undertake long overdue reforms in his Government, including vigorous anti-Communist measures. The tendency since mid-1958 has been to judge them as ineffectual has-beens, incapable when they had troops, money, and a strong military position of utilizing any of them advantageously, incapable now of ever staging a come back. The official judgment in Djakarta, as repeatedly pronounced by Bung Karno himself, is that they are "traitors," "criminals," "adventurers," "terrorists," "profiteers," "smugglers," "reactionaries," and "counterrevolutionaries." In fact, he declares, they are the "tools of the imperialists" and are bent upon "infecting the people with the sickness of <u>communistophobia</u>," not from any genuine anti-Communist conviction on their own part but merely as a ruse to gain SEATO support for a movement which they know is lost without it. To Bung Karno, the rebels represent "the antithesis of everything truly Indonesian" and are therefore a national disgrace and a national tragedy.

As usual, the truth probably lies well short of either extreme. There are individual PRRI leaders who are outstandingly competent, honest, and dedicated; but they share the weakness of other prominent Indonesian political leaders for personal intrigue and political feuding. There are others who are outright opportunists, yet who share the devotion of other prominent Indonesian revolutionary leaders to the welfare of the nation as they see it. As individuals, the insurrectionist leaders are in varying degrees, simultaneously and conflictingly, selfless patriots and feuding conspirators, revolutionary idealists and personal realists, brave fighters and timid fugitives. In case this judgment sounds too harsh to their supporters or too lenient to their opponents, this much at least can be agreed upon: they are men who have performed some of the most distinguished and honorable services for their country in the last two decades, whether as revolutionary fighters or as civil and military administrators; they have recently shown themselves to be unwise, inept, and divided in their efforts to force reform upon the Djakarta Government; they have set in motion an uncontrollable chain reaction which threatens now to lead not to their announced objective of a truly democratic Indonesia but to totalitarianism or chaos. Few Indonesians except Bung Karno profess to believe that in them the Indonesian Revolution has spawned a whole platoon of Benedict Arnolds. Most Indonesians, including many in Djakarta who gave tacit but equivocal support to their cause, regard them as one large and important segment of Indonesian national leadership which found itself completely frustrated in attempting to achieve any rational results by working from within the central Government and then equally frustrated in working from without.

The mere roster of top PRRI leaders, while it disposes of Bung Karno's thesis that these men are disreputable adventurers, does not explain why, if they rebelled at all, they did not rebel more successfully. The nine principal leaders are:

> Sjafruddin Prawiranegara: onetime Acting President of the Republic
> (1949); often a Cabinet Minister; Governor of the Bank of Indonesia;
> now Prime Minister of the PRRI.

> Dr. Sumitro Djojohadikusumo: Indonesia's leading economist; often a
> Cabinet Minister; Dean of the Economics Faculty of the University
> of Indonesia; now Minister of Economic Affairs and of Communications, and overseas agent of the PRRI.

> Mohammad Natsir: onetime Prime Minister of the Republic; often a
> Cabinet Minister; longtime head of the Masjumi Party; now adviser

to the PRRI, and since June 1959 Deputy Prime Minister.

Burhannudin Harahap: onetime Prime Minister of the Republic; now Minister of Defense and Justice of the PRRI.

Col. Maludin Simbolon: hero of the revolutionary army; brigade commander in the crack Siliwangi Division; longtime Commander of the North Sumatra Military District; now Foreign Minister of the PRRI.

Lt. Col. Ahmad Hussein: hero of the revolutionary army; Commander of the Central Sumatra Military District; a prime mover in the insurrectionist movement in Sumatra.

Col. Dahlan Djambek: hero of the revolutionary army; onetime Military Attaché in London; Third Deputy Chief of Staff of the Indonesian Army; now Minister of the Interior of the PRRI.

Col. Kawilarang: hero of the revolutionary army; longtime Commander of the Siliwangi Division, and Commander of the West Java Military District; Military Attaché in Washington; now troop commander and overseas spokesman for the PRRI.

Lt. Col. Ventje Sumual: hero of the revolutionary army, and once a favorite of Bung Karno; Commander of the Moluccas Military District; the prime mover in the Sulawesi insurrection.

Col. John F. Warouw: hero of the revolutionary army; Commander of the Moluccas Military District; Military Attaché in Peking; now Minister of Industries for the PRRI.

Of the four civilians, Sjafruddin, Natsir, and Sumitro must be numbered among Indonesia's ten or twelve most prominent leaders; all of the five military men are among its top twelve or fifteen commanders. One might reasonably have expected that under such leadership the insurrections would be well planned, well co-ordinated, and well conducted. They were not. They were a ruinous display of miscalculation, mismanagement, and misunderstanding on the part of the top leaders themselves.

The major miscalculation concerned Djakarta's willingness and capability to mount any strong military attack or even to take any effective nonmilitary measures. The rebel leaders, on the basis of their own long experience within the central Government, probably reasoned thus: A) The Djakarta Government is constitutionally incapable of taking decision, or if it does take a decision, it fails to act on it. In any event, strong proinsurrectionist elements within the Government will contrive impediments. B) The Djakarta Government will attempt, if anything, economic retaliation and political intrigue, never military action. A "war of brothers" is anathema to both sides; and in any event, prorebel elements within the Djakarta Headquarters will effectively sabotage any punitive expedition. C) Djakarta will never risk further exacerbation of the already serious anti-Djakarta sentiment in the provinces, or, if it does, it will arouse insurrection even in the provinces which are still under its control. D) For economic reasons, if no other, Djakarta cannot afford to take decisive action. Major segments of its two most vital dollar-earning industries--oil and rubber--can be readily denied to it. With the national economic position already most precarious, a military campaign would be prohibitively expensive, and to pursue the campaign through the inevitably long-drawn-out mopping-up operations would be ruinous.

The rebel leaders, by being too rational, erred in their calculations. The Djakarta Government had already shown by its action in closing out Dutch enterprises (December 1957) that it would indeed risk chaos rather than practice restraint, and it did so again. Beginning on March 12, 1958, it launched military action which quickly demonstrated, to the dismay of the rebels, that the Headquarters staff was capable of a campaign which was both well conceived and well executed. The PRRI leaders themselves, on the other hand, proved to be maladroit administrators, propagandists, strategists, and fighters. To be sure, they had had only about a year in which to try to reorganize and rehabilitate areas which had been deteriorating steadily for years past; many of the principle leaders arrived late on the scene and found few local persons with either the training or the competence to assist them; and final preparations to resist attack had to be made hastily and under pressure of threatened action from Djakarta. Their problems and their handicaps were enormous; but undeniably they had misread their own strength almost as badly as they had misread Djakarta's weakness. Even allowing for the extreme difficulty of the situation in which they found themselves, their record was not impressive.

The specific record of mismanagement shows in civil administration, military operations, and propaganda policy. In civil administration, it swiftly became apparent that the PRRI had a government in name only. It had a "cabinet" of ministers without anything approximating ministries. It relied for routine administration upon the same creaky old provincial machinery which had not worked well under the central Government and which worked even less well in these new circumstances. It relied heavily upon the military command which, in the insurrectionist regions as elsewhere in Indonesia, imposed its authority at will upon the civil administration without at the same time accepting responsibility for its actions.

The weaknesses of the rebel administration showed up especially in two vital and interrelated areas: first, the implementation of rehabilitation plans; second, the collection and distribution of revenues. The insurrectionists announced, immediately upon taking over authority in each of the areas, that they would provide the people and the troops with the facilities which the central Government had denied them--schools, hospitals, barracks, and roads being highest on the priorities list. They made a few brave starts, but schools and barracks, naturally, could not rise overnight, hospitals were out of the question on the short-term basis, road building and road repairs petered out after a few kilometers, funds were chronically short, and community work projects failed to catch on.

One major reason that funds were short and that volunteer labor projects were not popular was that the PRRI followed some of the same official and unofficial practices which had blackened the reputation of central Government officials and created public skepticism regarding their interest in public welfare. The insurrectionists, in effect, requisitioned what they could of the export produce of the area, sometimes, as in the case of the copra crop of North Sulawesi, paying for it in military scrip rather than in currency. The produce was then smuggled abroad through the ineffectual Government blockade, and there either bartered or sold for hard currency. The rebels used the major part of the proceeds to acquire large quantities of military arms and equipment. They also used part of it to support their own agents overseas and to maintain the wives and children who had fled abroad to safety. They made an effort also to procure the consumer goods needed by the population of their areas, but delivery was difficult, supply was inadequate, and prices in the shops were the long familiar black market prices.

The Djakarta Government, which maintained an extremely large and active group of intelligence operators in Indonesia and abroad, did not fail to circulate reports which would cause suspicion and dissatisfaction within the rebel areas and among the rebel fighters. The wives and children of the rebel leaders, according to Djakarta, were living in "luxury hotels and apartments" in Singapore; they were purchasing "luxury goods" for their own use or for shipment back to relatives and friends in Indonesia. Furthermore, PRRI military leaders had appropriated all of the ready cash in the Medan and Makassar branches of the Bank of Indonesia (over one hundred million rupiahs in each instance), and a rebel sympathizer, the Indonesian Ambassador to Italy, had made off to Switzerland with $500,000 of Embassy funds. What had become of these several windfalls, for which full public accounting was never made? It was too much, of course, to expect publication of an auditor's report in the heat of an insurrection; but it was also too much to expect the public to credit the PRRI leaders with absolute personal integrity in the face of widely current rumors and of undeniable facts--indeed, some of the rebel leaders and their wives did have access to large sums of money for which there was little apparent accountability.

The military mismanagement of the PRRI showed up as soon as the Djakarta attacks started. The PRRI had at its disposal perhaps ten to fifteen thousand trained troops who had brought with them central Government arms and equipment, and had managed to acquire from abroad surprisingly large additional quantities of modern arms and ammunition. They had made bold announcements about training "thousands" of volunteers, preparing impregnable positions, and issuing orders to fight to the death.

When military operations actually started, the rebels were repeatedly caught by surprise by Djakarta's attacks--which they had thought were not coming at all or were coming at other times and places. They abandoned position after position, with scarcely even token resistance--as, for instance, the Pakanbaru oil fields (Caltex) which for a few tense days the international world expected them to blow up. They surrendered in large numbers with full equipment intact. At times, indeed, whole rebel units defected to the government forces, before, during, or after engagements. It must be allowed that at times they fought very bravely but were outnumbered, outgunned, and outmaneuvered by the Djakarta forces which could stage naval bombardments, paratroop drops, and mobile pincers movements. Furthermore, they had counted from the very first, if worse came to worst, upon guerrilla rather than positional warfare. They finally withdrew the remnants of their forces into the inaccessible jungle areas to which they would have been better advised to withdraw in the first place.

As propagandists, as has already been noted, the insurrectionists failed to arouse consistent or active public enthusiasm. They failed also to arouse as much international sympathy as they might well have done, partly because they refrained--in line with Indonesia's "independent" policy which Sukarno accuses them of betraying--from any really vigorous effort to enlist foreign aid and recognition. They preferred to do it themselves with their own resources, buying arms and even planes as funds permitted. Only a couple of times, and then not very loudly and much too late, did they ask for direct aid from the West--such as might, of course, have precipitated open Communist bloc aid to Djakarta. They failed even in the minor but still important function of at least informing or helping to inform the outside world what was really going on in the rebel areas. Foreign correspondents encountered almost as much official indifference and obstruction in Padang as they are likely to encounter in Djakarta. Rebel news bulletins were unreliable and at times proved false within hours of dissemination. Rebel spokesmen overseas were ill-informed about events at home, as was understandable under the circumstances, but, as was less understandable, were prone to make rash guesses.

So far as the outsider is concerned, the misunderstandings among the insurrectionist leaders themselves are more a matter of conjecture than of factual information. Conjecture is supported, however, by highly credible reports that as the rebel position deteriorated, tensions and frictions mounted among the leaders and still continue to do so. It is also supported by the record of little counter-coups within coups, and counter-counter-coups within counter-coups--witness, for instance, the Medan situation. Colonel Simbolon there carried out a swift and bloodless coup on December 22, 1956. Colonel Gintings, his presumably loyal second-in-command, five days later deposed him. A year later, a presumably loyal junior officer deposed Gintings for a day, invited Simbolon to return, and was then himself deposed to make way for Gintings again. The lines of loyalty within the Medan command, originally a stronghold of insurrectionist sentiment, were confused enough; outside Medan, among the battalion commanders of the various regions, the lines of loyalty were and are impossible to disentangle.

The story of miscalculation, mishandling, and misunderstanding, and of the consequent tragedy both to the rebels and the loyalists, can best be illustrated in a brief reconstruction of the actual course of the insurrection. The story falls into three phases: first, the 1956-57 phase of build-up to active hostilities; second, the March-June 1958 period of military action; and third, the mid-1958 to mid-1959 period of continued guerrilla fighting. It necessitates geographic leap-frogging from Djakarta in Java to Medan and Palembang in Sumatra, to Bandjarmasin in Kalimantan (Borneo), and to Makassar and Menado in Sulawesi, with recurrent backtracking between the various centers. It requires special emphasis on the attempted coalition of the insurrections in the two key cities which happened to be remotest from each other, as far as effective communications were concerned, namely Padang and Menado.

The first phase of the insurrection, to which there had been a long background of relatively minor uprisings throughout the archipelago, began in mid-November 1956 with the attempt of onetime Deputy Chief of Staff, Col. Zulkifli Lubis, in collaboration with a powerful group of Headquarters and regional officers to overthrow the Djakarta Government. The coup miscarried, a large number of the officers involved were put under arrest, but Lubis himself made his escape, presumably to Sumatra. The Government and the nation were alerted that a military bid for outright power, long speculated upon, had been attempted and might soon be attempted again. On December 4, a group of 48 leading military officers of the North and Central

The Lake Toba area near Medan, center of scattered fighting between PRRI and government troops, still imperfectly "pacified."

Sumatran Commands, meeting in Padang, took an oath to carry out "radical changes" in their areas, in order to "improve the deplorable condition of the country and the people." The military had already in the last several years subscribed to a succession of oaths, charters, and guiding principles. This new expression of military intent, accordingly, was not taken very seriously in Djakarta until about two weeks later when there occurred the first of a long series of regional military coups and attempted coups.

Actual and declared insurrection began on December 20, 1956. On that day Lt. Col. Ahmad Hussein, Commander of the Central Sumatra Military District, announced the formation of a mixed military and civilian "Banteng (wild buffalo) Council" in Padang and Bukittinggi. He declared that henceforth the Council and not the Djakarta Government would exercise the real administrative authority in the area. On December 22, Col. Maluddin Simbolon, Commander of the North Sumatra Military District, staged a parallel coup in Medan and formed a "Gadjah (elephant) Council." On December 27, however, Lt. Col. Djamin Gintings, Deputy Chief of Staff for the North Sumatra Military District, after originally declaring his loyalty to Simbolon and his adherence to the Padang oath, acted on Djakarta's prompting to depose Simbolon in a bloodless counter-coup. After some little conflict as to whether he or a rival had earned the position, and whether regional battalions would be loyal to either, Gintings was confirmed as the new commander. Simbolon fled into the jungle with a few hundred followers and presently joined the Padang group.

During January and February 1957, Lt. Col. Barlian, Commander of the South Sumatra Military District, with headquarters in Palembang, acting more cautiously than Hussein or Simbolon, moved to detach his region also from Djakarta's control. On March 8 he announced that a new "Garuda (mythological eagle) Council" would henceforth be responsible for South Sumatra's administration. Barlian never broke as completely with Djakarta, however, as did Hussein and Simbolon. He tried to act as an intermediary between them and the Djakarta command. He was caught in the special predicament that while he believed he could rely upon the loyalty of about half of the officers and men in his area, he knew that he could not be sure of the other half--Javanese troops under strong Headquarters influence. While he avoided the rash impetuousness of Simbolon who gravely misjudged the strength of his own position, he failed to achieve even the appearance of confidence and solidarity. He earned the hostility of his insurrectionist associates by withholding outright military support at the crucial time. As soon as Djakarta felt strong enough (April 30), Barlian was disciplined by being relieved of his command and fetched back to Java.

Meanwhile, in the eastern islands, Lt. Col. Sumual, Commander of the Moluccas District, on March 2, 1958, kidnapped half a hundred leading officials of Makassar. He held them overnight, until he had persuaded them to sign a "Permesta (universal struggle) Charter" and to form a "Permesta Council." In the name of the Council, he issued a Permesta Charter in which he announced an inclusive program of regional reforms and development. Djakarta expressed shock at his insubordination but announced that it could "condone" the Charter, since there was a great deal in it that was "constructive." Djakarta's tolerance was stretched almost to the breaking point when Col. Sumual and his officers removed from the Makassar branch of the Bank of Indonesia something over a hundred million rupiahs in cash with which to finance their reforms. But Sumual was not having everything his own way in Makassar. He was confronted with a peculiar situation in that there existed a parallel military command in his own area--the East and South Celebes Pacification Command, charged with putting down Kahar Muzakar's Darul Islam guerrillas. Sumual's opposite number, Col. Sudirman, had not been invited to the kidnapping, had not signed or approved the Charter, was not enthusiastic about defying Djakarta, and although the two made a public parade of amity, the situation was tense. Sumual was constrained to negotiate with Djakarta military headquarters. The compromise solution was reached that both Sulawesi commands would be dissolved, to be replaced by four new commands, and that Sumual would be responsible for implementing the reorganization. Sumual accordingly on June 7 relinquished his command in Makassar, then took leave of absence to visit his ailing father in Menado. Once he arrived in Menado, he announced that the Permesta Charter and Council were reactivated in the North and Central Sulawesi areas, that he himself claimed paramount military authority over the whole region of East Indonesia, and that it would be administered independently of Djakarta's directives.

These various Sumatran and Sulawesi insurrectionist movements gathered momentum during the next few months, while Djakarta's military and civil officials hustled about the archipelago holding conciliatory conferences, or invited the insurrectionist leaders to confer with them elsewhere, generally in Palembang. For a time, it looked as though Kalimantan would join the insurrection. Lieutenant Colonel Abimanju, Commander of the South Kalimantan Military District, had shown himself as early as November 1956 a potential rebel. He had then indicated his disapproval of Djakarta's mass arrest of officers suspected of being implicated in Col. Lubis' attempted coup, by ordering the retaliatory arrest of any high Djakarta official, either civil or military, who might set foot on Kalimantan. But Col. Abimanju, like Barlian later, wavered and compromised. He obeyed Djakarta's order to report to Headquarters for conferences, and there he found himself quickly maneuvered out of his command. He was later (October 1958) tried in Surabaya and sentenced to six months' imprisonment.

There had meanwhile appeared in Kalimantan among Abimanju's adherents a "Lambungmangkurat (reform) Council," modeled presumably on the others. Reports from Kalimantan are so sketchy and inconclusive, however, that it is difficult to determine whether any insurrectionist movement did more than just barely get under way. So far as the main insurrectionist leaders were concerned, Kalimantan, like North Sumatra, seemed lost to the cause. South Sumatra was on the fence. The real strength of the movement centered in two cities fifteen hundred miles apart and accessible to each other's representatives only by difficult and devious travel routes--the cities of Padang and Menado.

The two separate but related insurrections managed to achieve a greater degree of co-ordination at the beginning of 1958 than at any later period. Colonel Sumual then flew to Tokyo to deliver an ultimatum to President Sukarno, on holiday in Japan, at the same time that Lt. Col. Hussein publicly announced the same terms in Padang. Sukarno rejected the ultimatum and refused to form a new Government. The rebels thereupon (February 15) declared themselves the Revolutionary Government of the Republic of Indonesia (PRRI), named their joint cabinet, and announced themselves ready to govern and to fight until such time as Djakarta acceded to their terms.

Phase two of the insurrections began on March 12 when the central Government, after preliminary warning and shelling, launched an air, sea, and land attack (perhaps one or two thousand men), not upon Padang, as the rebels had earlier expected, but upon the Pakanbaru area of Sumatra. The Djakarta forces captured Pakanbaru and its vital oil fields within seven hours of the opening of the attack. They suffered, according to official reports, only one casualty. The rebels--a force of some five to eight hundred men, according to various reports--fired a few shots and then withdrew. The government forces moved to consolidate their hold over the whole of the Central Sumatra area and to threaten the approaches to Padang itself.

At the same time, in Medan the central Government suffered a brief reverse. Major Boyke Nainggolan declared himself a supporter of the insurrection and seized and held the city and the airfield for about 24 hours (March 16-17). Then, under pressure of government forces advancing from the interior and from the seacoast, he withdrew into the jungle, taking with him a few hundred troops, a considerable quantity of arms, and some one hundred million rupiahs from the Medan branch of the Bank of Indonesia. The second major rebel effort to take the crucially important city and area of Medan had failed. Extremely complicated and confused fighting in the next few weeks among various small forces in the Tapanuli-Atjeh region resulted, for the most part, in reassertion of Government control.

Padang, meanwhile, prepared for the inevitable invasion. The rebel leaders announced that they had set up an impenetrable barrier of spikes and rails on the airfield and impregnable mortar installations on the shore and in the hills. The Djakarta forces started with a preliminary naval bombardment on April 16, then at dawn on April 17 launched sea, air, and land attack. By late afternoon of the same day they had occupied the city. Loyalist troops deployed to cut off the logical route of rebel retreat into the mountains toward Bukittinggi, then drove the rebel forces into traps set for them along the coast to the south. On May 4, after a few small-scale clashes on the mountain road to Bukittinggi, the loyalist troops entered the city without encountering any further resistance.

The gorge outside Bukittinggi, representative
of the rugged terrain in which guerrilla troops
now hold out.

The PRRI had had perhaps four or five thousand troops in the Padang-
Bukittinggi area, plus a few thousand volunteers, mainly students, who had
received a minimum of training in operating the arms which they were issued.
Djakarta committed perhaps ten thousand men to the operation. The majority
of the PRRI troops surrendered, delivering over considerable quantities of new
arms and equipment which the Djakarta military spokesmen declared to be
superior to their own. A couple of thousand, in all, escaped into the jungle to
conduct guerrilla warfare--and on various occasions to emerge from the jungle and stage raids upon the city of Bukittinggi itself. The PRRI had lost its
Sumatran stronghold and had been greatly reduced in numbers and strength;
some of its leaders (Sjafruddin, for instance) just barely escaped capture as
they fled into the jungles or to foreign countries; and the rebel-ruled urban
areas returned once more to Djakarta's administration.

Simultaneously with the attack on Central Sumatra, the Permesta
forces had begun to meet with reverses in Sulawesi. Partly as a result of
the disastrous experiences of their allies in Sumatra, however, they were
preparing to put up a stronger fight and to stage some surprises of their own.
Actual fighting in Sulawesi began on March 29, 1958, when loyalist elements
among the rebel forces staged a little counter-coup and took the Central Sulawesi seaport town of Donggala. Rebel forces counterattacked and regained
the town, but in a few days' time the loyalist forces definitely re-established
their hold. By early April, after regaining Donggala and capturing the nearby
airfield at Palu, the loyalists were in control of a strategic area of Central
Sulawesi from which to stage an attack upon Menado.

Then came the rebel surprise. On April 13 unidentified aircraft raided the Government's Mandai airfield near Makassar. A few days later strange aircraft began to attack Indonesian and foreign shipping in the seaports of eastern Kalimantan. By late April the mystery planes had extended their area of operation as far as Ambon in the Moluccas and had demonstrated, therefore, their capability of staging a raid on Java, perhaps even on Djakarta.

The PRRI, it was clear, had acquired itself an air force. To underscore their achievements and their challenge to Djakarta, the rebels staged sudden sea-air raids in late April upon the islands of Morotai and Halmahera. They occupied abandoned World War II B-29 bases and were consequently in a position, as the central Government presently admitted, to dominate the air over East Indonesia. On April 30, Prime Minister Djuanda explained matters to the Indonesian Parliament and to the public. The rebels had acquired their planes--World War II bombers and fighters--in Taiwan; they had also acquired quantities of modern automatic weapons, in addition to aerial bombs; they had engaged Taiwanese and American pilots and crews; and furthermore, since no aviation fuel had been available in Sulawesi and no adequate ground facilities were available until the Halmahera and Morotai fields were put into operation, they must have received assistance from nearby countries--by implication, the Philippines. "Vexation," declared the Prime Minister, "has cropped up in circles of the Armed Forces as well as among the common people which, if permitted to take its own course, would adversely affect Indonesian-American relations." "Vexation" changed to anger and protest on May 18 when Indonesian Government forces shot down one rebel bomber over Ambon and found that the pilot was one Allan Lawrence Pope, an American citizen, whose papers showed that he had been a member of the U.S. armed forces not long since, and that he had recently been in both the Philippines and Taiwan.

Meanwhile, however, the central Government forces had staged some surprises of their own which rapidly altered the strategic situation in East Indonesia. On May 1 they shot down two rebel planes. On May 10 they began a series of air raids on rebel airfields. Again and again, inexplicably, they seemed to take the rebels completely by surprise. In raids on the airfields near Menado, central Government pilots caught half a dozen rebel bombers and fighters on the ground and obliterated practically the entire remaining rebel air force. In attacks beginning May 20, they recaptured the airfields on Morotai and Halmahera and thus practically eliminated the possibility that the PRRI air force would be reinforced by additional planes reportedly already purchased in Taiwan.

The central Government had already launched its major invasion of rebel-held areas in Sulawesi, and as in Sumatra it managed repeatedly to deceive the rebel military commanders as to the actual time and place of attack. On May 14 it staged an invasion of the seaport town of Gorontalo and one week later, after what was probably the bitterest fighting of the whole campaign, it had consolidated its hold upon the town and the adjacent areas in the face of repeated rebel counterattack. On May 16 it began landing troops on beaches in the Menado area, the initial landings going unnoticed by the Menado garrison. By June 26, after considerable fighting, it had occupied the city itself. From Gorontalo and Menado the government troops fanned out into the countryside, but here their victories were less clear-cut and less permanent. The rebels managed to establish themselves in the mountain and jungle areas. They managed to stage counterattacks in the city areas, even recapturing the Menado airfield a few miles outside the city, holding it for months before yielding it again to loyalist attack, and making it unsafe even yet for central Government use.

Phase three of the insurrection set in with the rebel defeats at Padang, Bukittinggi, and Menado. Since mid-1958, government troops have been engaged in "mopping-up operations" in both Sumatra and Sulawesi. They have announced victory after victory, only later to admit reinfiltration by rebel guerrillas and disruption of local government, production, and communications by land or sea. According to a Djakarta report on September 29, 1959, a year of intermittent operations has resulted in loss to the government of 983 killed, 1,695 wounded, and 154 missing, as compared with rebel casualties of 6,373 killed, 1,201 wounded or captured, and 6,057 surrendered. But the rebels continue to hold out in their mountain-jungle positions, to acquire the arms and food necessary to sustain guerrilla forays, and even to recruit replacements. The government forces seem unable, unless they are greatly reinforced, provided with much new equipment, and supported by large-scale jungle-clearance and road-building programs besides, really to eliminate the guerrilla bands.

It seems relatively safe to assume that the rebels now have from ten to fifteen thousand full- or part-time professional or volunteer fighting men, scattered through the rebellious areas of Sumatra and Sulawesi, that the central Government has 50,000 out of its total of 200,000 troops scattered through the same areas, and further, that the central Government is deterred from sending really powerful reinforcements not only by reason of logistical problems but because it lacks confidence in the loyalty of the troops or their commanders, once they get far removed from Djakarta's control. On the basis of the record in nearby Malaya, for instance, where a few thousand ill-equipped and ill-supplied jungle guerrillas tied down tens of thousands of government troops for ten years and necessitated enormous military expenditures on the part of the Government in order to dislodge them, it seems that the odds in Indonesia are not so heavily against the PRRI guerrillas as might seem from the 1958 record. By merely surviving and continuing to disrupt government operations, the guerrillas can continue to inflict upon the Djakarta regime enormous losses altogether disproportionate to their own strength.

"Don't think we're finished," a rebel spokesman told me recently.

"We have the will, and the money, and the arms, and the men, and the leadership to continue the struggle just as long as it takes. That will be until Sukarno goes and someone else comes into power in Djakarta. It must be someone who is willing to work with us to eliminate the Communist menace and build an Indonesia that is really free and prosperous."

"We may not be able to stamp them out," a Djakarta government official told me, "just as we haven't been able to stamp out the Darul Islam movement and others like it. And we will run into increasingly serious political and economic crises because we can't. But at least we have totally discredited them, both at home and abroad, and whatever new leadership may eventually emerge in Indonesia, it won't be the rebels."

To the best of my own belief, however, both the rebel and the official spokesmen misread the real situation. The rebel leaders are by no means completely discredited. The names Sjafruddin, Natsir, Sumitro, Simbolon, Kawilarang, Sumual, and others still command widespread respect today, even in Djakarta, but respect which is more than a little tinged with disappointment that their cause has seemed to fail and they themselves have seemed no more capable than other top national leaders of giving new content and vitality to the revolutionary movement. On the other hand, when and if the Sukarno regime collapses, whether or not as a consequence of the insurrections, it seems improbable that Sukarno's successor will be any more acceptable to the rebel leaders than Sukarno himself, or they to him. It is an impasse all too unhappily typical of Indonesian developments in the last few years, and the sequel seems predictable only in that it will involve a great and tragic waste of national and human resources.

Willard A. Hanna

[All photographs courtesy Ministry of Information, Djakarta.]

American Universities Field Staff

REPORTS SERVICE

BUNG KARNO'S INDONESIA

Part VIII: The Irian Irritant

by Willard A. Hanna

October 20, 1959

This publication is one of a continuing series on current developments in world affairs written by associates of the American Universities Field Staff. It is distributed by the AUFS as a useful addition to the American fund of information on foreign affairs.

AUFS Associates have been chosen for their skill in collecting, reporting, and evaluating data. Each has combined long personal observation and experience in his foreign area with advanced studies relating to it.

WILLARD A. HANNA, the author of this report, is based in Kuala Lumpur to write about Southeast Asian affairs. Before joining the AUFS in 1954, Dr. Hanna had spent a total of more than ten years in East and Southeast Asia as a teacher, administrator, and writer.

Publications under the imprint of the American Universities Field Staff are not selected to accord with an editorial policy and do not represent the views of its membership. Responsibility for accuracy of facts and for opinions expressed in the letters and reports rests solely with the individual writers.

"From Sabang to Merauke, Indonesia shall be free!" "Irian Barat is our national claim!" With these slogans, Bung Karno generates a high-voltage emotionalism which serves at once to distract national and international attention from Indonesia's critical domestic problems and to rally the "vital, progressive" forces of nationalism against the "decadent, dying" forces of capitalism and colonialism.

Only the imperialists and the capitalists, says Bung Karno, fail to recognize the justice of the Indonesian national claim to Western New Guinea. Only they "allege that it is Bung Karno himself who is causing all that noise about Irian Barat." But no, he declares: "West Irian is written with burning letters in the hearts of every Indonesian,"--the 85 million Indonesians who have the support of 2,000 million "progressive people" everywhere. "Reactions in Peking," he says "have been excellent. . . .There have been excellent reports from Moscow, too," and "from Cairo." But "the American attitude in this matter is always connected with what attitude she has to take towards the Netherlands. . . .That is why the Indonesians start to look in another direction; to put it frankly: Indonesia starts to look with sympathy at Moscow. Actually, you'll discover that it's in Moscow where they justify Indonesia's claim on West Irian. It is there that the Asian-African Conference was

[WAH-19-'59]

accorded full support. It is there that our independence policy has been justified. Were we to request for a financial loan, well, in a few minutes the money
is there. Although I as President say that everybody is good, the fact remains
that one shows a wavering attitude while the other discloses clarity in vision."

"What do I care about Irian?" one ordinary Indonesian said to me without any prompting, one who was, perhaps, too ignorant and impoverished to be
able to afford clarity of vision. "What I want is food and clothing and the chance
to work. I know nothing about Irian. I'm not angry with anyone about Irian. I
don't want to fight in Irian or for Irian. I hear Bung Karno talk about Irian,
and I shout 'Merdeka.' Then I go home and my children ask for rice and I forget Irian."

"Never underestimate the popular support for Bung Karno's campaign
to get Irian Barat," one highly sophisticated Indonesian told me. "There is no
doubt about it. Irian is ours and we are going to have it--or crack up trying
to get it. Besides, would you have suggested that Americans didn't want or
need Oregon?"

"Personally," one Dutch official told me, "I wish we'd let them have it
years ago. Lots of Dutchman have argued that we should give it to Indonesia,
or anyhow get rid of it. God knows, it's no good to us. But don't you see, we
can't just hand it over to them now, not after Bung Karno has blackmailed us
for all he can get--and make no mistake about it, he'll blackmail you too.
Besides, you must understand that the Dutch as a nation have a sense of
responsibility and a sense of mission. We're either Catholics or we're Cal-
vinists, and in either case we're obstinate. We've promised to Christianize
and educate Irian and prepare it for self-determination, and we're not going
to hand it over now to an Indonesian colonialism that would be a lot less
enlightened than Dutch colonialism ever was!"

"There must be some reasonable compromise," an American official
told me, "and heaven knows there are enough Dutchmen and Indonesians who
would like nothing better than to save face by being maneuvered into one. A
UN trusteeship, maybe. Only it would be better if someone other than us did
the maneuvering."

"And after Western New Guinea," an Australian official asked me,
"then what? Australian New Guinea? And after Australian New Guinea,
British Borneo? Of course Portuguese Timor is scarcely worth claiming,
but don't forget: Indonesia hasn't a shred of a legitimate claim on New Guinea
but it does have quite a strong historic claim on Borneo and Malaya--and for
that matter, a case of sorts could be made even for parts of Indochina!"

"We have no territorial claim except Irian Barat," the Indonesian
Foreign Office insists.

"All Borneo belongs to us," Ministers of State Mohammad Yamin and Chairul Saleh have at times been heard to declare. Dr. Yamin is the prize promoter, next to Bung Karno, of an Irian Barat Irredenta, and Chairul Saleh is one of the organizers of an Indonesian mass action movement for the "liberation" of Irian Barat.

"If you Americans would just show good will toward us on the Irian problem," an Indonesian official told me, "then we could get it, and after we got it we could get down to the serious business of putting Indonesia in order."

"And where will you find the administrators for Irian, and the capital? And what about all the doctors, teachers, engineers, or for that matter, peasants and laborers?" I asked. "They don't like to transmigrate even to Sumatra or Kalimantan. How enthusiastic are they going to be about pioneering in New Guinea?"

"All in due time," he replied. "First, we must get it, and we won't rest until we do. So long as the Dutch remain in Irian Barat, Dutch colonialism is being perpetuated right inside Indonesia. We can't and we won't tolerate it. Would you tolerate Russian colonialism in Alaska?"

"We managed to tolerate British colonialism in Canada," I said.

"But that's different."

"I thought you implied that it wasn't."

"No friend of Indonesia's would suggest that the Dutch have any right to be in Irian Barat, or that Indonesia will ever be complete without it."

As for myself, of all the international disputes I have been personally familiar with, that over Irian Barat leaves me with the greatest sense of futility and fatigue. For the sake of Netherlands New Guinea, the Dutch have forfeited a good $2 billion worth of properties in Indonesia--although, as they point out, they might not have held onto them much longer in any event. They have seen some 10,000 Dutchmen expelled from Indonesia where they were gaining a good and useful living. They have assumed an administrative and financial burden of some $15.5 million per year and seem most unlikely soon to recoup unless by vast new development of oil or of some as yet undiscovered mineral deposit--uranium, for instance. For the sake of Irian Barat, the Indonesians, for their part, have courted national pandemonium and Western opprobrium by long-continued harassment and vilification of the Dutch. For the sake of both airing and sparing Dutch and Indonesian sensitivities on Western New Guinea, the United Nations and the United States have repeatedly let themselves in for the most stereotyped nationalist-communist-democratic debates. They have tended at the end of each round of debate to assume stances of self-righteous impartiality which serve only to exasperate both the Dutch and the Indonesians.

Two years ago, replete with debate over Irian Barat by persons who have never seen it, I decided to have a look for myself. My report, to telescope insofar as it is possible to telescope this vast semicontinent, must be made in Texan idiom. Irian Barat is roughly half as large (130,000 sq. mi.) as the State of Texas. (The whole island of New Guinea is 15 per cent bigger than Texas.) It is the vastest expanse of the most superbly beautiful mountain-jungle-swamp wilderness, populated by the most thinly scattered bands of the most primitive people living in the remotest and most inaccessible areas that have been least explored and developed, reportedly the most meagerly endowed with soil, mineral, or other natural resources--except timber--of any major unexplored portion of the earth's surface. Western New Guinea in particular, as contrasted with the rather more developed eastern (Australian) half of the island, seems at first, second, third, and even later glance, as many involuntary wartime American visitors, including Texans, will agree, to be huge, hot, empty, rough, and for civilized men all but uninhabitable.

The Dutch have bulldozed small stretches of mountain, swamp, and jungle to build up a few little European enclaves (total Dutch population, 17,000), inhabited mainly by government servants and their families, plus representatives of the few Dutch business firms which regard New Guinea enterprise as worth the huge effort required to get government permits to operate there. The Dutch have extended a generally tenuous sort of jurisdiction over some 350,000 of an estimated total population of 700,000 Papuans, most of them Stone Age people who live in semisettled groups and speak mutually unintelligible languages, only a few of whom have begun to become aware of the advantages--and disadvantages--of civilization. They have put some 30,000 young people into primary school, another 200 or so into secondary school, and there are working upon them an amazing transformation of body and mind by introducing nutritional and intellectual stimulus. They have also put about 16,000 Papuans to work in government offices or in modern enterprises like the building trade, a small shipyard, a small lumber mill, the oil fields, and some small-scale experimental projects like a mechanized rice polder and a fisheries co-operative. They are training a few dozen higher level civil servants, including one group of some twenty young Papuan men who are now attending school in Holland, one in the University of Leiden. They are operating many hundreds of missionary centers, both Protestant and Catholic (a few supported and staffed by Americans), an increasing number of hospitals (now about 20), clinics (now about 100), and various welfare projects. They are developing agriculture by operating small experimental stations and encouraging the production of copra, cacao, fruit, and vegetables. They are busily exploring mineral and other resources, in co-operation with scientists from Australian New Guinea. They are awaiting the day when a population which now subsists almost exclusively upon sago palm or sweet potatoes, and clothes itself, if at all, with a shell, a gourd, a g-string, or a strip of fringed cloth, is finally ready for "self-determination." When that day comes, some of the Dutch will admit with what seems almost like eagerness, the new Irian may invite the Dutch to depart by the earliest available transportation and vote to join Indonesia.

Western New Guinea now costs about US$32 million per year in administrative costs, about $17 million of which is recovered in revenues, mostly through company tax, income tax, and import duties, the burden of which falls to a very large extent, of course, upon the Dutch civil servants. Of its exports, valued at about $8 million per year, oil is by far the most important; it accounts for about two thirds by value of the total export but is dropping off in quantity each year, whether for economic or political reasons is difficult to determine. Except for nutmeg, copra, mace, crocodile hides, copal, and scrap metals, the latter from a huge but now greatly depleted World War II legacy of Japanese and American wreckage, Western New Guinea's exports are significant not for quantity or value but for embellishing the area's balance of trade tables with one of the world's more exotic sets of statistical items: sharks' fins, stag horn, massory bark, lawang oil, trepang (sea slugs), dammar, seashells, and bird-of-paradise feathers.

The foreign enclaves in New Guinea seem for the most part a bureaucratic triumph in making the worst of a bad situation. In Hollandia, the Dutch civil servants have recently been enabled at least to move out of the rusty quonset huts which they inherited from General MacArthur. The Governor himself has vacated MacArthur's transported and reassembled wartime "palace"--regarding which U.S. Congressional investigators raised questions of "extravagant" spending on "luxury quarters." He left the premises just as the termites were succeeding in making the place uninhabitable even to themselves, and moved into a new Government House built high on the mountain overlooking Hollandia's magnificent Humboldt Bay. All about him, however, are new little concrete-block bungalows for the civil servants, boxy facsimiles of each other designed, it would seem, expressly to admit heat and mosquitoes but to exclude air and view. Missionary designers who put up more attractive and more comfortable houses at lower cost were ordered to desist, since they were creating jealousy and discontent within the civil service. The Dutch administrators, despite their unimaginative quarters and a diet so monotonous that tinned spam and fruit cocktail constitute delicacies, exhibit a remarkable degree of zeal and dedication to their jobs. They are, for the most part, men of high professional qualifications. A good many of them have previously held bigger and better jobs--in Indonesia, for instance--so they are understandably nostalgic for a more cosmopolitan milieu, while at the same time determined to improve New Guinea.

The Chinese constitute the second largest alien group in New Guinea, numbering now about 18,000. As elsewhere in Southeast Asia, they run small retail enterprises and serve as middlemen in the collecting and marketing of produce. But even the Chinese have not been able really to prosper in New Guinea--a sobering factor in appraising the area's economic potentialities. The third minority consists of Eurasian immigrants from Indonesia, mainly former employees of the Dutch Government or of Dutch business firms, or former members of the Dutch armed services, most of whom have attempted to supplement their meager pensions by establishing little fruit, vegetable, or dairy farms. The Eurasian experiment has not been a success. These ex-soldiers and ex-clerical workers took over lands which had been settled, then abandoned by Dutch peasant transmigrants in the 1930's, and most of the new proprietors would now gladly abandon their forlorn little farms if only they could. Some of their children, no more interested in farming than their parents and most of them no better equipped, are beginning to find a natural place for themselves in government offices and in the new industries--ship-building, lumber milling, bottling works, biscuit factories, and the like. They often work side by side with the educated Papuans and may prove to be a much more vital and hopeful element in the new country than have their parents.

A fourth minority is made up of Indonesians, mainly from the Moluccas and mainly, of course, sympathizers with the Dutch. They serve as mission-aries, teachers, and workers in the oil fields, and tend to think wistfully of the old days in Indonesia and of the particularly beautiful island of Ambon from which many of them originated. Needless to say, none of the minority groups --Indonesian, Eurasian, Chinese, or Dutch--see any future for themselves in New Guinea if the area should be handed over to Indonesia.

Such, in brief, is Dutch colonialism in Netherlands New Guinea today. Indonesians find it "intolerable provocation," "exploitation," "oppression of the native peoples," "arrogant Dutch disregard for Indonesian nationalists' rights and aspirations," and "a threat to national security." Indonesian resent-ment does not diminish each time new rumors circulate that fantastic riches in oil and uranium have been discovered, or are about to be discovered; or that Indonesian or Papuan rebels against Dutch rule have been arrested, imprisoned, or even executed; or that Dutch land, sea, and air power is being built up; or that the Dutch in New Guinea are planning an armed attack upon Indonesian islands--or at any rate are lending aid and comfort to the Indone-sian insurrectionist movements.

"The Dutch are converting Irian Barat into a SEATO base inimical to Indonesia," report Indonesians in all seriousness. "The Indonesians are wheedling ships, planes, and arms out of the United States, Great Britain, Russia, Yugoslavia, and whoever else will supply them, for the ultimate pur-pose of mounting a campaign against us," say some of the Dutch. "It is cruel and delusory," suggest a few Indonesians, including Bung Hatta, "to build up a liberation of Irian campaign. How are our flaming youths going to get there--swim?"

So, among the Dutch, the policy has become one of going slowly, cau-tiously, and, if possible, economically in New Guinea. Among the Indonesians, the policy has started at least to shift to revitalizing the Indonesian nation itself rather than inflaming the public over the Irian issue. And abroad, the hope is that maybe, after all, this uproar over New Guinea will gradually die down, especially if no one listens.

Both the Indonesians and the Dutch have encountered, in the course of the dispute, rather more than the usual degree of international disinclination to listen patiently to the interminable arguments. They have encountered also a pronounced inclination on the part of other nations to line up on the Irian issue on the basis of instinctive reaction to anything presented as a nationalism-vs.-colonialism conflict. The Afro-Asian politicians present an almost but not quite solid front in support of Indonesia's nationalist demands; the Communist-bloc politicians, naturally, find in Indonesia's claims a convenient pretext to revive every bromide about colonialism, capitalism, and imperialism. The Latin American nations have tended of late, as they start thinking of establishing closer relations with Indonesia, to slide over to the Indonesian side. The Western European nations, plus Australia and New Zealand, nations with political and economic investments to protect in colonial or ex-colonial areas, side with the Dutch. The United States, which finds such issues peculiarly complicated, has sided with no one and has gained no friends in return. The United Nations, when last the matter came up for a vote (the tenth, on November 29, 1957), failed even to adopt a compromise resolution calling upon the Netherlands and Indonesia to reopen negotiations between themselves. Forty-one nations voted in favor of the resolution, 29 against it, and 15--including the United States--abstained. Nevertheless, Bung Karno now declares, 2 billion out of the world's 2.6 billion people have placed themselves on the side of the "inevitable victory of Asian nationalism" and the inevitable defeat of "the imperialists." Unofficially, a great many responsible Dutchmen have favored transfer of Irian to Indonesia at the earliest possible moment, and with no conditions attached; unofficially, also, a great many responsible Indonesians would prefer that the Government did not have to cope with Irian's problems, while having to cope with more urgent problems in the other islands. But officially, both Governments have been adamant.

The Indonesian and the Dutch official cases can be summarized briefly.[1] The Indonesian Government argued originally--and with no little originality--that geographically, racially, culturally, and historically Western Guinea constitutes an integral part of the Indonesian archipelago. The Dutch have pointed out, with massive evidence to support them, that geographically, racially, culturally, and historically Western New Guinea constitutes no such

---

[1] For more detailed analyses, the following works are suggested:

Bone, Robert C. Jr. The Dynamics of the Western New Guinea (Irian Barat) Problem, Ithaca: Cornell University, Interim Report Series, Modern Indonesia Project, 1958, 170 pp.

The Question of West Irian in the United Nations, 1954-1957. Ministry of Foreign Affairs, Republic of Indonesia, 490 pp.

Western New Guinea and the Netherlands. Government State Printing Office, The Netherlands, September 1954, 23 pp.

thing. The Indonesians later shifted their main argument to the legalistic grounds that during the course of negotiations on transfer of sovereignty over the Netherlands East Indies, the Dutch implied a promise to yield Western New Guinea which has been in theory a Dutch possession since 1828, in practice a Dutch administrative area beginning only in 1898, and disputedly an integral or a nonintegral part of the Netherlands East Indies. The Dutch quote exactly the same imprecise record of official, semiofficial, and unofficial conversations of the 1945-48 period to show that they made no promises regarding Western New Guinea. The Indonesians have again shifted ground in the last several years to the position that Dutch retention of Western New Guinea constitutes an intolerable colonialistic provocation within Indonesian waters and that good Indonesian relations with the Netherlands (and with the Western world in general, by not always veiled implication) are contingent upon Dutch accession to Indonesian demands. The Dutch, in what is perhaps an excess of urbanity, considering the incendiary effect upon nationalistic sentiment of foreign derision, have branded the Indonesian position in toto as "disingenuous," "fanciful," "changeable," and a "nationalistic extravanganza." They have declared further, with much unhappy evidence to point to, that the Indonesian Government has made a shambles of its own political and economic system and that New Guinea would be subjected to a chaotic Indonesian-style colonialism which would be sheer disaster not only for the Papuans but for the Western world's strategic interests as well. The Dutch declare that they themselves, on the other hand, are preparing New Guinea for the day--how distant, no one says--when it can exercise "self-determination," opting then, if it choses, even for Indonesian rule.

The Indonesian Government, in retaliation for Dutch refusal to yield and UN refusal to bring pressures to bear, took measures in late 1957 to achieve its goals by "another course," as Bung Karno had earlier threatened. It began its campaign to expel 10,000 Dutch subjects and their families from Indonesia and to seize some $2 billion in Dutch properties, making vague promises of some sort of "compensation" once the Dutch see the error of their ways. The move, the Indonesian officials asserted, would hit the Netherlands where it hurt: it would disrupt the Dutch economy and bring the nation to its knees. The Dutch, who had already liquidated a part of their holdings in Indonesia and hedged on others, were hard hit as individuals and deeply stirred as a nation, but only slightly shaken economically. Today, the Netherlands exhibits every sign of political and economic stability, and the Indonesian situation grows appallingly worse. The Dutch now tend to say: "What is to be gained by any concession?" The Indonesians say, in effect: "Better to collapse as a nation than to retreat on a national claim." But the danger of collapse has become so real and immediate that even in Indonesia sounder counsels may have begun to prevail on the Irian issue. Instead of raising the question again in the United Nations and instead of whipping up monster "Liberate Irian" rallies at home, some government leaders are cautiously attempting, with how much success remains to be seen, to convert the "Liberate Irian" into a "Regenerate Indonesia" cause.

The Irian question, like a good many other international issues, seems likely to remain unresolved for quite some time and to give comfort only to those interested in international conflict rather than in co-operation. United States policy makers find themselves in the not unaccustomed position of being unable to find a policy which seems both prudent and opportune. Their position is especially difficult since there seems so little grounds, in this instance, for sympathy toward the aspirations of a newly-independent nation, and so much to be lost by withholding support. The Dutch find themselves saddled with the thankless job of developing a remote area which can really be developed only with infinitely greater investment of capital, skill, and altruism than the Dutch seem capable or willing to expend. The Indonesians, on the other hand, find themselves saddled with an uncompromisable national claim which, it seems, a good many Indonesians would gladly forget. The United Nations, even if it decided it was able to rule on the Irian issue and to enforce its ruling, could hardly come forward with any better proposal than for an international consortium. Those serving in such a consortium would almost certainly find Irian Barat, because of its political and physical discomforts, one of the world's least desirable or rewarding assignments.

The initiative on the Irian issue has long been in the hands of the Indonesians and has been used for the most inflammatory national and international propaganda. The initiative could now, conceivably, be taken by the Dutch. Should they somehow achieve what they have long failed to achieve--that is, a new and imaginative policy regarding Irian Barat, one which would remove the stigma of colonialism and preclude the excesses of nationalism--they would be performing pioneer political exploration in the mid-20th century comparable to that they achieved geographically in the late 16th. Meanwhile, for reasons explainable only on the basis of the emotional appeal of an Irredentist cause to a highly sensitive but frustrated people, the Irian problem remains to Indonesia a flaming symbol of the iniquity of colonialism and the righteousness of nationalism.

Willard A. Hanna

SOUTHEAST ASIA SERIES
Vol. VII   No. 24
(Indonesia)

American Universities Field Staff

REPORTS SERVICE

BUNG KARNO'S INDONESIA

Part IX: The Spoils of Oil

by Willard A. Hanna

October 23, 1959

This publication is one of a continuing series on current developments in world affairs written by associates of the American Universities Field Staff. It is distributed by the AUFS as a useful addition to the American fund of information on foreign affairs.

AUFS Associates have been chosen for their skill in collecting, reporting, and evaluating data. Each has combined long personal observation and experience in his foreign area with advanced studies relating to it.

WILLARD A. HANNA, the author of this report, is based in Kuala Lumpur to write about Southeast Asian affairs. Before joining the AUFS in 1954, Dr. Hanna had spent a total of more than ten years in East and Southeast Asia as a teacher, administrator, and writer.

Publications under the imprint of the American Universities Field Staff are not selected to accord with an editorial policy and do not represent the views of its membership. Responsibility for accuracy of facts and for opinions expressed in the letters and reports rests solely with the individual writers.

Indonesia has the biggest oil reserves of the Far East. It has a well-established, albeit predominantly American, British, and Dutch-operated, oil industry that is poised to run production and export graphs steeply upward. It has an advantageous location from which to serve the fast growing Southeast Asian markets. It also has a collapsing domestic economy which huge transfusions of oil--into both domestic and foreign markets--might rather swiftly help to revive. What could be more logical--from the Western point of view, of course--than that the Indonesian Government should embark, with joyous Western co-operation, upon a crash program of oil exploitation?

Indonesian officialdom, however, seems to prefer it otherwise, and the word "exploitation" gives the clue. The oil industry, the Indonesian Government reasons, must be rigidly controlled in order to prevent foreign exploitation of Indonesia's wealth, and to divert concessions, management, and profits as swiftly and completely as possible from Western into Indonesian hands. Development for foreign sales must be restricted until the Indonesian Government is in a position to collect more of the proceeds. Domestic needs must be met by the oil companies at prices below production cost because Indonesian purchasing power is low. If the Americans, the British, and the Dutch don't like it that way, they are free to pull out at any time--

[WAH-20-'59]

leaving their installations behind them, of course. The Russians, the Chinese, the Germans, the Japanese, and many others are eagerly awaiting the chance to move in. They might prove willing to teach the Indonesians all of the "secrets" of oil so that the nation can soon run its own industry--secrets which might have to include how to achieve increased supply and profit from diminishing wells.

Over a period of years, the foreign companies have been arguing their case and supporting it with Western logic and mathematical calculations. Unless they get new development rights, production will fall off. Unless they get assurance of an equitable share of the profits, other oil-producing areas are going to look more attractive for new investment. Unless they get price increases in the local market, they cannot maintain distribution facilities. Unless they get Government co-operation, they can scarcely recruit, train, and retain competent Indonesian staff to take over operations and management.

The Indonesian Government, faced with a financial crisis which in-creased oil revenues would do much to remedy, faced with economic disinte-gration which domestic shortages and a black market in petroleum products do much to aggravate, faced also with scientific demonstration that the situa-tion is likely to grow worse, not better, has done practically nothing to put the industry on a sounder basis. Indonesian officials, it must be admitted, are probably well advised to regard altruism as secondary on the list of for-eign company motives and to look twice at market projections which empha-size substantial losses. On the other hand, it is the Indonesian Government and the Indonesian people, far more than the foreign companies and share-holders who stand to lose most--a state of affairs which does not make for increased cordiality either in continuing operations under the present set-up or in negotiating a change.

Since the days of Mossadegh vs. the Anglo-Iranian Oil Company, there has been no neater or sadder example of Nationalism vs. Rationalism--or, should one say, of exploitation of the "exploiter" vs. exploitation of the "ex-ploited"? In the case of Sukarno et al vs. Shell-Stanvac, the real issue is obscured by much greater sophistication and subtlety on the nationalist side, and overshadowed by greater tact and restraint on the rationalist side. The real issue is this: can a virtually insolvent nation which is unable to exploit its own rich oil reserves afford to entrust them to foreign Western concerns? Or conversely, can it afford not to?

Background Facts on the Oil Industry

The Indonesian oil industry is divided mainly among four companies. American companies have controlled 68.4 per cent of recent (1958) production --Caltex 45.6 per cent and Stanvac 22.8 per cent. British, Dutch, American, and Indonesian government interests have exercised joint control over the

Shell Oil Company (Batavische Petroleum Maatschappij), Djakarta office.

other 31.6 per cent--the Shell combine of mixed British, American, and Dutch ownership; and a Shell subsidiary, Permindo, a joint Shell-Indonesian Government venture. (Because of the large British and American equity in ownership, Shell installations were not touched when the Indonesian Government seized Dutch concerns in late 1957.) A fifth company, Permina, owned by the Indonesian Government and supervised by the Army, operates wells in North Sumatra seized by the Indonesian Republican Government during the Revolution and subsequently nationalized. Its position in the industry has been of little consequence until it began this year to feature in local sales and to export as well, with an American oil concern supplying it with equipment and marketing its produce abroad.

Total foreign investment and total income from past investment in the Indonesian oil industry is impossible to calculate with any exactness, but investment over the last half century must total well over half a billion dollars and profits a very great deal more. Postwar investment in rehabilitation and expansion of installations badly damaged by war has come to at least $100 million on the part of each of the major foreign companies. Shell and Stanvac were formerly the really important producers, but Caltex is at present in by far the most advantageous position. Although Caltex got into the competition late, shortly before World War II it acquired rights to oil fields which are just now coming into full production. These wells account for the major part of the increase in Indonesian output in the last several years and of the anticipated increase in output in the near future. Caltex has the further advantage that it produces exclusively for the foreign market and therefore enjoys hard currency profits without absorbing the rupiah losses which, as will be noted later, are the penalty upon Shell and Stanvac for having developed a local distribution system. Shell, Permindo, and Stanvac have none of them been able to acquire new exploration and development rights sufficient to offset long-range decline in production of existing wells. All three are faced with the unhappy prospect that as production begins soon to fall off seriously, greater and greater quantities of their oil are being diverted from the lucrative foreign into the money-losing local market.

The total output of Indonesian oil wells now comes to about 16 million tons per year, of which about 7.4 million tons are exported as crude oil (the entire output of Caltex, plus .2 million tons from other companies); 4.2 million tons are exported as refined products (about 45 per cent each of the Shell and Stanvac output); and about 3 million tons (after refining) are left for local consumption. This 16 million tons per year represents a 100 per cent increase over 1952, and production may double again by 1966, largely as a result of Caltex increases. In absolute terms, the production and export figures look good and the graphs healthy. In relative terms, however, the situation is by no means so favorable. Indonesia's oil output is not keeping pace with world oil production or demand; Indonesia is not really taking advantage of its known oil deposits or encouraging exploration for new ones; it is not even holding its own in the Southeast Asian market which it is advantageously located to supply; and it is developing an exceedingly unhealthy home market in which, as a result of artifically depressed prices, demand far exceeds supply, and development of the oil industry itself or of other industries dependent upon oil is critically handicapped.

Indonesia's known oil resources are modest, to be sure, as compared with those of the Middle East, but they are huge in terms of known resources in nearby areas and they could be a tremendous factor in the Indonesian and Southeast Asian economies in general. Indonesia produced 3 per cent of the world's oil in prewar years; it is producing only about 2 per cent today. It supplied well over half of Australia's oil imports in prewar years; it supplies less than a third now. Its domestic oil consumption has increased 700 per cent over prewar years, while its output has increased only about 100 per cent. Its oil exports, to be sure, have increased greatly in recent years, and its oil revenues have gone up accordingly; but both increases seem to have been accomplished more in spite of government obstruction than because of government encouragement. Meanwhile, by way of comparison, in the tiny nearby State of Brunei in colonial British Borneo, oil production has increased from negligible prewar figures to one third of Indonesia's total; direct and indirect state revenue from oil has increased so enormously that, try as it will, Brunei can spend only about 50 per cent of its income.

The Current Crisis in the Domestic Oil Market

Neither the Indonesian Government nor the oil companies are happy about the present situation, but for rather different reasons. The prevailing Indonesian point of view, of which the Government must, of course, take cognizance, seems to be that oil company profits still border on the astronomical and the extortionate. The contrasting company point of view--which some influential Indonesian spokesmen have come to share--seems to be that Indonesian policy regarding oil now borders upon the suicidal. Both points of view have been expressed, with appropriate restraint on the part of officials but with less restraint upon the part of press and public, in the course of recent negotiations (late 1958 and early 1959) between the Indonesian Government and the foreign companies. The basic point at issue was the domestic pricing policy. Shell and Stanvac claimed that they were losing tremendous sums in their local retail business. The Indonesian Government remained unpersuaded, or at least noncommittal, but Indonesian commentators tended--with notable exceptions among newspaper editors--to declare categorically that the companies were not really losing money, or that they could afford to do so, or that they were deliberately creating the crisis they said was crippling them, or all this at once.

Shell and Stanvac, which have heretofore been exceedingly cautious about airing their case, began in the course of their representations to the Government publicly to bare their souls and, what was more, their balance sheets. The company performance had about it certain elements of the strip-tease, since none of the public revelations included such vital disclosures as exactly how large a cut the Indonesian Government gets in the foreign exchange proceeds of the industry, or exactly how far company profits in foreign currencies are offset by losses in rupiahs. The Indonesian Government's performance, on the other hand, as is usually the case when it is dealing with financial and economic matters, had about it certain elements of hallucination --as though it hadn't really been there after all when the facts and figures were being presented. The Government's own facts and figures on profit and loss on oil, whether in foreign currency or in rupiahs, are quite incomprehensible. Nevertheless, it requires only a very little firsthand observation of the Indonesian domestic oil market and a rough-and-ready calculation of Indonesia's foreign currency profits to lead the Western observer at least to a very cynical conclusion. The present Indonesian oil market demonstrates how by the exceedingly adroit feat of profiteering from its own bad management and at the risk of killing the goose that greases the wheels of the nation, the Indonesian Government has managed over the last few years both to have its oil and sell it too.

By way of illustration, one can cite the gasoline marketing situation[1] in the Lampung area of South Sumatra, not far from the oil-producing and processing center of Palembang:

Stanvac sells to the dealer at the government-controlled price of Rp. 1.16 per liter--approximately US$0.40 per gallon at the former official rate of exchange for the rupiah; US$0.10 per gallon at the new official rate; something in the neighborhood of US$0.04 at the black market rates of recent months. Since supply rarely meets demand--largely as a result of distribution difficulties to be described later--dealers contrive to sell as little of their stock as possible at the official retail price of Rp. 1.22 per liter. A great part of the gasoline gets into the black market where it sells for

---

[1] Figures are for late 1958. Official prices have remained unchanged since then; black market prices have fluctuated; the basic problem remains the same.

Stanvac
employees
attend
a
typing
class
during
working
hours.

Stanvac's Sungei Gerong installation at Palembang.

Berlitz-method English instruction
for Stanvac employees, Palembang.

Housing for Indonesian
employees, Palembang.

Interior of Stanvac housing
for Indonesian employees.

Rp. 7.50 per liter (approximately US$2.00, $0.50, and $0.20 at the above rates of exchange). The black marketeer thus takes a profit of almost 700 per cent which he must split, naturally, with various associates in the enterprise, including, not uncommonly, civil and military officials. The Government takes a tax of Rp. 0.55 per liter, which Stanvac pays out of the Rp. 1.16 it collects from the dealer. Since actual production cost, plus tax and transport, comes to Rp. 1.58, Stanvac itself takes a loss of Rp. 0.42 on each liter it sells.

Elsewhere in Indonesia, the difference between official and black market prices of gasoline is not commonly so extreme as in the Lampung area, and shortages are only sporadic although increasingly frequent. In Djakarta and other seaport cities, for instance, where distribution facilities are relatively good, the black market ranges between two and three times the official price. But if gasoline constitutes no critical problem as yet to the Djakarta consumer, kerosene does, as it also does in other Indonesian cities where it constitutes a primary cooking fuel. The basic calculation on kerosene, again using the Lampung situation as illustrative, is as follows: company wholesale price, Rp. 0.60 per liter; black market selling price, Rp. 4.50; government tax, Rp. 0.07; company loss, Rp. 0.44.

In total, on gasoline and kerosene sales combined, Stanvac and Shell (including Permindo) calculate that they lose approximately Rp. 1,600 million per year (US$130 million, $33 million, or $15 million, depending upon the exchange rate). In order to make up these losses, they have to transfer profits from other sectors of the operation, converting them from hard currency into exceedingly soft rupiahs at an exceedingly unattractive rate, presumably about 30 to 1 in the past, about 45 to 1 at present.

The accusation is frequently heard in Djakarta that the oil companies are withholding oil products deliberately from the local market and are thus themselves creating the serious shortages and the black market. They do so, the argument runs, first, because they wish to sell for dollars rather than rupiahs; second, because they want to bring pressure to bear upon the Government. The oil companies, on the other hand, argue as follows: the shortages are caused by breakdown of the distribution system. Breakdown of the distribution system is the result of deterioration of storage tanks, lighters, tank-cars, trucks, and pumps. Wholesale replacement of such equipment will not be authorized by the company stockholders so long as the domestic market shows a loss rather than a profit. Under the circumstances, company spokesmen point out, as more and more equipment wears out and fewer and fewer replacements arrive, the distribution system is certain to grow worse and not better.

Shortages at present are already so acute that the whole national economy is feeling the effects. Black market prices of gasoline, for instance, are driving the costs of transportation sharply upward--by 100-300 per cent, for instance, for the riders of the "opelettes," the Djakarta jitney buses. Black market prices of kerosene are throwing household budgets completely out of joint, cooking fuel alone accounting for 10-20 per cent of a government employee's salary. Manufacturing industries, which are already experiencing difficulties enough in procuring a steady supply of raw materials, frequently have to close down for lack of fuel to operate their generators which are themselves essential because electrical current is scarce and unreliable.

As shortages have grown more acute and the effects more readily apparent, oil company requests for reconsideration of official pricing policies have begun to elicit some spirited support both in the press and among a few officials and private citizens. Nevertheless, two basic official objections remain insurmountable: that increase in domestic oil prices would seriously and adversely affect the whole Indonesian economy by greatly increasing living and industrial costs; and that the problem is one for the oil companies themselves to solve by increased efficiency of management and greater flexibility in balancing off apparent losses against certain profits.

The oil companies, in turn, have engaged in some careful cost-accounting. They came up during the latter part of 1958 with a proposal for a relatively modest increase in official prices which would enable the companies to operate at a profit and to maintain both supply and distribution at such a level that the black market would collapse. The companies suggested a fixed wholesale price for the Lampung area, for instance, of Rp. 1.78 per liter of gasoline, and retail price of Rp. 1.84. This would allow for an increase of the government tax from Rp. 0.55 to Rp. 0.58 per liter, a dealer profit of Rp. 0.03 (out of the Rp. 0.06 mark-up), and a company profit of Rp. 0.05 (as compared with its current Rp. 0.42 loss). The consumer, on his part, would realize a savings of Rp. 5.66 as compared with the black market price to which he is accustomed. On kerosene, the proposed price scale was: Rp. 1.17 per liter wholesale, Rp. 1.37 retail; no change in government tax; dealer profit of Rp. 0.10 per liter; and company profit of Rp. 0.05 per liter (as compared with a current loss of Rp. 0.44). The consumer would save Rp. 3.11 per liter as compared with the black market price.

The formula of simultaneous 50-100 per cent increase in price and 75-70 per cent resultant savings to the consumer would seem, in almost any other economy save the Indonesian, like the pitch not of an oil but of a snake-oil salesman. The Indonesian economy is capable, however, of compounding the contradictions. The official price of kerosene is exactly what it was in 1953; the price of gasoline is 2 per cent higher. The Indonesian rupiah, meanwhile, has been inflated almost to the bursting point. Prices and labor costs --but not salaries--have risen in proportion, or, to be more strictly accurate, in disproportion. A few key index figures, calculated as of mid-April 1959 on the basis of 1953 as 100, are as follows: rice--400; eggs--350; sugar--235; tea--625; firewood--200; charcoal--225; tires--300. The price trend continued sharply upward from mid-April until the drastic financial measures of late August set them to wavering uncertainly. That the general situation is not improved is to be deduced from even a few key indicators: sugar, which is grown and processed locally, has virtually disappeared from the legitimate market; and tires, also manufactured locally from local rubber--when imported chemicals are available--have become a medium of hoarding.

The oil companies, in suggesting in late 1958 a mere 50-100 per cent increase for their product, were running grave risk of having their proposals accepted and then being stuck with a newly increased and hence adamantly adhered-to official price during a period when the swift inflation of 1959 was making the whole price structure a fiction. The proposals were not accepted, however, They met with the accustomed Indonesian bureaucratic indifference, indecision, and obstruction. They met with obstruction also on the part of the increasingly large number of important persons and organizations that profit from the black market in oil. They met with obstruction also from the many persons who believe, whether from conviction or expediency, that the oil industry misrepresents its rupiah losses and conceals its dollar profits and, in any event, that after all these years of extracting great profit from Indonesia, the companies can afford virtually to donate enough gasoline and kerosene to tide the nation over its present crisis.

The oil industry, therefore, is faced with the continuing problem of sustaining serious losses and having to maintain a nation-wide distribution system which, incidentally, the Government has been trying to shift to Indonesian hands, with no very eager takers unless the companies themselves agree to underwrite the expense. Such is the method and the temper of the Djakarta Government today that the companies may find themselves confronted at any moment with an ultimatum either to solve the supply and distribution problem by their own unassisted efforts or to face nationalization. The prospects for sympathetic Government consideration of realistic revision of price structure are distinctly poor.

The Continuing Crisis in the Oil Industry

Until the domestic price issue recently became the focus of attention and, according to Indonesian suspicion, the lever for new negotiations not only on domestic pricing policy but on other questions as well, it was two other matters which constituted the main issues between the Government and the companies. One was the problem of division of foreign-exchange revenues; the other was the problem of granting of new concessions and of authorization for further exploration and development of the old.

On the subject of division of revenues, neither Government nor companies like to be very specific. For one thing, as a result of the infinite number of extras and variables which the Indonesian regulations introduce, the bookkeeping is so excessively complicated that it is virtually impossible to arrive at any figures that can be agreed upon as being even approximately exact. For another, the Government does not like to invite criticism from ultranationalistic elements for "selling out too cheap," and a company does

not like to invite comparison in other oil-producing nations which may feel
Indonesia is getting an extraordinarily good deal. It is possible, however, by
applying a little inductive reasoning to some figures released by the Government and the companies--fragmentary and obscure though they may be--to
arrive at an estimate of the Indonesian Government's net take from the industry. The figure of US$100 million per year from exports cannot be far wrong,
if only because it is in line with international standards. Where the Indonesian
Government really makes its killing, however, is in bringing off the politically
and financially athletic triple play of semiconfiscating US$75 million worth of
the oil for local consumption, collecting Rp. 600 million in direct taxes upon
it, and requiring the companies to convert some millions of dollars into rupiahs
in order to make good on their losses of one to two billion rupiahs. As a measure of urbane counterexploitation on the part of a long-colonialized nation now
dictating the terms to the capitalists, the feat, if deliberately calculated, cannot but command reluctant admiration. But it seems, in fact, more accidental
than deliberate, and in any event very few Indonesians have any personal comprehension of it. The prevailing opinion is that whatever the Indonesian Government and nation gets from the oil industry, it is much too little, and that if
only Indonesian negotiators play their cards right, they can force the rapacious
foreign capitalists to disgorge considerably more, as, indeed, they may.

Rancor over foreign profiteering from Indonesian oil, plus Indonesian
bureaucratic procrastination and indecision, has resulted in the situation
already referred to regarding exploration, development, and new concessions.
The oil companies have encountered such constant interference and prohibition
regarding exploration and development of new deposits even in areas over
which they already hold concessions--an inheritance from the Dutch colonial
administration--that they have virtually suspended all such operations. New
fields now coming into full production, mainly under Caltex but partly under
Shell development programs, are the result in the main of projects originated
before 1950. Applications for new concessions have been held in abeyance
since 1951 when the Indonesian Parliament passed an act prohibiting the granting of new concessions pending the completion of a new mining act. The new
mining act has been in process of preparation and debate ever since, with
little evidence that it is likely to be adopted in the near future. Even if a new
mining act should by some miracle be drafted and accepted, there is reason
to believe it would be little more explicit in its terms or more encouraging
to foreign, Western interests than was the Foreign Investments Act passed in
1958, an act which seems to the Western reader far more admonitory than
permissive.

The fantastic situation with regard to the oil industry is not, unfortunately, atypical of the general situation of foreign enterprise in Indonesia--
for for that matter, Indonesian enterprise. In all fairness, one must report
that both discrimination and favoritism would seem at times to be purely
accidental. The partly Indonesian Permindo oil company, curiously enough,
shares in the dilemma of Shell, and American Caltex, which got into operation

too late to compete for local market sales now finds itself in the exceedingly
fortunate position of not having built up a local distribution system. The over-
all situation is not improved by some complicated maneuvering in which both
Westerners and Indonesians engage. Shell, for instance, has begun vigorously
to advocate, much to the distress of Caltex, that Caltex now be granted its
proportionate share in the local market. And Permina, the Indonesian Army-
controlled company which has repeatedly managed to set fire to its wells,
conducts a continuous flirtation with the American oil concern which now
markets its product and with Japanese firms which would like to do so. It
also welcomes bids from international oil interests in general--East and West
German, Russian, and Czech--which think they might be able to make out
better than Shell, Stanvac, and Caltex in developing the undoubtedly rich Indonesian oil deposits. The Indonesian inclination, of course, is to reserve them
for strictly Indonesian development--which may be possible ten to twenty
years hence, whereas the world's need for oil and Indonesia's need for cash
is right now.

Willard A. Hanna

[Photograph page 3, courtesy Ministry of Information, Djakarta.]

SOUTHEAST ASIA SERIES
Vol. VII   No. 25
(Indonesia)

American Universities Field Staff

REPORTS
SERVICE

BUNG KARNO'S INDONESIA

Part X: Bankers' Quandary

by Willard A. Hanna

October 24, 1959

This publication is one of a continuing series on current developments in world affairs written by associates of the American Universities Field Staff. It is distributed by the AUFS as a useful addition to the American fund of information on foreign affairs.

AUFS Associates have been chosen for their skill in collecting, reporting, and evaluating data. Each has combined long personal observation and experience in his foreign area with advanced studies relating to it.

WILLARD A. HANNA, the author of this report, is based in Kuala Lumpur to write about Southeast Asian affairs. Before joining the AUFS in 1954, Dr. Hanna had spent a total of more than ten years in East and Southeast Asia as a teacher, administrator, and writer.

Publications under the imprint of the American Universities Field Staff are not selected to accord with an editorial policy and do not represent the views of its membership. Responsibility for accuracy of facts and for opinions expressed in the letters and reports rests solely with the individual writers.

Almost two years ago, Sjafruddin Prawiranegara, then Governor of the Bank of Indonesia, departed from Djakarta for Sumatra to join and presently to head the rebel movement against the Sukarno Government. He had previously submitted report after report in which he declared, in effect, that Indonesia's economic and financial ills were induced largely by political interference in economic and financial matters. He had tried for eight years to cope with Indonesia's deteriorating financial situation while political interference mounted to intolerable proportions. Then, disguested with the Djakarta Government in general and with Bung Karno in particular, Mr. Sjafruddin went on leave to Sumatra and wrote back a blistering letter denouncing government policies. He identified himself with the regional insurrectionists, got himself discharged from his post in Djakarta and branded as a traitor, almost got himself captured by loyalist troops during the military action against Bukittinggi, and now, as Premier of the PRRI government-in-hiding (Revolutionary Government of the Republic of Indonesia), he waits it out in the jungles of Sumatra, observing from a distance, it may be assumed, the quandary of his successors.

According to public announcement on August 31, 1959, Mr. Lukman Hakim, long-time colleague and rival of Mr. Sjafruddin and his successor

[WAH-21-'59]

as Governor of the Bank of Indonesia, was relieved of his post "at his own request." Mr. Hakim, during the early period of his tenure as Governor, had espoused the theory that Indonesia's economic ills resulted in large part from the fact that "Indonesia's economic development has inadvertently gone the way of individual enterprise." The difficulty, he thought, could be remedied by transferring major segments of the nation's enterprise to government control. During the latter period of his tenure, however, he swung toward the point of view that Indonesia's economic problems were the result in even greater measure perhaps of dangerous inflation brought on by large-scale government spending, especially that occasioned in putting down the regional insurrections. But the inflation, he insisted, was something which had to be accepted as an unpleasant reality from which there was no quick or easy "way out."

Mr. Hakim was not consulted when President and concurrently Prime Minister Sukarno, together with First Minister Djuanda, devised a quick but by no means easy "way out"--the sudden devaluation by 90 per cent on August 25, 1959 of 47 per cent of the nation's outstanding paper currency, the freezing of 90 per cent of bank deposits in excess of Rp. 25,000, and the scrapping of existing import-export regulations, all this to be followed, it was announced, by follow-up measures yet to be devised. Mr. Hakim was still, in theory at least, Governor of the Bank of Indonesia when virtually all business and banking came to a standstill on August 26, 1959, and the nation began to ask how and when, exactly, they were to be started up again.

The case of Mr. Hakim is both enlightening and baffling. Just what mixture of political and economic thinking went into the solution to sack him, or at least to circumvent him and thus make sure of his resignation, may never be revealed. On both political and economic matters, he had stood for quite some time with Bung Karno and the Sukarno-Djuanda Government and never overtly opposed them. His ultimate error, if error it was, seems to have been to insist upon expressing a banker's outlook on banking problems. Two years ago, Mr. Hakim provided a good deal of the economic and financial rationale for measures which Mr. Sjafruddin opposed: outright dismissal of the Bank's staff of Dutch financial experts; outright seizure and operation of Dutch properties in Indonesia; and continued large-scale deficit financing by the Bank of Indonesia as achieved by the simple device of ordering up new bales of banknotes from the engraving plant. But he seems to have come around, eventually, to very much Mr. Sjafruddin's point of view about what admixture was admissable of political expediency into financial accountability. Mr. Hakim's resignation, it was officially announced, had nothing whatsoever to do with the new financial and economic measures. Mr. Hakim, however, was not available for any detailed comment. His annual report for fiscal 1958-59, coincidentally, was just off the press and was actually released the day his resignation was announced. His report of the previous year was still available for comparison with the new one. Taken in combination, the two documents provide an important commentary upon the economic and financial rationalizing which has been going on in Indonesia in the last few years.

Mr. Hakim's report for 1957-58 affords significant clues to the economic and financial theory which lay back of many of the practices of that critical year. His report for 1958-59 provides similar clues to the reason those practices led the nation to the verge of economic collapse. It provides also, since it is in effect disclaimed by the release of Mr. Hakim from his post, the clue that these same practices are being pushed today to their logical and illogical conclusions, despite Mr. Hakim's own reconsideration and modification of his stand.

The texts and the detailed statistical tables of the Bank of Indonesia reports will bear out the thesis which, by mid-1959, had become a commonplace among all economic analysts, Indonesian and foreign alike, and had for months been accepted even by Bung Karno himself whose interest in economics has generally been perfunctory. The nation, in Bung Karno's words, was "deteriorating economically and financially" and, indeed, in every other way, so fast that only "the most drastic measures" could save it from "disaster." The financial method adopted by Bung Karno was to strip both the alien and the Indonesian capitalists and entrepreneurs of the large part of their liquid assets. Already in late 1957 and early 1958, in retaliation for Dutch refusal to yield Western New Guinea, he had prompted the seizure and in effect the nationalization of vast Dutch holdings in Indonesia. In late 1958 he had prompted the nationalization of the important holdings of Chinese allegedly sympathetic to the Taiwan regime. Then, in mid-1959, in an effort swiftly to deflate the currency, he either drained off or froze a major part of the liquid assets of the remaining entrepreneurs. At present, the next scheduled move is to convert a major segment of the remaining private Chinese enterprise into Indonesian-owned co-operatives. The swift and clear national trend is toward substitution of state for private enterprise at virtually all levels. The great majority of firms doing business in Indonesia, whether originally Dutch, Chinese, Chinese-Indonesian, or Indonesian in ownership, are being placed under direct state control or are being made dependent upon government loans. Most other concerns are seriously weakened financially and even more seriously threatened politically. Notwithstanding the commonly accepted fact that the history of Indonesian state enterprises to date is one of extravagance and mismanagement, a state enterprise economy has been the objective of a large and powerful group of Indonesian politicians for the last 15 years and now seems to be on the point of realization. Mr. Hakim's own writings, as of a year ago that is, give the apologia.

"The time has come," wrote Mr. Hakim in mid-1958,[1] "to subject our economic philosophy to a thorough and exhaustive examination, since Indonesia

---

1 Report of the Governor of Bank Indonesia for the Financial Year 1957-1958. G. Kollf and Co., Indonesia. 262 pp. Excerpts from pp. 22-24.

will enter upon a new era if and when [sic] the present political crisis is overcome as anticipated.

"Generally speaking, Indonesia's economic development has inadvertently gone the way of individual enterprise and has followed individual lines of
thought. The liquidation of the colonial economy has been interpreted as a
replacement of Dutch entrepreneurs by their Indonesian counterparts. The
fact has been overlooked that the Indonesian people are poor and lack experience. In fact, it is doubtful whether national development can cope with a
great many obstacles if it is entrusted to individual enterprise which lacks
capital and skill. In actual practice, entrepreneurs in need of capital take
the view that the Government is duty bound to provide them with their requirements. This occurred in the past and the oddness of this attitude should be
realized, since Government money is public money, which, if utilized, should
benefit the whole public and not the individual. Supplying capital to individual
entrepreneurs implies that any loss will come to the charge of the public as
a whole, while any profit will be to the advantage of the entrepreneur concerned. Such a policy--which, I reiterate, has generally not been pursued
intentionally--actually leads to the growth of a national capitalist group,
which does not come into being through its own efforts and through carrying
its own risks, but thanks to Government aid.

"I doubt whether our revolution had as an object the creation of a group
of individual entrepreneurs living on the money of the people--the creation of
a small, though national, group growing prosperous by the sweat of people. I
also doubt whether the system of bringing our country to development through
individual energy and effort is in keeping with our condition. It has become
clear that the individual is weak in Indonesia and he needs the support of the
Government, while the Government has to bear the losses and does not share
in the advantages reaped. It is obvious that Government support is indispensable in present conditions. This, however, poses the question why, if this is
actually the case, the Government itself should not undertake national development. Of course, there are risks. But then, Government support to private
enterprises does not eliminate such risks, while any profits will fully come to
the benefit of the Government--that is, to the benefit of the public in general
and not to the benefit of a small group--if the Government engages in such
enterprises for its own account. This will bring the Government-implemented
work of development closer to the fifth principle of Pantja Sila, the ideology
of our State. Furthermore, I think it more in line with the conditions of our
State if the work of development is implemented by the Government. The skill
our people lack due to century-long colonial domination, can more easily be
acquired by the Government than by individual entrepreneurs since the necessary foreign experts prefer Government guarantees to the guarantees of a
private entrepreneur. Thus, the Government is in a better position to overcome the shortages of capital and skills. For this reason I firmly believe
that the Government must play the leading role in the work of national development.

"Besides, conditions abroad have developed in such a manner that private enterprise in the sense of the 19th-century liberal capitalist philosophy has practically disappeared. The economy in socialist countries is obviously in the hands of the Government, while private entrepreneurs in Western countries have associated into large units, such as the European Coal and Steel Community, the gigantic enterprises in the United States, etc. . . .

"This is one more reason why it would seem inexpedient to me if Indonesia, as yet weak, should counter the formidable foreign economic units--in the west as well as in the east--by insignificant units based in individual enterprise still lacking strength due to inadequate capital, skill and experience.

"If Indonesia aims at rapid and sound development, it must supersede the small units which so far have been the vehicles of economic development.

"I do not mean that all economic activity in Indonesia should be in the hands of the Government. But, it is my strong belief that the Government must play the leading role in national upbuilding, while private enterprise should only be carried on if those small units are run on co-operative lines, or combined into large-scale associations.

"As a matter of fact, the economic philosophy just set forth is supported by a principle that has been alive in our society for centuries and forms part of the Indonesian national identity. I refer to the principle of "gotong royong" (mutual help). Any weakness has always been overcome in Indonesia by combining potentials under the "gotong royong" principle. Our sovereign national Government has been the most outstanding achievement of the "gotong royong" system of our people."

This analysis, coming from the Governor of the Bank of Indonesia, has elements of astonishing naiveté. The pious references to the Pantja Sila and "gotong royong" are to be expected; in fact, they are politically inescapable. But the simple trust in the ability of a small clique of inexperienced or little experienced Indonesian businessmen--for there are virtually no others--to accomplish in operation of state enterprises what they have been unable to accomplish in operation of private concerns: this was scarcely to be expected. Blindness to the plain fact that state interference has led to stagnation of private enterprise, and confidence that more state controls would result in more, not less efficiency of operation: this, however, was to be expected of a state socialist, even one who recognized that the objectives and methods of state socialism had miscarried badly in the past.

Mr. Hakim's analysis, while it exhibits naiveté, exhibits also in certain respects both penetration and courage. Mr. Hakim points out quite frankly that individual Indonesian enterprises in the past have operated on the very unsound basis of personal profiteering with public funds. The typical Indonesian private businessman has been the politically well-connected individual who has maneuvered for himself unsecured government bank loans, plus thick sheaves of official licenses, permits, and requisitions, and has then set himself up in extravagant style with the bank absorbing the losses and himself taking the profits, when and if there are any. Mr. Hakim points out with equal frankness that the ordinary Indonesian concept of liquidating alien holdings has been for private Indonesian citizens to move in, take over, and divide up the properties and, so long as they last, the profits as well.

The economic and financial developments of the year 1958, as described in the 1957-58 Bank Report and in a continuing flow of press reports from Indonesia, show how the state enterprise philosophy advocated by Mr. Hakim was indeed applied and how it led to results at least as deplorable as those of the former "individual enterprise" system which continued to exist in part alongside it. The huge Dutch companies, for instance, were placed under Indonesian Government and Army management to be operated as state enterprises. To be sure, there was bitter intramural dispute as to whether they should not be carved up and parcelled out, but on the whole, not only was the principle of "corporate integrity" preserved but the abhorred Dutch practice of company monopoly was actually reinforced. The "Big Five"--firms which operated estates, engaged in import and export, and served as agents for dozens of corporations abroad--were increased, by the addition of three basically Indonesian state-financed concerns, to the "Big Eight." To the "Big Eight" were assigned exclusive import-export privileges over essential goods, including textiles, and upon them, consequently, converged the business and the business agents that had previously been divided among hundreds of smaller organizations. Into managerial positions in the "Big Eight" moved a population of young Indonesians--many of them Army officers on active duty, others being businessmen whose own concerns were experiencing difficulties. And promptly, from the headquarters of the "Big Eight," came well-confirmed rumors of extravagance, mismanagement, personal enrichment of individuals at the expense of the companies and of the state. The earlier group of "national capitalists" was being replaced and supplemented by a new group of "state agents." The practical difference, however, was extremely hard to detect; in many cases the faces were the same, and instead of new enterprises flourishing, the old languished.

Indonesia's economic troubles, far from being diminished, were being redoubled. The reason, as of mid-1958, according to Mr. Hakim's report, was to be found in a combination of external and internal factors. The chief external factors were: decline in world prices for raw materials, and recession in the United States and Western Europe. The chief internal factors were: the Indonesian inflation resulting from huge Government expenditures to put down regional insurrections, and loss to the Government of substantial sums in foreign exchange profits as a result of direct "barter" trade between the rebel-held areas and the outside world. In all, Mr. Hakim concluded, "Indonesia's economic position. . .shows a highly unsatisfactory picture. A foreign exchange position which, in March 1958, only sufficed to finance about one month's imports is far from satisfactory, the less so in view of the continuing dullness of exports. Meanwhile the revenues of the National Exchequer decreased, while outgoings continued at the same rate and even increased. In spite of aid from Japan (war reparations), from Russia (credits), and from the Chinese People's Republic (credits) [Note: no mention here of U.S. and other Western aid], the economic position remained critical."[2]

When it came time to write his report for 1959, Mr. Hakim acknowledged that the situation not only remained critical but that in the course of the year, despite some favorable indications, the nation had on the whole suffered further setbacks. The crucial factors, he now pointed out, were continued recession in prices of raw materials and unforeseen difficulties in the production and marketing thereof, also continued inflation, and difficulties arising out of the take-over of Dutch enterprises. His report exhibited certain striking inconsistencies in its various sections with regard to the question whether the recession was or was not past, whether world prices for Indonesian raw materials had improved or deteriorated, whether Indonesian production had or had not held up as well as might be expected, and more especially whether the take-over of Dutch enterprises had or had not on the whole proved to date to be a good thing. "It goes without saying," he wrote with regard to the necessary adjustments in production and marketing resulting from the expulsion of the Dutch, "that for the time being such adjustments had rather affected the smoothness of production and trade, while new methods and channels needed improvements.

"Action against the Dutch enterprises should be continued until Indonesia could be entirely freed from Dutch domination in the economic field and viewed from a long-term viewpoint, the take-over and supervision of all Dutch enterprises would only result in Indonesia's benefit."

In all, the report tended to indicate that while things might be improving, then again they might not. In any event, Mr. Hakim declared, "we should do everything possible to avert economic deterioration to a level. . .which can not be accounted for in relation to the situation of the people as well as to that of production because if it already reached such a state it would be difficult to intensify the country's economy again after the security situation has already been restored."

Whatever else the above may mean, Lukman Hakim makes it quite clear it means this: "In efforts to safeguard Indonesia's economy, we should take the reality as the starting point." This implies: "Firstly, inflation really posed a big danger which threatened the country's economic development and therefore it should be surmounted as soon as possible. Secondly, on the other hand, it can not be expected that the dreadful inflation can be wiped out overnight in the present situation, particularly in view of the Government's actions

---

2 Op. cit., pp. 20-21.

in the security field. Thirdly, the Indonesian State, people, and economy are vital enough and have adequate strength and wealth to overcome the danger and the difficulties."3

Mr. Hakim's 1958-59 report, obviously, was that of a seriously perplexed and troubled man. Undoubtedly he had gone into these problems and his proposed resolution of them with the Cabinet and presumably with President Sukarno. Undoubtedly, also, he had the gravest misgivings about swift, rash moves in the financial and economic fields--moves toward which, as everyone in Indonesia was aware, pressure was building up. Reduce government expenditures, he said, in effect; increase interest rates; concentrate on increased production and exports; reduce consumption and imports; rationalize the whole economic and administrative structure; take all the conventional, unpleasant, professional steps to check inflation and revitalize the economy: but don't look for any easy politician's nostrum.

President Sukarno and First Minister Djuanda chose to dispense with the services of Mr. Lukman Hakim and to adopt a nostrum. They also announced a drive to effect government economies, to increase production, and much else besides; but first of all, they applied the nostrum of devaluation and virtual confiscation of wealth. It remains to be seen whether the bankers' misgivings about fancy manipulation are well or ill founded, and whether the audacious political approach to financial problems will indeed provide the new spirit and the new stimulus which Indonesia requires. President Sukarno and First Minister Djuanda, in the last two years, have rejected the counsels of the nation's two top bankers. One of them, Mr. Sjafruddin, they came to regard as "reactionary" and "Dutch-minded." The other, Mr. Hakim, they seemed to regard until rather recently as truly "revolutionary," although, it appears, not nearly revolutionary enough for what is happening in Djakarta these days. If present trends continue, and there is no reason to believe they will not, then what is in store for Indonesia is a fuller and swifter implementation of the policy of state ownership and management than Mr. Hakim ever envisioned. The consequences upon the state economy and finances are certain to be drastic. It is conceivable, of course, that the bankers are wrong and the politicians are right and that the consequences will be not only drastic but salutory.

Willard A. Hanna

---

3 Quotes from the 1958-59 report are from excerpts and summary printed in The Times of Indonesia, September 1, 1959.

SOUTHEAST ASIA SERIES
Vol. VII   No. 26
(Indonesia)

American Universities Field Staff

REPORTS SERVICE

BUNG KARNO'S INDONESIA

Part XI: Engineers' Venture

by Willard A. Hanna

October 25, 1959

This publication is one of a continuing series on current developments in world affairs written by associates of the American Universities Field Staff. It is distributed by the AUFS as a useful addition to the American fund of information on foreign affairs.

AUFS Associates have been chosen for their skill in collecting, reporting, and evaluating data. Each has combined long personal observation and experience in his foreign area with advanced studies relating to it.

WILLARD A. HANNA, the author of this report, is based in Kuala Lumpur to write about Southeast Asian affairs. Before joining the AUFS in 1954, Dr. Hanna had spent a total of more than ten years in East and Southeast Asia as a teacher, administrator, and writer.

Publications under the imprint of the American Universities Field Staff are not selected to accord with an editorial policy and do not represent the views of its membership. Responsibility for accuracy of facts and for opinions expressed in the letters and reports rests solely with the individual writers.

Indonesia's economic development has tended to date to bog down in vague plans that don't seem to stabilize long enough to be carried out, or in crash projects which turn out to be not very well thought through. The nation's First Five-Year Plan, for instance, took well over five years to write, then more than two years to put through Parliament (September 1956-November 1958). It turned out in the end to be merely a general statement of intent rather than a blueprint for development, and even before being approved by Parliament it had already been virtually set aside by reason of the political, economic, and military crisis through which the nation was passing. A $200-$300 million, multipurpose Asahan Project in Sumatra, conceived as the answer to many of Sumatra's power, industrial, and irrigation problems, remains after ten years merely an enticing mirage. A "private" trading company, established with 100 per cent government capital for the purpose of seeking new markets for Indonesia's exports and for importing materials critically needed for Indonesia's new industries, finds itself operating consistently at a loss because it can't get priorities on local materials and transport facilities and because it can't get import licenses for the machinery and industrial supplies it seeks to bring in. A government-subsidized bicycle tire factory, to take an example of a small-scale project, has had to restrict production repeatedly

[WAH-22-'59]

for lack of imported chemicals, and textile mills, built on government loans, rarely operate at more than 50 per cent capacity for lack of imported yarns.

Such frustrations, of course, are endemic in an underdeveloped, overly-nationalistic nation, and constitute, it seems, some of the major hazards through which such nations must pass on the road to progress. It is reassuring, therefore, to discover that whereas the vast, over-all plans tend to melt away and the little projects to hit big snarls, there are instances in which planning and operations prove relatively effective. One of the most significant of these in Indonesia is to be found in the mountains of West Java, about half way between Bandung and Djakarta--the Djatiluhur Project.

The Djatiluhur Project combines hydroelectric, irrigation, inland fisheries, and recreation aspects, and constitutes a sort of miniature, tropical TVA. It is designed to throw a 100-meter high, 1,800-meter long dam across the Tjitarum, the largest river in West Java. It provides for installation alongside the dam of a power plant consisting of six generators of 25,000 kw capacity each, with a total output of 700 million kwh per year, thus doubling Java's present total power supply. The dam will back up a body of water 3 billion cubic meters in volume covering an area of 8,000 hectares (19,760 acres). The lake will be used for fish farming, producing an estimated yield of 800 tons of fresh-water fish per year. The overflow will irrigate 240,000 hectares of land; since it will allow for conversion of much nearby dry land into rice paddies and for two crops per year instead of one, it will mean a theoretical increase of 300,000 tons of rice annually--approximately one half the amount which Indonesia is at present forced to import. The hills over-looking the lake will be converted into a holiday resort area to attract local and perhaps international vacationers, and the new bungalows now occupied by foreign workers will become a source of rental income. Since West Java suffers from an acute shortage of electrical power for industrial and other development, and since population pressure has created serious problems of land and food supply, the Djatiluhur Project should contribute measurably to over-all improvement of the area. It is one of the largest projects of its kind yet undertaken in Southeast Asia, and in the course of a very few years should yield returns much greater than its approximate US$70 million cost.

Preliminary surveys for the Djatiluhur Project were begun by the Dutch in 1945. Large-scale operations, however, began only in 1953 and 1954. The target date for completion, first set for 1961, has now been reset for 1964. Work has been divided into three phases, of which at the present time one is complete, one is well under way, and one is about to start. The first phase, begun in 1953 and now completed at a cost of Rp. 200 million, was the acquisition of land rights and the construction of access railroads, roads, and a housing area for the employees. The second phase, started in 1956, is the construction of a diversion tunnel 300 meters long and 11 meters high, and of the dam itself. Work on the diversion tunnel will be completed in the next few months and work on the dam is about to start. The third phase will

be the construction of a glass-enclosed tower and installation in it of genera-
tor equipment, with work to start presumably in 1960.

        The Djatiluhur Project has been financed to date by Indonesian govern-
ment funds, but completion of the project--most specifically the procurement
and installation of the generators--will require an international loan, presumably from the International Bank to which application has been made.
Construction is being carried out on a contract basis by two French engineering firms, Compagnie Francaise d'Enterprises and Coyne-Bellier, which supply an assortment of heavy equipment, largely French in manufacture, a corps
of about 140 French engineers and technicians, and a labor force of about 40
Italians--mainly miners for the tunnel construction job. Foreign employees

Work in progress at the dam site.

total about 180; Indonesian
laborers on the project number
about 2,000; and three Indonesian
engineers are kept by the Government at the construction site
in a supervisory-liaison capacity.

        The mere statistical
details do not serve, however,
to give the real dimensions of
the project, or to measure
either the difficulties or the
achievements. I had myself been
reading and hearing about the
project for years, and had accumulated conflicting evidence
that it promised to be a great
success and that it threatened
to be a dismal flop. I was eager,
therefore, to see it for myself,
and I recently managed to do so
with the very helpful assistance of the Government Information Office in Bandung. My brief visit to the project site served to convince me that this is no
minor, routine engineering operation, but a major adventure and a very prom-
ising gamble.

        The project site is one of the most beautiful in scenic West Java, a
cool mountain valley through which rushes the Tjitarum River. Upstream,
where a new lake will soon submerge their homes, live a few thousand country people who now make a large part of their living by cutting timber and
bamboo. They float their produce in rafts down the Tjitarum to the seacoast.
The narrowing of the riverbed at the dam site is now making the feat much
more hazardous than before and rafts on the river are beginning to interfere
with work progress, but the country people defy all orders that the traffic

View upriver toward the dam site
and the mountains.

View downriver. (Bungalows for
European staff at upper right.)

must cease. They are going to
prove an even bigger problem
when the day comes for flooding
their land. They have already
been compensated for the land,
but at a rate which bore little
resemblance to the real value,
and they have long since spent
the proceeds or seen their savings devalued by inflation. The
hope is that these few thousand
people will find ready employment in the new industries of
the lowland area; but the shock
of eviction is going to be severe
and both the expenses and the
hardships of resettlement are
likely to prove serious.

On the hillside above the
river, at a spot just below the
dam site, is built a new village
of about 150 concrete-block, tile-
roofed bungalows intended for
the foreign employees and eventually for tourists. Here lives a
French-Italian colony of about
300 persons, some 40 of the
higher paid European employees
having brought with them their
wives and children. This little
European enclave is provided
with a church, hospital, school,
club house (in which are also
quarters for the Indonesian
engineers and for official visitors), and commissary--the
latter being one of the wonders
of West Java with its impressive
stock of French and Italian foodstuffs and wines.

Whereas the Europeans
live in attractive little hillside
bungalows (cost, about Rp. 60,000
each before the recent inflation),
surrounded by small gardens

planted with trees and flowers, the Indonesian laborers live at the foot of the hill in "row houses" built of bamboo and matting on hurriedly bulldozed terraces adjacent to dusty service roadways. Whereas the European families are provided with modern furniture, ample electrical supply and equipment, and some of them with Renaults and Fiats, the Indonesian employees and laborers, except for those few at the very top, are living at close to subsistence level with little in the way of amenities or privileges. The workers' homes are a dingy room or two per family, plus a small porch front and back and a little packed earth space for children, chickens, and an occasional papaya tree. The workers' wages are about Rp. 10 per day, and clerical employees draw little more than twice as much. The European employees, on the other hand, draw up to US$30 per day, 60 per cent of it in foreign currency for remittance abroad, 40 per cent of it--coming to about Rp. 100-200 per day at the former rate of exchange--for local expenses. The European employee receives full educational, health, and commissary privileges. The Indonesian employees have a school, to be sure, but of a much more modest type than the European. They are given treatment in the hospital on the site; but they have no insurance coverage, safety regulations are not well enforced, and the rate of accidents has been high. They have no special commissary privileges, and both supply and price of such staples as rice, sugar, cooking oil, and tobacco have been matters of major concern to them, as to all Indonesians of modest means, over the last few months.

On the whole, the surprising fact about the juxtaposition of two such diverse enclaves is not that a considerable degree of suspicion has prevailed between the two, but that no overt troubles have developed. But if clashes have not occurred, rumor has been busy and can clearly be heard as far away as Bandung and Djakarta. Rumor is concerned in large part with the manner in which Europeans or Indonesians or both have taken advantage of the emergency situation which prevails here, as elsewhere in Indonesia, with regard to the handling of funds, procurement, storage, and accountability in the matter of supplies and equipment. Europeans and Indonesians are implicated, to varying degrees, in widespread allegations. Of the cost of the Djatiluhur Project, it is widely thought, a very large percentage is chargeable against bribes, gifts, and favors; of supplies presumably stored or used, a very large percentage has either been purchased at exorbitant rates involving kickbacks or has been diverted into black market channels; and if any real audit or inventory were held, it would disclose irregularities on a scale to compare with the more openly aired scandals that recurrently shake Djakarta.

One factor which has threatened at times to slow or even stall operations on the project is the presence nearby--in fact, just across the river from the housing areas--of armed Darul Islam guerrillas whose intentions toward the Government and Government projects like these are not amicable. The D.I. guerrillas have staged a series of minor infiltrations and one major raid upon the project itself. Late one Saturday night (July 26, 1958), while many of the European employees and their wives were relaxing in the club house, a gang of some 50 well-armed guerrillas staged a surprise raid. They entered the club house and stripped the guests of their money and valuables; they broke into the offices at the dam site and made off with portable valuables they found there; and they entered private houses and thoroughly ransacked them. In the course of the raid, one Italian laborer was shot and killed, even though he apparently offered no resistance.

Since that D.I. raid, the dam site has been strongly guarded and patrolled by Indonesian troops. Nevertheless, considerable apprehension prevails, more among the Indonesian employees, it appears, than among the Europeans. The Indonesian enclave, it is relevant to mention, is more favorably situated than the European for its residents to observe the lighted torches which show at night in the hills just across the river, where no country man, unless he were a part-time guerrilla, would think of moving about after dark.

Nevertheless, despite D.I. raids, accounting irregularities, interracial friction, and tremendous difficulties of engineering and logistics, the Djatiluhur Project is moving visibly toward that day, conceivably in 1964 as announced, when the dam will be completed. If not in 1964, then not long afterward, it seems that the lake will be filled, the generators will be operating, the fish will be growing, and the rice crops on the surrounding lowlands will be flourishing. If so, the bungalows of the project area itself will then be occupied by week-end visitors; the handsome modern office building on the edge of the dam will be operating as a hotel and restaurant and as the terminal and overlook point for sight-seeing buses which will follow the new asphalt highway even after nightfall without danger of guerrilla attack.

View from the balcony of the administration building, one day to become a hotel.

It is projects like Djatiluhur, despite all its defects, which give some
reason for optimism that for Indonesia the year 1964 could be considerably
happier than the exceedingly troubled year 1959. Unfortunately, there are
all too few such projects, not so much for lack of resources and assistance
with which to develop them as for lack of government policy and decisiveness.
Djatiluhur, in itself a major national effort and expenditure, constitutes no
more than a fraction of one per cent of what the nation really requires. Still,
to be sure, it is a beginning.

Willard A. Hanna

[Photographs, courtesy Ministry of Information, Djakarta.]

SOUTHEAST ASIA SERIES
Vol. VII   No. 27
(Indonesia)

American Universities Field Staff

REPORTS SERVICE

BUNG KARNO'S INDONESIA

Part XII: Sports, Aid, Tourism, and Politics

by Willard A. Hanna

October 26, 1959

This publication is one of a continuing series on current developments in world affairs written by associates of the American Universities Field Staff. It is distributed by the AUFS as a useful addition to the American fund of information on foreign affairs.

AUFS Associates have been chosen for their skill in collecting, reporting, and evaluating data. Each has combined long personal observation and experience in his foreign area with advanced studies relating to it.

WILLARD A. HANNA, the author of this report, is based in Kuala Lumpur to write about Southeast Asian affairs. Before joining the AUFS in 1954, Dr. Hanna had spent a total of more than ten years in East and Southeast Asia as a teacher, administrator, and writer.

Publications under the imprint of the American Universities Field Staff are not selected to accord with an editorial policy and do not represent the views of its membership. Responsibility for accuracy of facts and for opinions expressed in the letters and reports rests solely with the individual writers.

Indonesia is scheduled to play host in Djakarta to the 1962 Asian Games. Between now and mid-1962, therefore, Indonesia must prepare a huge new sports area, build an "Olympic Village" for some 3,000 athletes and officials, prepare accommodations for thousands of foreign and tens of thousands of Indonesian visitors, greatly improve transportation facilities, and co-ordinate the planning for an elaborate international event. Besides that, if it expects to make a favorable impression upon visitors, it must engage in a major housekeeping job of scouring, polishing, painting, and refurbishing its now dilapidated capital. For a city so disorganized and overcrowded that the arrival of the Harlem Globetrotters or a Russian acrobatic circus induces a series of flaps over performance bookings and hotel accommodations, impresarioing the Asian Games is no small order. How well prepared the city is going to be by 1962 to cater either to contestants or spectators is a matter for a good deal of skeptical conjecture among Indonesians and foreigners alike. Yet national prestige is at stake, the Government is determined to make an all-out effort, and even a minor success would be a major triumph.

There are three points of view which are now being expressed among Indonesians themselves about the 1962 Asian Games. One: the project is a reckless extravagance, certain to cost the Govern-

[WAH-23-'59]

ment not just the estimated Rp. 750 million (about US$20 million at the present exchange rate) but at least Rp. 1 billion, perhaps quite a lot more. With an anticipated budgetary deficit of Rp. 18 billion this year, and with over-all national development stalled because the nation is virtually insolvent, there are a lot of better uses for a billion-odd rupiahs. Two: the project is exactly the incentive and the discipline the nation and the city need to start pulling themselves together. Indonesia in general and Djakarta in particular have been deteriorating steadily in recent years, not for lack either of means or of energy, but for lack of purpose. Now national pride will dictate that decisions be taken and co-ordination achieved and projects completed. The beneficial effects will be felt not only in Djakarta but throughout the nation as a whole. For that the price is cheap. Besides, the major part of the expenses can be recovered by sale of film rights, concessions, buildings--and through foreign aid. Three: the project is a potent catalyst whereby Indonesian resources plus foreign aid can be applied harmoniously to one great national undertaking, with consequent advancement of Indonesia's policy of promoting not just Indonesian development but the easing of international tensions. The project calls for a tremendous outlay of Indonesian money and effort, but already the Russians have anted up $12.5 million to build a stadium, the Japanese have anted up $8 million to build a hotel, and the Americans, the British, the Australians, the Chinese, the Czechs, and the Hungarians--who have already mentioned provision of "some hundreds" of diesel street buses--are not going to let themselves be shown up as pikers. The spectacle of everyone working amicably together, or for that matter the spectacle of everyone competing vigorously both in aid and in sport, is likely to be both nationally and internationally inspiring.

Extravagance, incentive, inspiration, or all three combined, the Asian Games project is getting off to a slow start. The invitation was extended and accepted over a year ago--with Pakistan, incidentally, the only other bidder and not a very enthusiastic one. Mid-1962, distant as it may now seem, is not half distant enough, a good many Indonesians think, for all that must be accomplished in the meantime. The developments of the last year, while they include some surprisingly and gratifyingly easy solutions to some of the main problems, further complicate others, as will appear from the survey below.

The Problem of the Games Site

For the Asian Games, Djakarta requires a big new sports area, something far more impressive, spacious, and accessible to traffic than the downtown Ikada Stadium which was thrown up in 1951 in a 93-day crash program. President Sukarno himself, reconnoitering the city area by helicopter, chose the new site--a big tract of land lying between Djakarta proper and the new residential suburb of Kebajoran. The area is advantageously located, but its development as a games center, as now envisioned, will not be quick, cheap, or painless. Djalan Djenderal Sudirman, the four-lane highway connecting

Djakarta and Kebajoran, must be widened and turned into a parkway--with consequent razing of hundreds of modern buildings and thousands of squatter shacks. In the main games area, to the west of the road, long-established villages of both permanent and squatter housing must be leveled before new construction can start. To be sure, the improvement of Djalan Djenderal Sudirman is a must for a growing city; the construction and design of some of the permanent buildings in the area leaves much to be desired; and the squatter settlements have been built in defiance of all land, construction, fire, and sanitation ordinances. But some tens of thousands of individuals who invested in property here in good faith stand to take very serious losses. These persons include some of Djakarta's estimated 750,000 squatters, most of whom had no alternative save illegal occupancy and illegal property trans-actions since the Government could never get around to devising a land tenure policy for new low-cost housing developments. Government plans of assist-ance and compensation seem quite incommensurate with the loss and the need.

By way of illustration, I can cite one case with which I am personally familiar, one which is no less apposite for pertaining not to Djalan Djenderal Sudirman but to the Pasar Minggu Road, parallel to the Bogor highway, like-wise to be widened as part of the games project. A young Indonesian, married, the father of five small children, sold off a bit of inherited rice land about eight years ago to buy a tiny four-room house of wood frame, woven bamboo side walls, earth floor, and tin roof. Since then, he has invested in the house all the money that he could save or borrow in order to raise it above flood level, lay floor and roof tiles, acquire a little furniture, and at one point to buy out a tenant who occupied it during a period when he and his family were living in the country. His total investment is impossible to calculate, since it was made in small amounts over a period of years in the midst of rapid inflation. He was offered Rp. 45,000 for the house a few months ago and declined the offer. Some weeks later, he was served with a municipal notice that he would have to vacate the premises before the end of the year. So far as he can now determine, he will receive compensation at the rate of Rp. 5 per square meter of land--a total of about Rp. 500; he is promised assistance in removing any salvable materials to a new building site; he is promised also an allocation of new land. He is understandably skeptical, however, about the purchasing power of his Rp. 500, when and if he receives it; about the reliability of municipal assistance in the moving operation; and about the terms on which new land, if any, will be provided. Besides, even if he can solve all the complicated logistical and construction problems of moving, he will be five to ten miles distant from his job, with no assurance that public transportation will either be available or within his means.

The Problem of the Stadium

The central feature of the Asian Games site will be a huge new sports stadium, intended to outdo Tokyo's new stadium for the 1958 games, which seats 70,000 and cost $4 million. What Indonesia needed, the sponsors decided, was a stadium to seat 100,000 and therefore approximately Rp. 500 million with which to build it. Since Rp. 500 million is twice the annual budget of the city of Djakarta and approximately twenty times the amount the city has at its disposal for schools, roads, bridges, and other public improvements, it was obvious that the nation would have to tap some extraordinary source of funds. President Sukarno, according to informed report, put the proposition to the Russians, and the Russians, with scarcely a moment's hesitation, increased their $100 million loan (extended in 1956 but definitely accepted only in 1958) to allow an additional $12.5 million for the stadium. They then sent a special mission which conducted on-the-spot surveys and has now returned to Moscow to prepare plans and blueprints. They will put an eminent Russian engineer in charge and assign to him a team of 20 to 40 Russian technicians. Construction will begin early in 1960, to be completed well before the still unannounced date for the opening of the games.

This USSR $12.5 million landmark--the first fixed Russian installation to supplement the jeeps, jets, ships, and bulldozers that began to pour in last year--will tend to overshadow a good 14 years' worth of American projects totaling about $500 million since 1945. What the Americans and other Western peoples are going to do to compete with this massive Russian advertisement is a matter for much interested conjecture in Djakarta today.

The Problem of Accommodations

What the Japanese are going to do has already become fairly clear. They are going to provide money, materials, and perhaps technical assistance in the construction of the new 14-story Hotel Indonesia which has remained earth-bound since the first piles were driven three years ago. The Japanese are by no means as enthusiastic about their share in this international venture as are the Russians. The record speaks for itself. Indonesian spokesmen put out a series of statements that the Japanese were going to take on the hotel project within the framework of the Indonesian-Japanese reparations payments and reparations loans agreement of 1958, about the implementation of which there has been some little acrimony. Japanese spokesmen put out a series of tactful denials. President Sukarno talked with the Japanese Ambassador in Djakarta, also with Japanese trade delegations which were very much interested in arriving at understandings about Japanese participation in development of Indonesian petroleum, minerals, and shipping. Both governments presently put out statements that Japan would pick up the checks on the hotel.

The Hotel Indonesia, when completed, will provide some 300 rooms, all equipped with the modern conveniences such as air conditioning, modern plumbing and telephones which Djakarta in general lacks. The hotel does not at the moment, and it has not for the last few years, looked like a self-liquidating proposition. The Japanese have therefore been reluctant to go into it on a loan or even semiloan basis, and everyone else, including Mr. Hilton, has exhibited only the briefest interest in this--or for that matter, in any other hotel-building proposition in Indonesia. Indonesian hotel rates are rigidly controlled at a figure which makes even breaking even on operating costs extremely chancy and return on capital investment virtually out of the question, especially any foreign exchange returns. Djakarta, accordingly, will gain 300 hotel rooms from this Hotel Indonesia project, but it will still fall short by at least 2,000 rooms of its minimal normal requirements, let alone its special requirements for the Asian Games period.

The situation in the Hotel Duta Indonesia (formerly the Dutch-owned Hotel des Indes) indicates why hotel investment and management is not particularly attractive in Indonesia these days. The Hotel Duta Indonesia, Djakarta's best, has a total of 200 rooms and 533 beds. Ninety per cent of the rooms are occupied on a long-term basis by high-ranking government officials and military officers for whom no other housing is available. Some of the rooms are occupied by families numbering as many as seven persons. Most of the families have installed make-shift cooking and laundry facilities on the premises. The new management, the Indonesian Tourist Council, which accused the Dutch owners of deliberately allowing the hotel to deteriorate from its high prewar standards, now finds itself saddled with the same problems: unwanted semipermanent residents whose official rentals are even lower than the public rates; chronic difficulties with regard to service, utilities, and repairs; a memorably bad cuisine; and lack of any profits to plough back into the operation. The situation in Djakarta's other hotels is even worse. Unless there is some major new housing and hotel-building program in prospect, the situation in the new Hotel Indonesia could quickly become as bad. The Japanese, like many others, are understandably reluctant to associate themselves with such a project.

Aside from putting the pressure on the Japanese to build the Hotel Indonesia, the Government has given little evidence that it appreciates the dimensions of its problem or contemplates any realistic measures to deal with it. The only other relatively big project is the construction of an Olympic Village of some 200 houses, each to accommodate ten or more athletes and officials during the period of the games and then to be sold to the public when the games are finished. The Olympic Village, it appears, is to be built in the neighborhood of Bogor, about 40 miles away in the cool, scenic foothills.

The Problem of Communications

The mere provision of transportation to contestants and officials, not to mention the general public, necessitates major renovation and expansion of Djakarta's totally inadequate public transportation system. The new projects contemplated at present are the building of a new road to Bogor and the procurement of new diesel buses, and/or the building of a new interurban

line to Bogor and procurement of electric or diesel equipment, with road and
railway link-up with the seaport, the airport, the downtown districts, and the
sports area. None of these projects is as yet at all clearly defined, but obviously they involve big-scale contracts for construction and equipment. The
Hungarians, as already noted, have indicated their willingness to provide
diesel buses. The Japanese, so far, have been the most energetic competitors
in submitting plans and contracts for an interurban line and stand to gain a
good deal of the business which, unlike the hotel, could turn out to be distinctly
profitable because it would be self-liquidating.

        The very mention of a special Djakarta transportation gridwork neces-
sary for the Asian Games raises a much bigger question to which, as yet,
very little attention seems to have been given. The problem is not by any
means restricted to the Djakarta and Bogor metropolitan area; it is the nation-
wide problem of inadequate, antiquated, overburdened public transportation
systems. Tens of thousands of persons from all over Indonesia are certain

Street

scenes

in

Djakarta,

during

traffic

lulls.

to want to attend the games; thousands of visitors from abroad are certain to want to see more of Indonesia than Djakarta and Bogor. Clearly, a very great deal more needs to be done than merely renovate and expand Djakarta's sea-port, airport, bus, tram, and rail facilities. The itemization of what needs to be done is staggering.

Railways: Java's railroads, both roadbeds and much of the rolling stock, are in a state of advanced deterioration which has led recently to a series of serious accidents, one of them a major disaster. First- and second-class tickets are procurable with great difficulty, if at all, and do not give any assurance that a reservation has actually been made or that the coaches will not also be packed to suffocation with standees. Third-class tickets on the express trains are procurable only by those willing to stand in line for many, many hours, frequently to return the next day to start standing in line all over again.

Airways: Garuda Indonesian Airways has drastically curtailed its flights since the departure of Dutch pilots and technicians. It now has new crews in training, new planes on order, new airport expansion programs planned. At the present time, however, it is unable to handle more than a small percentage of those wishing to purchase tickets, and while its expansion program may be sufficient ultimately to meet current demand, it does not allow for increased demand.

Shipping: Since the enforced suspension of Dutch KPM services, inter-island shipping in Indonesia has been disrupted so seriously that the remoter ports see a ship only once in three or four months. Even the island of Bali is accessible by sea only to those who have the most extraordinary patience or influence, or who can make a running start from Singapore and pay their fare in foreign currency. By 1962 the Indonesian Government hopes to have assembled a fleet adequate to replace the ships which it required KPM to withdraw; but KPM at best was able to provide service to only a few thousand passengers per year and not to a few thousand in a matter of weeks.

Highways: Indonesia's roads have been in bad shape for years. The main highways on the island of Java, at least, are now generally in relatively good condition, although there are still stretches which are ruinous to a motor vehicle, and other stretches where it is inadvisable to travel because of guerrilla troubles. Public transportation on the highways is for the most part minimal, irregular, and uncomfortable. At the present time, at least, the gasoline shortage if nothing else makes private transportation unreliable.

Other facilities: Only Bandung and Bali are even reasonably well pro-vided with hotels of a standard which will not send the average foreign visitor off again by the quickest available transportation. Although Indonesian home cooking is excellent, public eating places, except for some of the Chinese restaurants, serve food which, to the foreigner at least--including many

Asians--is either indigestible or downright dangerous. Public comfort stations are the roadside. Public postal, telephone, and telegraph service is slow and unreliable.

The Indonesian Tourist Bureau calculates that Indonesia will have a record number of tourists this year--perhaps 8,000 as compared with 6,000 in 1958, 4,000 in 1957, and 2,500 in 1956, most of them, of course, Bali-bound and only too eager not to be delayed in Djakarta. To contemplate the influx of a modest 10,000 additional foreign visitors for the Asian Games at the same time that Indonesians themselves are traveling to and from Djakarta in unprecedented numbers, is to contemplate an increase by one thousand times over of the convulsions through which the city now goes daily in providing for its visitors--or, conversely, the convulsions the visitors go through in not being provided for.

The Problem of Politics

The problems of too many visitors for the 1962 Asian Games may be solved in part at least by the reverse effect of the problem of politics. As Indonesia starts to get ready for the Asian Games, both official and unofficial Indonesian spokesmen have got themselves involved in a couple of international disputes which, although they have now died down, could mar the spirit of Olympian serenity and also cut down on attendance.

Dispute number one arose over the inclination of unofficial spokesmen, particularly newspaper editors, to declare that while certain nations would be welcome as participants, certain others would not. At the top of the unwelcome list were Nationalist China and Israel--Nationalist China because Indonesians in general believe that Communist China should be invited instead; Israel because they believe the Arab nations would object. There arose also questions as to accreditation of North or of South Korea, of North or of South Vietnam, and of invitations to the Asian Republics within the USSR. Spokesmen from nearby countries--the Philippines and Malaya in particular--were quick to point out that sport was sport, and politics was politics, and that if Indonesia proposed to bring the two together, it would do better to let someone else be host. Furthermore, they stated, it was the business of the Asian Games Federation, not Indonesia, to determine who would participate, and that some of the questions raised by Indonesia were irrelevant anyhow, since Communist China, North Vietnam, North Korea, and the Asian Soviet Republics had never applied for membership. Then, not long afterward, Nationalist China was boycotted by the International Olympics Commission. It seemed that politics did apply after all in the big league, so why not in the little league as well; and with the USSR building the Djakarta stadium, what would be more natural than that Asian Soviet Republics, if not other Communist Asian countries, might yet apply? For the time being the problem is in abeyance.

Dispute number two arose over Indonesia's status vis-à-vis the Asian Football Confederation which Indonesian representatives helped to found in Manila in 1954. The Confederation announced some months ago that Indonesia had persistently failed to reply to communications, that it had never paid its dues, that it had never paid the Confederation the agreed-upon percentage of all international matches played in Indonesia, and that it must now either conform or face a football boycott by all Confederation member neighbors. Indonesia replied that it had never actually joined the Confederation, that it had frequently and fruitlessly requested copies of the constitution and other pertinent documents so that it could come to a decision, that consequently it was not liable for any dues or percentages. Indonesian official and unofficial spokesmen intimated that they had objections to some of the other members of the Confederation--specifically, Nationalist China and Israel--and that as for the Confederation's "disciplining," Indonesia was much too important a nation in international matches for the Confederation to afford to boycott it. This dispute, like the other, has simmered down for the moment, but it could boil up again rather speedily, and football is a major item on the Asian Games agenda.

                *   *   *   *   *

It is s.o.p. in Indonesia for there to be prolonged delay and dispute, then a furious and confused last-minute rush, resulting as often as not in a final production which goes off as though there had never for a moment been any doubt that it would actually occur or that it would be a smashing success. But there are slip-ups, too, and the 1962 Asian Games are a tremendous undertaking which can scarcely be left to last-minute luck and ingenuity.

The one comparable previous production in Indonesia was the 1954 Asia-Africa Conference in Bandung. In an astonishingly short time, after it seemed that delay and indecision had greatly prejudiced chances for success, the Government prepared a conference hall, renovated the hotels, assembled transportation, and organized a reception and administrative staff; it even repaired the highway to Bandung and dressed up Djakarta to welcome the delegates and speed them on their way. To be sure, it also evicted almost all private hotel guests, it requisitioned a number of private villas, it squandered tremendous amounts of money, and it provided little in the way of facilities for any except the official conference delegates. All the same, the Conference itself was well and smoothly run, a notable demonstration to skeptics that the Indonesian Government was able to make good on its invitations and its promises.

The 1962 Asian Games will be a production of quite another magnitude, however. There is much to be said for the point of view that if the Government really does what is necessary to make the games themselves a success, it will be making a very important start toward putting the city of Djakarta and the nation of Indonesia in reasonable working order. Benefits can accrue

not only in Djakarta and Indonesia but to Southeast Asia and the international
world in general. Relative success or relative failure in preparation for the
1962 Asian Games should constitute a fairly good indicator of Indonesia's
general state of health and its state of morale.

Willard A. Hanna

[Photographs, courtesy Ministry of Information, Djakarta.]

American Universities Field Staff   REPORTS SERVICE

BUNG KARNO'S INDONESIA

Part XIII: The Impact of Djakarta

by Willard A. Hanna

October 29, 1959

This publication is one of a continuing series on current developments in world affairs written by associates of the American Universities Field Staff. It is distributed by the AUFS as a useful addition to the American fund of information on foreign affairs.

AUFS Associates have been chosen for their skill in collecting, reporting, and evaluating data. Each has combined long personal observation and experience in his foreign area with advanced studies relating to it.

WILLARD A. HANNA, the author of this report, is based in Kuala Lumpur to write about Southeast Asian affairs. Before joining the AUFS in 1954, Dr. Hanna had spent a total of more than ten years in East and Southeast Asia as a teacher, administrator, and writer.

Publications under the imprint of the American Universities Field Staff are not selected to accord with an editorial policy and do not represent the views of its membership. Responsibility for accuracy of facts and for opinions expressed in the letters and reports rests solely with the individual writers.

"There's one 'way out' we haven't yet explored," mused an Indonesian friend of mine. "We might offer to hand over Djakarta to the Dutch in exchange for Irian Barat. But I suppose we'd have to throw in Bogor and the Puntjak before they'd even consider the deal, and we really wouldn't be any better off in the end."

"Amputate Djakarta," was another suggestion I heard. "It's malignant."

"No, just scrub it and disinfect it," was another. "Then put it out of bounds to politicians; convert the sentry boxes into public lavatories to replace the canals; disconnect the canals and build throughways; put in an elevated highway as far as Bogor, and build a million low-cost apartments into the foundations. That's all it would take."

"Djakarta's an acquired taste," said an American. "It has a flavor all its own. Like durian."

"Smelly, yes," said another. "But a flavor more like bitter almonds."

"What do you expect of a city whose popula-

NOTE: See also 300 + 37 = 429: A Biography of Djakarta (WAH-16-'59), an AUFS publication.

[WAH-24-'59]

tion has increased 400 per cent--who knows? maybe 800 per cent--in the last 30 years? It's been beat up by war and revolution. It was just a remote Dutch colonial outpost before the war. Now it's a new capital city. It's had to tackle overnight all the problems of the 20th century. It's got guts. Give it time."

"Gladly!" said a tourist. "So far as I'm concerned, it can have another 50 years. Then, maybe, I'll come back." The tourist was stranded in Djakarta on his way to Bali. No plane reservations were in sight, no hotel accommodations were possible, nobody was much interested in his problems. He had just spent two hours in a hot, shabby, crowded waiting room getting through quarantine, immigration, and customs. He had also been threatened with a humiliating strip-down in a body search for undeclared currencies, and he wasn't comforted much to learn that for the traveling Chinese it wasn't just strip-down but shake-down as well. Nobody knew what documentation he needed to travel even to Bandung-- only that it was going to be quite a production either to find out or to procure it.

"Djakarta isn't Indonesia," an Indonesian official insisted to me. "We got stuck with a run-down Dutch-Chinese city for our capital. The Dutch were always parsimonious. Look at what they left us in the way of electrical, water, and telephone facilities--enough for 100,000 people by the minimum standards of 25 years ago. The Chinese never had any civic spirit, only clannish collu-sion to get rich. That public strip-tease you Americans take photos of--that's because the Dutch left most of the population with only canals for laundry, bath, and toilet. That strip-down at the airport you object to--that's the way the Dutch controlled currency and we're just maintaining their democratic practices. Besides, it doesn't really happen very often, and how else are you going to throw a scare into the Chinese, who sew thousand dollar bills to their underwear to take them abroad? You don't like not being able to find a hotel room. How do you think we Indonesians like not being able to find a house for years on end? How do you think we like seeing rich foreigners pay big black market prices in inflated rupiahs for houses that smart Chinese build for them? I know one foreigner who bought a big house with the Rp. 1,000,000 he made by selling an automobile that cost him $2,500 and came in duty free. Do you suppose we enjoy having it pointed out to us that everything is modern and efficient over in Singapore, but that here we have nothing but one political crisis after another and an economy that's on the rocks? We're trying, and we're getting somewhere, but here in Djakarta, no matter how hard you try and no matter how much progress you make, people and problems just keep backing up on you. Get outside Djakarta, and you'll see--people are more relaxed and more is visibly getting done. And if you look closely even at Dja-karta, you'll see that everything isn't going down-hill. There are thousands of new houses, and lots of new office buildings, and schools, and clinics, and mosques, and even factories, but of course, not half enough."

Not ten per cent enough, was my estimate. Still, I had to concede, he had a point. If Djakarta is far more dilapidated and littered than it was two years ago, and if crowds are denser and tempers shorter and the dress and

diet of the ordinary people obviously poorer, still there are some impressive
evidences of advance. Yet the mere physical appearance of the city, the neglect and ramshackle congestion of once handsome business and residential
areas, relieved by occasional glimpses of new construction and evidences of
new spirit, all this is likely to pose to the thoughtful visitor the perplexing
question: if a little can actually be accomplished to reverse the general trend
toward retrogression, why can't quite a lot more?

One of the big accomplishments is a new University of Indonesia complex, consisting of half a dozen or more big new buildings. They will soon be
occupied by the nonscientific faculties of the University, leaving the old complex, into which had previously been packed all the faculties totaling over
10,000 students, once again to the medical school. But the new campus is
still quite inadequately provided with electricity and water. It is situated at

the end of a narrow, winding
street so packed with traffic
that a speed of ten miles per
hour is positively reckless,
and it still fails to meet the
real needs of a rapidly expanding institution. In the
old University complex, the
sheer extent of postwar construction and new activity is
once again impressive; but
at the Medical School hospital, for instance, where the
staff has been increased and
the facilities improved, the
out-patients must still queue
up early in the morning and
even then, after waiting for
many hours, they are likely
to have to return the following morning even earlier if
they wish to be sure to be

Main building of the Medical Faculty,
University of Indonesia.

seen by an overworked doctor for even a couple of minutes. To be sure, it is
expecting too much to think that one hospital could serve so large a percentage
of Djakarta's population, or to think that enough new hospitals could be built
and staffed within a few years to meet the steadily rising demand for modern
medical services; but it is not unreasonable to think that a patient might be
given some indication, before he has waited for ten hours, whether he really
is going to receive attention.

Private medical facilities are as acutely overcrowded as the public,
and despite some handsome new buildings, primary and secondary schools are
as inadequate to meet the real needs of the city as is the University. Mosques

have fared better on the whole; but while an expensive new private mosque is replacing the tennis courts in the Presidential Palace garden, the new national mosque remains a dream. The moldering Dutch fort which stands on the proposed site remains an unwelcome civic and historic landmark while being subjected to rather leisurely demolition. A new 14-story hotel, planned to provide the city with its first skyscraper, is still rivaled by a few new five or six story buildings of fairly uninspired design, of which the most striking feature, logically enough, is the sun-baffle. These are the new quarters of government ministries and government-subsidized business concerns whose underemployed personnel always seem to overflow whatever expanded quarters are provided for them. The hotel itself, which must perforce be finished for the Asian Games in 1962 and for which the Japanese have now reluctantly agreed to put up the money, has progressed after about five years to the point where foundation piles have been driven and a high board fence has been put up to keep squatters from reoccupying the grounds. The hotel seems to date more truly symbolic than the University of the ability of the national and the municipal governments either to lay plans or to carry them out.

From the site of the new hotel, one needs to drive out Djalan Djenderal Sudirman to the new suburban city of Kebajoran to observe in greatest concentration Djakarta's civic planning progress and problems. Long stretches of Djalan Djenderal Sudirman are bordered with dense settlements which supply shelter to a part of the 750,000 or more squatters who make up perhaps one fourth of the city's population. Mat-shed construction and shortage of electrical or sanitary installations create the double hazard of fire and epidemic. Other stretches of the roadway are built up with shops, small office buildings, workshops, and factories; but the chronic Djakarta shortages of equipment, machinery, and raw materials convert the proprietors of these establishments into nearly full-time procurement agents scouting for the wherewithall to stay in business. A bicycle assembly plant, for instance, lacks assembly parts. A garage lacks both new vehicles and repair parts; a batik co-operative combats chronic shortages of textiles and imbalance of processing materials. Whether squatter shed or brick-and-plaster commercial property, however, a very great many of these buildings must soon come down. Djalan Djenderal Sudirman must be widened and beautified for the 1962 Asian Games. Large

The
new
Ministry
of
Industries
building,
Djakarta.

built-up areas, old as well as new, are to be leveled at a time when Djakarta's building problems, always acute, are more critical than ever before.

In the postwar suburb of Kebajoran itself there are thousands of new houses, many of them government-built and assigned to government employees for purely token rentals that amount to a couple of American dollars per month, a great many more of them built with "hot" money created by the inflation and renting for two to three hundred dollars monthly. Far too large a proportion of them are "luxury"housing to satisfy the demands of the newly rich or newly powerful, rather than the low-cost public housing which is desperately needed. Even for "luxury" houses, however, it may require months to get an electrical connection, a telephone is generally out of the question, and other public utilities and services in general are dismally short.

The greatest public improvement in Djakarta in recent years was undoubtedly the new water filtration plant, opened about two years ago. After a couple of early breakdowns in the system, the flow of water is now relatively dependable through both old and new city mains, for the first time since World War II. Even yet, however, the bulk of the population is without piped water supply and is dependent upon kampong wells; thousands must still resort for laundry, bath, or toilet, or all simultaneously, to the sluggish canals which are rapidly silting up with a slime that is best left undescribed.

Another major improvement in Djakarta three years ago was the introduction into service of about a hundred big diesel street buses, Australian gifts to Indonesia under the Colombo Plan. More than 50 per cent of these buses are immobilized these days by reason of reckless operation and lack of proper maintenance. Repair parts, supplied gratis from Australia, tend to get misplaced in customs godowns while the Government attempts to collect import duties upon them. The general traveling and commuting public still depends largely upon the little seven-passenger jitneys, the "opelettes," on which fares are rising by 100 to 400 per cent, or upon the trishaws, for which unending thousands of newcomers from the rice fields provide pedal power. Opelette and trishaw congestion makes a ride through Djakarta traffic both more deliberate and more hazardous than a ride in almost any other city of Asia.

Most visitors and most traveled Djakartans are likely to concur in the judgment that the city is the most uncomfortable and inconvenient if not the most downright depressing of any major city of Southeast Asia today. Only Rangoon is a runner-up in the competition, and Rangoon of late has experienced a fairly successful face-lifting operation. One cannot but be sympathetic, however, with Djakarta's enormous problems. The least enormous, in absolute terms, is its budget. Djakarta, a city of some 135 square miles with a population of some 3,000,000, has an annual budget of about Rp.230,000,000, or US$7,500,000 at the present official rate of exchange. The nearby island of Singapore, with an area of 210 square miles and a population of 1,500,000, has

a municipal budget of approximately US$40,000,000, a rural board budget of
US$1,750,000, and an overlapping state budget of US$70,000,000. The miracle
of Djakarta city management, perhaps, is that it is not far worse managed
than it is. In view of the budget of US$7,500,000, only $500,000 of which is
earmarked for building schools, roads, bridges, and maintaining other public
facilities and services, it seems unreasonable to ask that the city light or
clean its streets, that it provide parks and beaches, that it improve drainage
or combat mosquitoes, that it install a telephone exchange which will make a
phone call less exhausting than a trip through traffic to deliver the message
in person, or even that it provide an adequate police force so that householders
need not hire private guards to avoid being burgled.

It does not seem too much to ask, however, that the city's and the
nation's officials, underpaid and harassed as they undoubtedly are, and suffering far more than any visitor from the city's inadequacies and incoherencies,
should exhibit a little more interest in making life and business in Djakarta
just a little easier for themselves and for others rather than, as is their
wont, making it almost always more complicated. It is the constant complaint
not only of visitors but of Djakartans as well that the surest way not to accomplish what you set out to do, or at least the way to waste the most time and
energy in accomplishing it, is to go through prescribed official channels.
Two experiences of my own may serve to illustrate.

Example One: Immediately upon arrival in Djakarta four months ago,
I requested--experimentally--that the Ministry of Information set up for me
four presumably routine official appointments. In the course of the next five
weeks, I made at least ten trips to the Ministry to check up on progress.
Each time I had difficulty locating anyone who had any knowledge of the matter, or, if any knowledge, any interest in it. I kept repeating my requests
either orally or in writing, and in the end I came up with the following score:
one appointment made and kept, although there was a mix-up about hours; one
appointment made too late to be kept; one appointment vaguely and tentatively
made and by mutual and tacit consent allowed to lapse; one appointment never
heard from.

Example Two: Just before I arrived in Indonesia, the Military Command had put out a new regulation that all foreigners required travel passes
for any overnight trip outside Djakarta. I spent one whole morning searching
for the right office and waiting just to get a week-end permit. I was then
informed that the permit wasn't really valid until it was countersigned by a
guarantor, returned, and re-stamped. I talked my way out of that one, but I
still had to return the first permit and apply all over again in order to get a
second. The second took only half an hour and--after some persuasion--was
made valid for three weeks' travel to specified cities on specified dates.
Nobody ever once asked to see my permits after that, but to be sure, if anyone had asked, and if I hadn't had them, or if I hadn't had exactly the right
form with all the dates and chops and signatures and photographs exactly as

my interrogator thought they should be, I would have been liable to a year in jail or a Rp. 100,000 fine or both. (Or would I? I never could find out whether the regulation really applied to transients.) I wondered, incidentally, what purpose my visa served--it had cost the outrageous sum of US$20, and had taken nearly two months to procure. I wondered also what purpose the hotel registers served, for in logging-in a visitor must fill out exhaustive forms in duplicate in two sets of books, all in accordance with police regulations.

Once outside Djakarta, I should acknowledge, there was a remarkable change. In each city I visited, I was met on arrival by an agreeable, accommodating and efficient representative of the Ministry of Information. My problem was not to solicit favors but to avoid imposing upon official and even personal hospitality, and to keep from monopolizing official transportation and guide service. As for the police, I had no reason to believe they ever took any suspicious interest in me, not even when I showed up with a party of eight for a forbidden moonlight picnic on top of the Borobudur. Only in Djakarta was I made to feel like either a nuisance or a menace.

"Don't let it disturb you," Djakartans told me, not for the first time. "You went about it wrong. You should have come to us. We could have fixed it up."

"Fixing it up," or, if it can't be fixed, then bearing it; but in either case avoiding insofar as humanly possible the labrynthine challenges of bureaucracy and taking a certain antic pleasure in demonstrating that official controls are basically unworkable and personal satisfactions basically unencroachable: this seems to be the speciality of the 1959-model Djakartan. Like Indonesians in general, Djakartans are by nature both resilient and resourceful, much better, perhaps, at contriving emergency expedients than in devising or executing long-range plans. They exhibited the most remarkable courage and audacity in asserting their independence of the Japanese and of the Dutch, and then, with virtually no resources at hand, making their assertion stick. Their difficulties, including those with an almost totally obtuse government, are perhaps even greater today than in 1945. If so, their finest hour may be upon them. If Djakarta can just hang onto what is left of its sanity for a few more years, then eventually there may come progress too.

Willard A. Hanna

[Photographs, courtesy Ministry of Information, Djakarta.]

SOUTHEAST ASIA SERIES
Vol. VII   No. 29
(Indonesia)

American Universities Field Staff

REPORTS SERVICE

BUNG KARNO'S INDONESIA

Part XIV: The Bandung Perspective

by Willard A. Hanna

October 31, 1959

This publication is one of a continuing series on current developments in world affairs written by associates of the American Universities Field Staff. It is distributed by the AUFS as a useful addition to the American fund of information on foreign affairs.

AUFS Associates have been chosen for their skill in collecting, reporting, and evaluating data. Each has combined long personal observation and experience in his foreign area with advanced studies relating to it.

WILLARD A. HANNA, the author of this report, is based in Kuala Lumpur to write about Southeast Asian affairs. Before joining the AUFS in 1954, Dr. Hanna had spent a total of more than ten years in East and Southeast Asia as a teacher, administrator, and writer.

Publications under the imprint of the American Universities Field Staff are not selected to accord with an editorial policy and do not represent the views of its membership. Responsibility for accuracy of facts and for opinions expressed in the letters and reports rests solely with the individual writers.

Bandung, I thought, and not for the first time, is almost everything that Djakarta could be and should be but isn't. Of course, Bandung does have a head start, for it has climate and scenery in its favor. Located on a mountain plateau, Bandung is high, cool, and surrounded by some of the most beautiful scenery of all Indonesia. From almost any point in the city, whether from the busy downtown streets or from the quiet residential suburbs which climb the foothills to the north, one is aware of the mountains, their steep slopes tamed by terraced rice fields. Cocoanut palms, bamboo, and huge flowering trees--flame-of-the-forest, cup-of-gold, African tulip--luxuriant gardens, a vivid blue sky and clear mountain air: all these make Bandung not merely tropically idyllic but almost theatrically contrived. Djakarta, on the other hand, is flat, hot, and humid, and save for a few of the ex-colonial residential enclaves, affords little space for broad avenues or fine gardens. Nor does Djakarta seem to prize orderliness and sanitation, or allow for a morning and evening turnout of promenaders who look well dressed and well fed, unhurried and unharassed. But what really clinches the case for Bandung for a foreigner is not just that it is cool and clean and tree-shaded and beautiful, but that you can actually get a hotel room there--most of the time, that is-- and a good one; you have a whole street lined with shops that carry an inviting assortment of goods;

[WAH-25-'59]

and you have your choice of good
Chinese restaurants without having
to mount a major expedition to reach
them. Besides, there are golf and
swimming and riding within easy
range of the downtown area, and
there's even a country club.

It was while I sat comfort-
ably on the breezy terrace of the
country club, looking out over the
swimming pool and the splendid view
of the valley and the city below that
I began to ask questions. Was all
this as good as it seemed, and has
Bandung, unlike Djakarta, found a
rational solution to the problem of
living in an Indonesia that is in unending upheaval? And presently things
began to look not quite so good in Bandung either.

A country view, near Bandung

Take the country club itself. It was built by the Dutch in 1957, with
the money a former Dutch club received in compensation for its downtown
building which was requisitioned for the Asia-Africa Conference. It was
opened with much gaiety one evening not long before Christmas. It was
closed the next day when the Indonesian Government began to take stern
measures against the Dutch in retaliation for their refusal to give up Western
New Guinea, and ordinary Indonesian citizens were enjoined--under threat of
beatings by youthful gangs of vigilantes--not to sell a chicken or a banana or
a loaf of bread to the Dutch nor to provide any services, but rather to be
ready on call to help seize and "nation-
alize" all Dutch property. The club is
operated now under the control of the
West Java Military Command. It
seemed slightly less pleasant to relax
in when I recalled that I was in effect
an uninvited guest of absentee Dutch
hosts. And the handsome houses I saw
on the slopes below me--built perhaps
out of the profits of colonialism, to be
sure, but as a result of individual initiative and individual savings, too, and
not always to the detriment of the
nation--are now also expropriated for
others' use without much prospect of
compensation to the Dutch owners.
But then c'est la guerre, I had already
enjoyed involuntary postwar hospital-

Bandung street scene.

ities in Germany and in Japan, so my vague scruples were perhaps inappropriately censorious.

I experienced no such scruples when I returned to Bandung proper to visit a mammoth new swimming pool and poolside restaurant, both indubitably built by the Indonesian police force and open to the general public at the astoundingly low price of Rp. 3.00 per head. I refrained from any inquiry as to how the land had been acquired or who now owns the onetime Dutch villas that surround it, although one, I discovered incidentally, is the official holiday house of the Prime Minister. I felt a returning sense of uneasiness, however, when I returned to the Hotel Savoy-Homann where courteous waiters still serve in the spacious ground floor lobby-terrace and peacocks patrol the garden and an orchestra plays for dancing--but, as in the club, only until 10 p.m. and only a few times a week, for Western ballroom dancing, like the hoolahoop and rock 'n' roll, is regarded with suspicion by the military keepers of the public morals. The Homann, I recalled, is an immensely valuable property, one which was disposed of by its former Dutch owners a few years ago at all but forced sale and for a fraction of its real value. Political party funds and political pressures featured in the transaction, and there was a big scandal later about the purchase and about the money the Government put into the hotel to renovate it for the Asia-Africa Conference.

The new swimming pool.

It was better, I thought, to get out of town for a bit, to go to the big
resort hotel in nearby Lembang, one of the most scenic spots the tropical
mountains have to offer. But at Lembang there did not seem to be the accustomed bustle of visitors. The town had been raided the previous week-end
by a powerful band of Darul Islam guerrillas who fought--and didn't altogether
lose--a pitched battle with the armed forces. It seemed inadvisable to continue to Tangkuban-praoh where one can drive onto the very rim of a smoking
volcanic crater, for three months earlier a whole caravan of Sunday picnickers
had been held up by the Darul Islam forces and all were robbed and five were
killed.

Better to look at the constructive, the progressive, the hopeful. I
decided to visit the new teachers' training college a few miles from Bandung
city. It is located in a fortresslike hill-top villa, once the private home of a
Dutch newspaper publisher, repeatedly fought over and bombed out during the
Revolution and since 1954 restored at immense labor and cost by the Indonesian Government. It now provides a five-year, tuition-free training course
for some 1,500 students at a cost to the Government of about Rp. 70 per day.
The old villa is now the center of a thriving little community, with new class-
room and laboratory buildings just recently occupied and a cluster of neat,
modern bungalows for faculty residences. To be sure, the College is encountering great difficulties. It has trouble recruiting and retaining a teaching
staff, currently numbering about 250, including part-time instructors and

The main building of
the Teachers' College,
once a private villa.

One of the **prewar** university buildings, Bandung.

12 foreign teachers sponsored by American and other aid programs. It can't keep within its budget in these days of wild inflation; its Indonesian teachers are faced with the difficulty of trying to live on Rp. 1,500 per month; and its graduates look forward to the unappealing prospect of having to work for the Government for a fixed number of years at much lower salaries. Nevertheless, there is a spirit of pride and confidence about the establishment which goes far to counteract such minor annoyances as the cost of textbooks being out of reach of the ordinary student, transportation to and from Bandung being chancy, and the curriculum being highly variable and experimental.

At the University of Bandung, the Technical Faculty, like the Teachers' College, must be judged a major administrative triumph over recurrent and critical difficulties. Centered still in the old Dutch university complex, but now provided with handsome new buildings and vastly expanded in enrollment, the University has been gradually solving its formidable problems of shortage of equipment, lack of qualified teachers, and incoherence of a too swiftly expanded curriculum. The Indonesian staff, plus a University of Kentucky professorial staff of about a dozen, plus various other foreign experts, have managed, in the course of the last three years, to rescue the institution from its really critical plight of not being able to graduate more than about five per cent of the students who entered. If the university situation has improved vastly in the last few years, it has also become more complicated, for there have appeared in Bandung two splinter and competing universities, not very soundly planned or administered as yet. At least, however, they serve the purpose of enabling teachers to hold down appointments in two or three institutions at the same time and thus to earn two or three salaries, which still are all too few to provide a decent living.

Having seen the new Indonesia at its best and most hopeful in the Teachers' College and University, I decided I should see it, or at least hear of it at its worst, so I headed for the home of a trusted Chinese informant. As I had suspected, things were very bad indeed. My Chinese friend had lost his downtown properties--squeezed out, he said; it had been a question of selling out for whatever he could get, or of having the properties requisitioned by the military. He had lost his business phone--taken out, he said, by the military which had decided that someone else needed it worse than he did. He's still in business but it's mainly quick buy-sell, turning rupiahs over fast in order to keep up with the inflation, and putting profits not into any business development but into scarce goods which can safely be hoarded while prices rise. He still has one small retail shop, and he has some distinguished customers. He named some names. "Of course," he added, "they don't pay their accounts, and it isn't smart to present bills."

In a few months, he continued, things are really going to get tough. Chinese who now live and do business outside the major cities are being forced to dispose of their properties; they tend, naturally, to concentrate now in a city like Bandung. They are already starting to bid on any attractive properties--and to offer bribes to the civil and the military officials to help them get them. My friend is going to have to match their offers if he wants to hold onto what he still has. The Chinese aren't exhibiting much esprit de corps, he says. After all, they're all in the same trap and they should stick together. The really smart Chinese are getting out of Indonesia altogether. But it isn't just the Chinese who are suffering. Any Indonesian who is trying to do real business instead of merely operating a racket is in the same fix.

Deciding that I had better get an Indonesian reading on the subject, I visited an Indonesian friend who is engaged in a variety of businesses. At first he wasn't inclined to talk. He had been up for daily questioning by the military police not so long before. He doesn't know why--he never could find out. It was during the regional insurrections and a lot of people were being questioned, so perhaps it was just routine. Of course the Chinese are having their troubles, he admitted, warming up a bit. But the Chinese troubles are no worse than his. He hadn't been able to get an import license for six months, and the last shipment of goods he had received from abroad he had to sell to the military below cost. If things keep on as they are, he has just enough capital to keep him in business until the end of the year, no longer. He doesn't even have a house or a car of his own which he could sell to raise money in order to hang on for a few more months. Fortunately, his parents have a house in Bandung--they got a residence permit to occupy quite a handsome house that belongs to a Dutch businessman. He can always live with his parents, and they can always meet basic living costs--unless things get very much worse indeed--by renting out a few rooms.

I then tried another Indonesian friend who has turned tea planter. "Sure, it's theoretically a good thing," he said; but was I aware of some basic economic facts? Labor costs are rising; production is falling. If you need a new truck or a new jeep, you must go through the most incredible amount of paper work, then wait six months to a year for the vehicle even to be ordered from abroad. Meanwhile you must maintain your own intelligence and bribery system to make sure it isn't sold to someone else or requisitioned by the Army. Do I know of the case of the Swiss-owned estate, not a tea estate like his, to be sure, but a rubber estate on which the situation was comparable? Things had become just too much for the Swiss owners who decided simply to abandon their holdings--over 4,000 acres of what were once immensely valuable plantings. After their departure, the laborers first took over, about two thousand of them. They continued operations on their own and demanded continued company compensation. Then the Government took over. It is continuing operations--at a loss, of course--and it is making various claims against the Swiss company and its Dutch agents. He hopes it won't come to anything like that on his tea estate, but he can't make enough profit to pay the laborers a living wage. Have I had a look at the estates hereabouts to see what is happening? How instead of keeping things up, as they are paid to do, the workers are neglecting or even cutting down the tea to plant patches of food crops?

I admitted that I hadn't looked very hard, but I made another trip out of town and this time I headed for a tea growing area. I saw what he meant. Whereas the tea used to be planted in beautifully trimmed green rows over a whole mountainside, it was now interspersed with patches of cassava and banana and sweet potato. The tea that remained looked badly tended--the bushes were overgrown, they were not kept weeded, and they looked as if they had scale disease. I stopped at the factory of what used to be an extremely well-run foreign estate. Half the machinery was out of order; the buildings were run down; the trucks that brought in the baskets of newly-picked tea leaves looked as though they hadn't many miles of service left. The processing and grading, even to my amateur eye, seemed slapdash. The estate, like many others in the area, had come under the supervision of the military command.

I had already arranged a couple of appointments with the military command, and I was beginning to wonder, in view of all I had been hearing about military interference and foul-up, just how stiff the going would be. I need not have worried. The appointments went off smoothly and agreeably. The military personnel I met exhibited both competence and urbanity. I talked, for instance, with the regional commander, an extremely self-possessed and forceful young man. To be sure, he seemed interested primarily in leading me into an explanation of the American proclivity for seeing all international affairs in terms of the Cold War and for judging Indonesia in particular as headed toward a Communist take-over. He was little disposed to give me any run-down on the local military situation, and on the political-economic situation he refused to comment at all. But he seemed a strong successor to the command of the West Java Military Region and of the crack Siliwangi Division which is based on Bandung. The Siliwangi Division, I recalled, had been vigorously anti-Communist in putting down the 1948 Madiun Communist Uprising; but the Siliwangi command now, like the rest of the Indonesian Army and Government, denounces anticommunism and declares that noncommunism is the only tenable position for a patriotic Indonesian. Some of the onetime top officers of the Siliwangi Division who professed open anticommunism have defected to the rebel cause and have both denounced and fought their former revolutionary colleagues in arms. I decided not to ask for any explanation.

I have heard it just as often as the present Siliwangi commander has heard the explanation of the American position.

I visited the noncommissioned officers training school which is operated by the West Java Military Command. There the commanding officer was again a prepossessing, energetic young man, recently returned from the United States, quite friendly toward the Western world. The staff was smart and able. The students, who had had only five weeks' training at the time I visited the school, were drilled and disciplined to the point where a Prussian officer would have been proud of their parade ground performance. They gave every evidence of being no mere automatons but smart, likeable, resourceful young men. As a military institution, the school was as impressive in its way as the Teachers' College and the University.

I spent some little time in Bandung with one particular young Headquarters' officer who was responsible for seeing that my appointments with the military went off without hitches. He exhibited the greatest determination that all should be at the same time militarily precise and socially cordial, and a few minutes' delay at any point or any slight evidence of stiffness in reception made him acutely uncomfortable. In the natural course of events, I came to learn a little about his private life. He had no house of his own. He owned no automobile. He was having an extremely difficult time making ends meet on his meager Army pay. So far as I could detect, he had no racket by which to supplement his salary.

My personal observations led me to think the military headquarters was running a good show. But then, from many persons--Indonesian, Chinese, and foreign--I began to hear that the Siliwangi Division is reputedly just as opportunistic and as corrupt and as uncertain in its loyalties as the Indonesian armed forces in general are believed to be. Some of the officers are widely believed to be getting rich by such illicit practices as putting the squeeze on the Chinese and exacting personal profits from the Army-controlled Dutch enterprises. Some of the men--those, for instance, who were sent many months ago to help put down the rebellion in Sumatra and are now getting letters from their wives telling them it is impossible to live on Army allotments --are said to be on the point of mutiny. These impressions and rumors were hard to reconcile. But then, in Indonesia today, few things do seem to add up.

What I needed was relaxation, a chance to let things slip into focus, so I went to a performance of wajang orang by a Central Javanese troupe in a mat-shed kampong theatre. It was spirited if rather tawdry theatricals, complete with highly stylized exchanges and posturings of the actors; garishly regal classical costumes; masklike make-up which, for the Indonesian spectators at least, immediately identified the characters and the Hindu legends in which they featured. The action took place on a Western-style stage, making use of such other modern innovations as footlights and a mirror box for the appearances and fadings of dream figures. Bottled soft drinks were being

Backstage at the theatre, Bandung.

On stage at the theatre: a <u>wajang</u> <u>orang</u> performance.

peddled at a brisk pace among the audience. I also attended a performance
of <u>wajang</u> <u>golek</u> where a narrator takes all the parts and manipulates dozens
of wooden puppets to suit the action, and the audience settles in to eat and
talk and watch and catnap from 8 p.m. to 6 a.m. I also tried the Chinese
restaurants, visions of whose menus sustained me through the longer mono-
logues at the theatre: gourame pond fish fried crisp and covered with herbs
and sweet-sour sauce, broiled frogs' legs sprinkled with lime juice and salt
and pepper, birds' nest soup with crab eggs, roast duck with black mushrooms,
Indonesian-style <u>sates</u>--bits of chicken or beef (varied by the Chinese to
include pork or shrimp) broiled over charcoal on bamboo skewers and served
with a sauce of ground peanuts, chilis, and spices.

　　　　　But still Bandung did not fall into perspective. It still left me with my
major question unanswered. How can things be so chaotic in Indonesia and
yet how can life--outside Djakarta at least--still be so good in so many
respects? How can so many extremely agreeable, intelligent, resourceful
people be getting themselves into an intolerable snarl, but yet remain agreeable, intelligent, and resourceful? At least Bandung does lend this perspective: it is mainly in Djakarta that the trouble originates; it is in Djakarta that
the effects show up most conspicuously and most discouragingly. So far as
Java at least is concerned, the farther one gets from Djakarta, the more one
can hope that things are not quite as bad as they seem.

Willard A. Hanna

[Photograph, top of page 2, courtesy Ministry of Information, Djakarta;
all other photographs, courtesy Office of Information, Bandung.]

SOUTHEAST ASIA SERIES
Vol. VII   No. 30
(Indonesia)

American Universities Field Staff   REPORTS SERVICE

BUNG KARNO'S INDONESIA

Part XV: The Jogja Corrective

by Willard A. Hanna

November 2, 1959

This publication is one of a continuing series on current developments in world affairs written by associates of the American Universities Field Staff. It is distributed by the AUFS as a useful addition to the American fund of information on foreign affairs.

AUFS Associates have been chosen for their skill in collecting, reporting, and evaluating data. Each has combined long personal observation and experience in his foreign area with advanced studies relating to it.

WILLARD A. HANNA, the author of this report, is based in Kuala Lumpur to write about Southeast Asian affairs. Before joining the AUFS in 1954, Dr. Hanna had spent a total of more than ten years in East and Southeast Asia as a teacher, administrator, and writer.

Publications under the imprint of the American Universities Field Staff are not selected to accord with an editorial policy and do not represent the views of its membership. Responsibility for accuracy of facts and for opinions expressed in the letters and reports rests solely with the individual writers.

When I got off the plane at Jogjakarta last July, I was almost immediately reminded of three impressions which have struck me many times before in this Central Javanese city. First, it is determinedly pushing ahead in spite of persistent difficulties and setbacks. It now has a handsome new airport building, one which contrasts sharply with airport facilities elsewhere in Indonesia which are the most dismal in Southeast Asia. Second, it is capitalizing upon its educational-cultural advantages to make itself both an Indonesian and an international cultural center. Just by way of emphasizing the point, the walls of the VIP waiting room in the new airport were then being adorned with large sculptured murals--not, perhaps, everyone's cup of sculptured tea, but "Jogja modern"--to greet the delegates to the Colombo Plan Conference which Jogja has lured away from Bandung and Djakarta. Third, the man behind Jogja's development is the Sultan, Hamengku Buwono IX, who combines inherited feudal authority with modern administrative status as governor. He was absent from the city during my visit, but work was being pushed forward at the airport building to earn his approval on his return, just as practically everything else in Jogja seems to hinge upon him.

I would not go so far as to say that Jogja is so atypical of Indonesia these days as to present a

[WAH-26-'59]

record of over-all coherence. I had no sooner arrived, for instance, than I
learned that the return flight on which I had reservations had been cancelled
and that no other flight would be made for at least a week. (As it turned out,
a special flight was routed through Jogja, for some reason, and what was
more, I was notified by special messenger well in advance.) During the ride
from the airport into town, I was informed that the gasoline shortage was
worse than in most other parts of Java; that the local batik industry was
languishing for lack of materials and because of inflated prices; and that in
this tobacco-growing center popular brands of local cigarettes were often
unobtainable. But you don't need a lot of gasoline in Jogja, one batik lasts
quite some time, and if pure tobacco cigarettes are scarce, one can fall back
on the clove keretek variety, or on betel nut.

Jogjakarta, happily remote from and relatively unmolested by Djakarta,
seemed not to be afflicted by the same sense of desperate emergency. The
country people, who live in some of Java's densest and most impoverished
agricultural concentrations, seemed nevertheless to have enough to eat and to
wear and were not packing into the city to join the jobless urban poor. Nor is
the city overflowing with squatters or with the nouveaux riches. There are
relatively few beggars, and so too there are relatively few ostentatious new
houses or shiny motor cars. There are, however, a lot of modest new suburban developments, and above all else, there are a lot of bicycles, carrying
scrubbed young students on their way to the proliferating primary and secondary schools and to the university. From the air, the Jogja rural landscape
seems to be dominated by a huge new sugar mill; but it is the big new university building which looms largest in the suburbs, and in the heart of the city
it is the rambling old Kraton of the Sultan which sets the tone and mood.
Jogjanese gentlemen, in their traditional dress of boldly striped jacket and
dark brown batik sarong, drive past in ancient horse carriages or walk
sedately along the tree-shaded lanes of the older parts of the city. While you
know that quite a good deal of feudal intrigue is going on beneath their tightly
folded batik headcloths, you feel inclined to regard it as a relief from Djakarta's nationalistic variety.

The Kraton shows little if any visible change over the years since the
Revolution. Its outer courts are still packed with overflow university classes.
Its inner reaches are still cool and spacious and quiet. Well-behaved parties
of visiting school children now scuffle up the gravel courts a bit and slide sur-
reptitiously on the marble flooring of the open pavilions. But they listen atten-
tively to the guards who recite the sonorous Javanese names for each of the
historic gamelins, exhibit the wedding palanquins and treasure chests and
royal portraits, point to the eternal flame that burns in the ceremonial bed-
chamber, and lead the groups of visitors through the succession of gates and
courts, each with its special ceremonial name and significance. The visitors
do not encroach upon the private quarters of the Sultan, where he lives in a
modified Dutch-style bungalow. He maintains the surviving splendors of the
past primarily, it would seem, for the pleasure of visitors, secondarily to

The Borobudur, 8th-9th-century Buddhist stupa near Jogja.

A pavilion in the Sultan's Kraton, Jogja.

Naga ornament, part of the symbol indicating date of construction of the Kraton.

Residence of the Sultan, within the Kraton.

give occupation to the now greatly diminished royal retinue that is now numbered only in the hundreds rather than the thousands.

If the Kraton seems changeless, the university, its counterpart as Jogja's second major urban landmark, does not. Ten years ago Gadjah Mada University, so far as its own physical plant went, was a series of brick and cement foundations, bravely started during the period of the Jogja Republic, but abandoned at the time of the Second Dutch Police Action. Three years ago, it was the scaffolded but accusing skeleton of a vast new administration building, apparently doomed indefinitely to remain unfinished since building funds, inadequate to begin with, had been embezzled. Today the building is complete --the biggest new building in all of Indonesia, say Gadjah Mada staff members with pride. It is an immense hollow rectangle which houses not only the administrative offices but several of the University faculties in quarters that are spacious, handsome, and airy--a combination rarely attained in modern Indonesia. Near the central building, others are soon to rise so that most of the University's 10,000 students will ultimately be accommodated on one campus.

A short distance away from the new building there is located a fast-growing residential area. Here the University provides neat apartments and bungalows for faculty and staff, including half a dozen Americans who are assigned to Gadjah Mada under various ICA, Ford Foundation, and other contracts. The residential complex has just been enlarged by addition of some 40 new bungalows, completed in time to house the delegates to the current Colombo Plan Conference and thereafter to provide additional faculty housing. All this is a major achievement, and the spirit of vigor and confidence is unmistakable among students and staff members alike. The spirit is dampened at times, to be sure, by the difficulties of life anywhere in Indonesia these days. But in Jogja, a higher percentage of the faculty members have decent places in which to teach and to live, and they have a better chance than academic personnel elsewhere in Indonesia of coming reasonably close to living on their salaries. Many of the students are accommodated in government hostels, and even if they room with townspeople they can get by on about Rp. 500 per month as compared with about Rp. 750 in Djakarta. Preoccupation with the economic and political debate of modern Indonesia is accordingly less, and attention to academic matters rather more than is the norm elsewhere.

I had particularly wanted to visit two new industrial establishments in Jogja, one a factory jointly sponsored by UNICEF, FAO, and the Indonesian Government for the production of powdered soy bean milk, the other an East German-built sugar mill. The soy milk factory was a project which had encountered long and complicated difficulties in getting started but seemed to me now to represent a real success story in international co-operation. The sugar factory had encountered even longer and more complex difficulties and seemed to me possibly to represent a success story in Communist bloc-Indonesian co-operation, also a reminder that Communist bloc projects seem to run no more smoothly than those sponsored by the West and perhaps for

some of the same reasons. The milk factory visit proved easy to arrange.
The sugar factory proved mysteriously impossible to schedule, so I had to be
satisfied with an outside view and secondhand report.

The East German sugar mill is a US$8.6 million installation, compris-
ing the sugar mill itself, a power plant, a housing project for higher level
employees, new transportation facilities and connections, and other minor
installations. The original contract was negotiated by the Sultan about five
years ago. Then began a series of delays and misunderstandings on all sides.
The machinery was shipped to Surabaya and lay there in storage for a year
or more while customs and transportation difficulties were being ironed out.
Indonesian government bank money with which the local expenses were to be
paid did not come through in the amounts or at the times agreed upon. Groups
of East German industrial experts made repeated visits, surveys, recommenda-
tions, and operational starts, only to encounter further delays. Dutch sugar
mill owners, whose mills the Sultan refused either to hand back or to restore
to operation under new management, argued that the whole project was unneces-
sary, that existing mill facilities were capable of handling any possible crop.
Opponents of the project in Jogja itself argued that the Sultan had been tricked,
and that in his eagerness to counterbalance Western with Eastern economic
aid, he had got into quite a lot more than he had bargained for.

Nevertheless, construction eventually got under way and continued on
the whole smoothly. A colony of some 100 East German engineers and technicians settled into Jogja to supervise the project and, incidentally, to make
themselves somewhat conspicuous not only in the industrial but in the limited
night life of the city. Finally, by mid-1958 the mill was built, but long behind
schedule, and no sooner had it started into operation on July 10 than it was
shut down again. Obviously, said the Germans, in a project of this magnitude
and complexity, it was necessary to conduct trial runs and then to rectify
minor shortcomings; and anyhow, a one-foot strip of iron had mysteriously
been fed into the mill along with the cane and had done considerable damage
to the machinery before it was discovered. Implausible excuses, said a great
many critics, some of whom should have known: the mill was in reality not a

The new sugar mill, built
by the East Germans.

cane sugar mill at all but for sugar
beets, and hence unsuited to Indonesia's needs. The sugar growers'
association, which calculated that
it might lose two to five per cent of
its crop by reason of these additional delays, entered suit against
the German builders to be indemni-
fied for losses. And then, finally,
the mill started up operations again,
unmistakably processing cane sugar.
It is now turning out a product which
has a ready market in Indonesia

where over-all sugar production has fallen off so sharply since World War II that rather than being an important export crop, as formerly, even domestic needs are not met. As I traveled through the Jogja district, I saw much cane being harvested and hauled off in the direction of the new mill. Outside the mill was a line-up of trucks and flatcars which indicated that there would be no problem at least in transporting the supply of raw material. An Indonesian staff now runs the mill, trained by the Germans before their departure, to be able to cope, it is assumed, with whatever new emergencies arise.

The story of the powdered soy bean milk factory was not altogether dissimilar. When I last visited Jogja three years ago, the Rp. 7.5 million factory building was empty, awaiting some US$380,000 worth of machinery. A polyglot assortment of international agencies and experts were still arguing about what and whose machinery was best adapted to a still experimental process. The machinery has now arrived and has been installed--an astonishing and astonishingly well-hitched-up assortment of equipment from the United States, England, Germany, and Sweden. The manufacturing processes and formulas have now been worked out, an adaptation and improvement by an Indian doctor of the FAO of basic formulas used in a couple of factories in the United States which the Indonesian manager and two technicians from the Jogja factory have visited. The soy beans are being delivered by the farmers, who have had to be encouraged to grow an improved variety for the factory, and the milk powder is coming out of the drying vats for tinning at the other end of the assembly line, enriched by additional carbohydrates, calcium, iron, and vitamins, and flavored with chocolate, vanilla, or banana to disguise the faintly unpleasant soy taste. But the factory is operating at about half capacity at best, producing about 1.5 tons per day. It is marketing only minute quantities of milk powder as compared with Indonesia's demands and imports. It is encountering difficulties such as would swiftly age any less resilient management--irregularity of supply of soy beans, inflationary prices asked by the farmers, shortage of fuel oil to run the factory's generator, necessity to purchase fuel oil at high open market rather than low controlled prices, necessity to distribute the product at an unrealistically low controlled price (Rp. 25 for a one-pound tin), dependence upon a government distribution agency whose energy and efficiency leaves a very great deal to be desired, difficulty in developing soy milk products which will appeal to the consumer and, if they do appeal, difficulty in providing a constant supply of the products. All the same, the factory is now actually in operation and is turning out a high-protein milk powder to supplement the national supply of fresh milk which is estimated at one tablespoonful per day per capita. It is creating new opportunities in subsidiary industries, such as those producing soft drinks, cakes, and candies.

The Jogja stories of steel and tobacco present in the one case more in the other case less clear-cut evidence of the almost prohibitive difficulties with which at times the local operators are faced. A small steel mill, once Dutch-operated and prosperous, then taken over by the Indonesian Government,

has now been closed down completely for constituting a
drain upon government money to pay for renovations,
wages, and extravagant sums in salaries and perqui-
sities for the management. A large-scale program to
plant, process, and market Virginia leaf tobacco resulted in the first couple of years in loss or deterioration of a very large part of the crop, also in rancorous
disputes with the British-American Tobacco Company
cigarette plant over quality and delivery; but now, if
the prevalence of healthy-looking tobacco plants as a
peasant's crop is to be taken as evidence, the program
seems well on its way to successful realization.

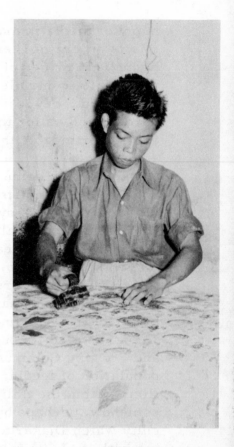

        Jogja's traditional industry is the manufacture
of batik, a textile produced by drawing or stamping a
design in wax, followed by repeated hand dipping to
apply the appropriate dyes to the appropriate segments of the pattern. Despite valiant efforts by
Jogja's Batik Research Institute, the industry today
has entered a slump from which it may not recover,
partly as a result of the over-all Indonesian economic
difficulties, partly because of the impossibility in this
case of converting traditional hand processes to modern mass production. The batik factories, mostly
small family industries, are now operating at no more
than half capacity at best. They are
concentrating either upon the cheapest product for ready sale or a very
expensive product suitable for hoard-   Wax is applied with a
ing against inflation. Imported cam-   copper stamp in the
brics, sold to the batik makers at   cheaper batik process.
low controlled prices--when official
controls are actually functioning,
that is--now prove to be much more
profitable to resell on the black market as unprocessed yard goods than
to convert into the cheaper batik.
The fine, completely hand-drawn
batiks, which require an average of
six months' time on the part of an
individual craftsman to complete,
represent a major investment in
which the risks are great and for
which buyers are limited.

        The future of the batik indus-
try is not viewed very hopefully by

The batik hand process.

many of the batik makers themselves. They point out, quite logically, that this is an era of cheap printed textiles and that as wages rise higher and higher and prices of raw materials are realistically adjusted rather than artificially controlled, even the ordinary batik becomes a luxury which few can afford. Few customers are prepared to pay a premium price for it abroad, and as for the foreign market in general, government export controls are so formidable that it is unlikely to flourish.

All the same, in Jogja today, as a couple of years ago, a visitor does not feel the cynicism and blank despair which so often pervades Djakarta. If old industries are dying out, new ones are getting started. In any event, educational and cultural activities constitute an industry in themselves. Thousands of students head for Jogja to attend the national schools, and hundreds more are coming to study both the traditional and contemporary arts for which big and little ateliers seem to multiply and flourish. Jogja, unlike Djakarta, seems able at the same time to keep moving into the progress and muddle of the modern world and to retain a degree of the stability of the old. To be sure, Jogja has also its built-in tensions among its feudal nobility; it has a large and growing Communist element, even among the aristocracy; it has the usual population of feuding politicians of the modern school; it has the usual conflicts within the military establishment and the government agencies. But somehow, perhaps by very reason of its distance from Djakarta and the difficulty which Djakarta bureaucrats experience in traveling to it or communicating with it, Jogja manages still to maintain at least the appearance of equilibrium.

Willard A. Hanna

NOTE: See also <u>Two Cities and Four Princes</u> (WAH-22-'56), an AUFS publication.

[Photographs courtesy Ministry of Information, Djakarta.]

SOUTHEAST ASIA SERIES
Vol. VII   No. 31
(Indonesia)

American Universities Field Staff   REPORTS SERVICE

BUNG KARNO'S INDONESIA
Part XVI: The Eloquent Betja Driver

by Willard A. Hanna

November 3, 1959

This publication is one of a continuing series on current developments in world affairs written by associates of the American Universities Field Staff. It is distributed by the AUFS as a useful addition to the American fund of information on foreign affairs.

AUFS Associates have been chosen for their skill in collecting, reporting, and evaluating data. Each has combined long personal observation and experience in his foreign area with advanced studies relating to it.

WILLARD A. HANNA, the author of this report, is based in Kuala Lumpur to write about Southeast Asian affairs. Before joining the AUFS in 1954, Dr. Hanna had spent a total of more than ten years in East and Southeast Asia as a teacher, administrator, and writer.

Publications under the imprint of the American Universities Field Staff are not selected to accord with an editorial policy and do not represent the views of its membership. Responsibility for accuracy of facts and for opinions expressed in the letters and reports rests solely with the individual writers.

"I do not understand," said my trishaw-man, "why everything is worse than before we had Merdeka."

I thought it was not my place to attempt to explain or to try to stop him.

"I work harder than I did before. I live in poorer quarters. I have less rice and fewer clothes. I have nothing else. No, I have my family."

"How many?" I asked.

"Five children."

"How many wives?" I asked.

"Tuan is joking! How could I afford more than one wife? But it would be very nice. Then I could have more children."

"How would you feed them?" I asked.

"Aduh! I could not feed them. But when I am old, they could feed me. I have four daughters, tuan, and one son. The daughters will marry, and I may not even see them again. My son will be a betja driver like me, and maybe he can help me for a time, but then he will have children of his

[WAH-27-'59]

own, and he won't be able to feed them, so how can he feed me?"

"How would it help, then, to have four more sons?"

"Maybe we could all earn money and educate one. Then he could support us."

"But your children are in school now, aren't they?"

"Two are in school, tuan. But I cannot pay the fees for the others. Soon, maybe, I cannot pay the fees for these two. It is only a little, but where am I to get ten rupiahs each month for school fees? And more besides for books and nice clothes. And much, much more after the first couple of years. Schools are hard to get into, tuan. You are lucky if you find a place. And now my oldest daughter is fifteen, and we have found a husband for her. But where am I to get the money for a new sarong and some gold earrings?"

"Let's see," I said. "You need maybe five hundred rupiahs this year for a wedding and one hundred rupiahs a year for school fees. You have only to save two to three rupiahs each day, and you have more than you need."

"Tuan is joking."

"Two to three rupiahs per day," I repeated. The price of four, maybe six cigarettes. You smoke cigarettes, don't you? How many?"

"When I have twenty cents and I am not hungry, I buy a cigarette--but a clove cigarette, tuan, not one of those other cigarettes that cost forty cents each."

"O.K.," I said, "the price of ten cigarettes."

"But I don't smoke ten cigarettes a day. So how can I save the price of ten cigarettes?"

"How much do you earn?"

"It isn't fixed, tuan."

"Let's start this way. How much do you pay to rent your betja?"

"Twenty-five rupiahs, tuan. One day and one night, twenty-five rupiahs."

"You share it with another rider, then. So it's twelve-fifty."

"No, tuan, twenty-five. I ride it until eleven at night. After that there are no more customers. And I begin at six in the morning. Twenty-five rupiahs."

"I agreed to pay you ten rupiahs for this trip. Say, then, a minimum of ten trips per day. That's one hundred rupiahs. You clear seventy-five. You could soon buy the betja and then you would clear one hundred."

"Tuan! A betja costs Rp. 3,000. The best ones Rp. 4,500. And I never see one hundred rupiahs in one day!"

"How many do you see, then?"

"If I am lucky, and if I get a rich foreigner, like tuan, sometimes after I pay the rent on the betja I have twenty-five rupiahs. Then we get by."

"How much do you spend for rice?"

"Six people eat three litres of rice a day. That's fifteen rupiahs for the poorest quality."

"That leaves ten rupiahs."

"No, tuan, because often I do not have enough for rice. Then we eat sweet potatoes. It leaves nothing."

"Then how do you buy clothes and meat and vegetables?"

"For one year, tuan, I have bought no clothing. How can I? The price goes up and up. The price of rice goes up too. Now perhaps we eat rice only once in two days, and we eat no meat, only sometimes a fish that my son catches in the stream, and a little vegetable. Fuel costs so much that my wife carries the cooking pot out to the trash heap where she finds scraps to burn. My clothes are in rags and my children's clothes are too. Does tuan think I would wear these shorts if I had anything better? It is two pairs of shorts, because there are holes in both, and I am ashamed. Now people who are rich don't want to ride with me."

"But there's plenty of food in the country, and clothes don't matter so much there. Surely you come from the country? Maybe it would be better to go back."

"Tuan is joking!"

"You aren't from the country?"

"I have lived in Djakarta for twenty years. I came to Djakarta because there wasn't enough land in my desa twenty years ago. People have less land now. How can I return to the country? Who would give me land?"

"Maybe things will get better."

"How will things get better, <u>tuan</u>. They always get worse. First it was the Dutch, and then it was, 'you must pay your tax, and you must build some roads, and you must stand aside if a white man passes.' But then we had food and clothes and work too. Only not after the Japanese came. They took every-thing and they made us work for nothing. The Japanese times were bad, <u>tuan</u>, but then the Dutch came back again and we fought them, and that was bad too, except that here in Djakarta we had food and clothes again. And then came <u>Merdeka</u>, and Bung Karno said everything would be different. Now we are free, and the big plantations belong to us, and the Dutch have left behind their fine houses and their fine cars and it all belongs to us. But I haven't a fine house, <u>tuan</u>. And I haven't a fine car or even a bicycle. I haven't even a <u>betja</u> of my own, and soon, I think, I will be too old to drive a <u>betja</u> anymore, and what will I do then, <u>tuan</u>?"

I had reached my destination and started to pay off my <u>betja</u> man, but he wanted to talk some more.

"You understand, <u>tuan</u>," he said, "I am not complaining. I do not dare to complain--the police don't like you to complain. But I don't understand. I have lived here for twenty years, and now the police want me to show them registration cards and housing permits and licenses for this and licenses for that, and if I don't have the proper papers, then I must go to jail. Or if I move around at night, then they think I am a terrorist--everybody knows I am no terrorist. I don't hate anyone, <u>tuan</u>, and I don't want to do anyone any harm. I don't even hate the Dutch. I don't hate the Chinese who owns my <u>betja</u>. Peo-ple say I should hate the Dutch, and I have been beaten because I say I don't hate them, but how can I hate them, <u>tuan</u>, when they are the ones who pay me a fair price, like <u>tuan</u>, for a <u>betja</u> ride? Bung Karno says I must fight the Dutch because the Dutch are in Irian. But I don't know where Irian is, <u>tuan</u>, and I don't want Irian for myself, because I think maybe it already belongs to some-one else. All I want is a chance to work and enough rice and maybe a little goat-meat and vegetable to eat and some decent clothes and enough money so that my children can have food and clothes and schooling. Bung Karno says I will have all this, but I must shout <u>Merdeka</u> and <u>Irian Barat</u> and <u>gotong-rojong</u>. So I shout, and everything is the same as before or worse. Bung Karno says I must work hard and believe in the Pantja Sila, so I work hard and I believe in the Pantja Sila. But I think, <u>tuan</u>, it is the will of Allah that things are as they are. That is why I can stand it. Only I do not believe it is the will of Allah that people should be suspecting and fighting each other the way they are."

I paid him twenty-five rupiahs, thus contributing to inflation, solving none of his problems, and making myself feel like a rich American tourist.

William A. Hanna

SOUTHEAST ASIA SERIES
Vol. VII   No. 32
(Indonesia)

American Universities Field Staff   **REPORTS SERVICE**

BUNG KARNO'S INDONESIA
Part XVII: The Ambivalent Intellectual

by Willard A. Hanna

November 4, 1959

This publication is one of a continuing series on current developments in world affairs written by associates of the American Universities Field Staff. It is distributed by the AUFS as a useful addition to the American fund of information on foreign affairs.

AUFS Associates have been chosen for their skill in collecting, reporting, and evaluating data. Each has combined long personal observation and experience in his foreign area with advanced studies relating to it.

WILLARD A. HANNA, the author of this report, is based in Kuala Lumpur to write about Southeast Asian affairs. Before joining the AUFS in 1954, Dr. Hanna had spent a total of more than ten years in East and Southeast Asia as a teacher, administrator, and writer.

Publications under the imprint of the American Universities Field Staff are not selected to accord with an editorial policy and do not represent the views of its membership. Responsibility for accuracy of facts and for opinions expressed in the letters and reports rests solely with the individual writers.

"A year ago we had a '<u>Karya</u>' (labor) Cabinet; now we have a <u>Kerdja</u> (work) Cabinet. Maybe soon we'll call it a <u>Kira</u> (guesswork) Cabinet, or a <u>Kura</u> (tortoise) Cabinet, and you still won't be able to tell the difference. As for me, I've been asked in the past to take government offices, but I'm waiting until we have a <u>Kintja</u> (cleansing) Cabinet--and don't be American and ask me whether I'm using the word in a Communist or an anti-Communist or a non-Communist sense."

"I won't," I said, studying the young intellectual, a onetime member of the Socialist Party, and wondering whether for all his intelligence and competence he would be able to accomplish much in or out of the government he persistently refused either openly to join or openly to oppose. "But tell me, how are you going to set about this cleansing?"

"First," he said, "We'll throw out the corrupters. That means everyone who has gotten rich and powerful by playing the political and economic rackets, like buying and selling import licenses and trading political appointments for friends."

"Who's that going to leave?" I asked. "I mean, who in any position of significance or with any experience?"

[WAH-28-'59]

"There are still some," he said. "You know and I know that for the last ten years the only way to get anything done in Indonesia has been to play the rackets. People had their choice between turning opportunist or accepting defeat. But there are a lot who have accepted defeat and for that very reason have still maintained their integrity and have even increased their determination, when the time comes, to run things another way."

"Has the time come?" I asked.

"No, not yet."

"When will it come?"

"When things get even worse. Much worse."

"As they will?"

"Yes."

"Soon?"

"This can go on for a long time in Indonesia. We aren't like the West. We don't force a showdown. Or if we do, it isn't really a clear-cut showdown, unless somebody miscalculates badly and takes up an unalterable position-- like the Sumatra rebels, for instance. We let a situation develop, and so far as we can't do anything drastically to change it, we don't waste our time trying. We adjust to it and wait until by reason of natural reaction the pendulum starts swinging our way. Then we take over and, I suppose, the other side begins making its adjustment and waiting its own time."

"Fatalism," I said.

"Certainly not. Realism. Of course, I don't mean we do nothing in the interval. We make ourselves ready. We read, and we think, and we talk, and we plan. We improve ourselves, if you like, and we try to improve those others who are willing to be improved. Then when the time comes, we are ready."

"That isn't how your revolution worked."

"It's exactly the way our revolution worked. We didn't really rebel until the strategic moment arrived in the summer of 1945. During the last years of the Dutch period and the years of the Japanese occupation, we were quietly getting ready--oh, some of us went to jail and there was a lot of oratory, but there was so little open evidence of revolution that the Dutch were taken quite by surprise and never got over their surprise. Even at that, we didn't so much fight the Dutch as just sit it out, refusing to admit defeat, although by any Western standards we were defeated from the outset. Obviously, though, the pendulum was swinging our way."

"It almost swung the way of the Communists," I said. "They were getting ready too."

"No American can see 20th-century conflict in any other terms than pro- or anticommunism. And since you Americans and the Russians--who are just as dogmatic in their way--are by far the most important factors in the dynamics of the modern world, you have imposed upon us a pro- and anti-Communist struggle of our own. We begin to find ourselves talking as though the really important point of disagreement among Indonesians was their stand for or against communism--the Sumatra rebels did, and that was their biggest mistake. They weren't primarily anti-Communist, as they claimed. They were anti the Sukarno brand of nationalism. It's nationalism that is the key factor here in Indonesia."

"Could you say then that the conflict is between the forces that are pro and anti the Sukarno brand of nationalism?"

"No, not exactly. Because whether you like Sukarno or not, Sukarno is a revolutionary nationalist, just as all the rest of us are. Personally, I think Sukarno is everything his unkindest Western critics call him--a demogogue, a libertine, an egomaniac. But if he is, why, so have been a great many other of the world's really great men. And he is no dictator, no Communist, and no puppet. When I meet him he can still make me feel that he is a warm and generous person and that he voices the real determination of the Indonesian people, which is to make Indonesia great. That's exactly what we are all dedicated to, the Nationalists, or the Communists, or the Socialists, or the religious party members, or any others. And we're all agreed that the institutions of the West aren't transferable to Indonesia but we have to work out our own--as we are now doing. The disagreement isn't whether we are more or less Marxist, or Communist, or Socialist, or democratic, because we are all of us all that in proportions that don't after all matter too much. The disagreement is whether we feel it is justifiable, under present circumstances, when the problems are so huge and the progress so slow, to take for ourselves a large share of the material advantages which obviously everyone can't yet have. Or whether we are willing to forego them for a while longer, even though in foregoing them we don't yet assure them just yet to anyone else.

"In other words, it's a question not of nationalism but of idealistic integrity versus realistic compromise."

"But that's what our real nationalism is--pure idealism. That's what makes you practical Americans dislike it and even fear it, because we don't like to compromise and let you run our business and even our government for us merely because we can't yet run it for ourselves. That's what our claim to Irian Barat is based on--the ideal that colonialism must be wiped out immediately and absolutely. We want a completely reorganized social system. You can't achieve that without upsetting an awful lot of vested interests. Only now a lot of our own revolutionary leaders have acquired vested interests, and that's why they can no longer sincerely promote the sort of absolute nationalism we require."

"Do you believe that any group of revolutionary nationalists, yourselves included, could avoid the same sort of compromise if you did take over?"

"Yes. We see what that sort of compromise has already led to. We have refused to have any more part of it than we can avoid. At least, we can make a fresh start. It has taken the present group of leaders ten years to get as corrupt as they are. It would take us twenty, and by that time we may be able to afford it."

"Have you ever read a favorite book of mine, The Autobiography of Lincoln Steffens?"

"No, I haven't. But you have recommended it to me before."

"Then let me recommend it again. Lincoln Steffens was a reformer. He started off thinking that by kicking the bad men out and putting the good men in you could make certain for a while at least of a government that was honest and efficient. He found that by putting the good men in, you formed a government which didn't know how to cope with the bad men all around it. Lincoln Steffens made me a lot more tolerant about judging politicians, and a lot more humble about thinking I knew better than they did."

"Have you read Arnold Toynbee?"

"No, I haven't. Not consecutively or completely, I mean."

"I have. And Arnold Toynbee puts up a case for a cyclical theory of history. We Indonesians and Asians in general are now riding the cycle upwards, no matter what the apparent reverses and even disasters; no matter, either, what happens to an individual government or an individual person. Bung Karno and our present politicians got us started and somebody will appear to take over from them. We're on our way--upwards."

"And we Americans?"

"Let me recommend that you read Toynbee."

Willard A. Hann

SOUTHEAST ASIA SERIES
Vol. VII   No. 33
(Indonesia)

American Universities Field Staff **REPORTS SERVICE**

BUNG KARNO'S INDONESIA
Part XVIII: The Case of Mochtar Lubis

by Willard A. Hanna

November 5, 1959

This publication is one of a continuing series on current developments in world affairs written by associates of the American Universities Field Staff. It is distributed by the AUFS as a useful addition to the American fund of information on foreign affairs.

AUFS Associates have been chosen for their skill in collecting, reporting, and evaluating data. Each has combined long personal observation and experience in his foreign area with advanced studies relating to it.

WILLARD A. HANNA, the author of this report, is based in Kuala Lumpur to write about Southeast Asian affairs. Before joining the AUFS in 1954, Dr. Hanna had spent a total of more than ten years in East and Southeast Asia as a teacher, administrator, and writer.

Publications under the imprint of the American Universities Field Staff are not selected to accord with an editorial policy and do not represent the views of its membership. Responsibility for accuracy of facts and for opinions expressed in the letters and reports rests solely with the individual writers.

Mochtar Lubis is Indonesia's most famous and its most controversial newspaperman. Between 1950 and 1956, as editor of Djakarta's crusading and muckraking <u>Indonesia Raya</u>, he was the most ingeniously persevering gadfly of the Indonesian Government. Since December 21, 1956, he has been under military arrest, for the first two weeks in a military prison, since then in his own home. These two sets of circumstances are not unrelated, although the military have so far brought no explicit charges against him or indicated any intention of doing so, or, for that matter, any intention of releasing him. Mochtar Lubis's cause has been taken up repeatedly by the Indonesian Press Association, by the International Press Institute, and by various Indonesian political spokesmen, all of whom say, in effect: charge him, try him, then convict him or release him.

The only effect all this has had upon the military command to date has been to make of the Mochtar Lubis case an issue on which, seemingly, for prestige reasons they will not and cannot make decision either way. To bring Mochtar Lubis to trial would undoubtedly result in exceedingly embarrassing revelations about the Army itself, and to release him would be to admit either to weakness or to error. Meanwhile, practically anything which Lubis's friends attempt to do for him merely increases official resentment against him. The

[WAH-29-'59]

regional insurrectionists, for instance, did him no service in singling him out for special mention in their manifesto of February 15, 1958, when they declared their independence of Djakarta and then went on to explain why, including in their specifications, the following:

"Mochtar Lubis, a journalist who has been particularly courageous in upholding truth and justice and has attacked tyranny and oppression at its very source, has already been under arrest for well over a year . . .without having been brought up for trial in court. One of the important personages against whom Mr. Lubis made charges, Mr. Ruslan Abdulgani, has been convicted by the high court on one charge which was proved against him, but then he was presently elevated to become Vice Chairman of the unconstitutional National Council."

The manifesto goes on to mention two scandalous cases which Mochtar had been instrumental in exposing. One was the case of Mr. Djody Gondokusumo, Minister of Justice in the first Ali Cabinet, who was sentenced by the courts to a year's imprisonment on one of a series of charges that he had accepted hundreds of thousands if not millions of rupiahs in bribes from Chinese seeking Indonesian entry permits. Djody Gondokusumo was very soon released by pardon of Bung Karno, and he then resumed his seat in Parliament. By way of contrast, a Police Inspector in Tjiandjur, who had to support a big family on a small salary, was convicted of having embezzled a few thousand rupiahs. He was sentenced to one year's imprisonment. His appeal to Bung Karno for pardon was rejected.

So far as anyone can determine, Mochtar Lubis remains under house arrest, first, because he gave offense to a great many very prominent people, including Bung Karno and members of the military command; second, because he is suspected, with or without any evidence, of having been not merely sympathetic but perhaps even helpful to the regional insurrectionists; and third, because any public trial would be likely to result in sensational revelations; fourth, because if he were released he would immediately resume his role of gadfly, one which the administration is not eager to have filled.

Lubis's penchant for causing embarrassment to the administration can be illustrated by itemizing a few of the exposés he ran in Indonesia Raya during the days when it was understandably the fastest growing and most eagerly read newspaper in Indonesia: a series on an official "hospitality committee" allegedly established to provide brothel facilities for delegates to the Asia-Africa Conference; a series revealing the marriage of Bung Karno to Hartini and the attempts made to deny and to conceal it and to falsify certain pertinent records; a series on the scandals, feuds, and frauds within the various Djakarta ministries; a series on the "antics" within Indonesian diplomatic establishments abroad, including allegations of personal corruption on the part of top officials; frequent articles on confusion and mismanagement within the armed services; a series on the amorous conduct of a high Ministry of Education official when he was host to an Indian cultural mission and presiding officer at an official conference; the original scoop on the "August 17 Incident" when the Army attempted to arrest the Foreign Minister; a series on corruption and embezzlement within the Information Ministry, and a follow-up series when, at his own civil trial for libel and for publication of "statements displaying hostility, hatred or derision of the Government," Lubis produced original documents, photostats of secret police records, and various other items of evidence conclusive enough to get the case against him dismissed (July 30, 1957) and to make a great many people wish it had never been started; and the first press story on the first of the Sumatran insurrectionist coups.

In the fall of 1956, many forces converged to bring Mochtar Lubis's career as editor of Indonesia Raya to an end. In the first place, he was then involved in the civil court case mentioned above. In the second place, a relative of his, Col. Zulkifli Lubis, attempted a coup d'état with the intention of deposing General Nasution, Army Chief of Staff, and then, when the coup misfired, vanished from Djakarta and was rumored to be "fomenting insurrection" variously in Java and Sumatra. Finally, on December 20 came the Padang coup. Mochtar Lubis carried the report in Indonesia Raya the next morning. That evening the military police picked him up and took him to jail. Military statements regarding the reason for his arrest were vague and conflicting. The implication was that Mochtar Lubis might somehow be mixed up in the insurrectionist movement and that he was certainly very deeply involved in the stirring up of public dissatisfaction with the Djakarta regime which was the basic reason for the Padang insurrection and the others which followed.

For two weeks the military police held Lubis in jail; then they placed him under house arrest. They escorted him several times to court to attend his own civil trial, but they rejected or ignored all suggestion that they bring him to trial themselves. In the period that he has been under house arrest, Mochtar Lubis has had the unhappy experience of seeing his newspaper first go into a marked decline as regards quality and circulation, then split into two rival papers of the same name when his staff quarreled among themselves, and finally collapse altogether. He has had time to write a couple of books-- which have not yet been published. His other writings, meanwhile, have disappeared from the shelves of Djakarta bookstores, whether because they were sold out or because they were withdrawn it is difficult to determine. He has occupied himself with the study of languages (Spanish and Italian among others), painting, photography, gardening, carpentry, and other hobbies. But he has ceased to enliven the Djakarta newspaper world, and his disappearance from the scene has not merely worked great personal hardship upon him, his wife, and three children, but has been a major loss to the cause of Indonesian journalistic enterprise.

The number of Indonesian newspapermen in addition to Mochtar Lubis who have been in trouble with the Government in the last several years is a bewilderingly large and shifting one. The military command has put out such frequent and inclusive regulations that virtually any independently written newspaper story or editorial regarding military, political, or economic matters, unless quite innocuous, can somehow be construed as infringing upon official verbotens. All stories regarding the military must receive Army clearance; any political or economic story likely to "disturb the peaceful atmosphere" is an offense. Any article at all critical of the President, at all conciliatory toward the rebel leaders, or at all skeptical regarding the effects of recent "reforms" can land an editor immediately at military headquarters for interrogation. But the military command clamps down irregularly, and, to a considerable extent, unpredictably. Half a dozen potentially objectionable stories may get by while an innocuous one leads to trouble--or seems to be the one that leads to trouble. Prominent Indonesian newspaper and news agency editors these days expect to be called in for military grilling at fairly frequent intervals. When they are summoned, they expect to be kept waiting for hours on end, then to be questioned repetitiously over seemingly irrelevant matters. They expect also to be called back again and again to go over the same old material with old or new interrogators, some of whom display no other discernable objective than to waste time and to annoy. On the other hand, they may receive at once a severe warning or reprimand. Disciplining, for the most part, consists of suspension of publication for a period of a few days.

Actually, the newspaperman who has received the harshest treatment to date is not Mochtar Lubis but S. T. Hsieh, an Indonesian citizen, correspondent for the Central News Agency of Taiwan and for Time-Life. S. T. Hsieh has been in jail for over a year, reportedly in a prison camp on an off-shore island, whether because he was regarded as a key figure in the Djakarta Kuomintang organization which was suppressed and its leaders jailed at about the time he himself was picked up, or because of unflattering Time coverage of Bung Karno, or for a combination of reasons, being a matter of mere conjecture. Injo Beng Goat, editor of the Socialist-slanted daily, Keng Po, has been subject to prison arrest, house arrest, and city arrest, and now finds it discreet to disassociate himself altogether from newspaper work. Charles Tambu, editor of the English-language Times of Indonesia has been repeatedly on the now well-worn military carpet. He has been brought into court by the Government for calling Nasser a "bootlicker" of the Communists and has been let off with a light fine (Rp. 300) and a warning. He has been called in recently to receive a stern reprimand and a brief suspension following an editorial critical of recent financial and economic measures. The news agencies Antara and PIA have each been suspended at various times. The presumed reason is that they carried stories about the military without advance clearance. For the most part, it has been the press that is basically friendly to the West which has been in difficulties, but the Communist press has had its turn too. The editors of Harian Rajkat, the official Communist organ, and Sin Po, a Communist mouthpiece, have been several times questioned and their papers have been several times suspended.

The over-all effect upon the Indonesian press is not to enhance its readability. Indonesian newspapers used to manage, despite their mere four pages of text, their small staffs, and their very modest budgets, to make out remarkably well. They never provided the detailed local news one expects of a metropolitan press, but they did manage among them to provide a composite political commentary which was frequently diverting and enlightening and at least as reliable as most. Today, the papers still maintain surprisingly good foreign news coverage--foreign news and commentary being safer than the local. Their coverage of Djakarta developments, however, leaves many gaps, even reports on Parliamentary debates being both spotty and sketchy. Thanks, however, to Indonesian editorial adroitness at putting both news and opinion between the lines, there is still a good deal to be gained by careful and intuitive reading. An editor will manage, for instance, on the day he publishes a new military exhortation to simplicity and even austerity in daily life, to publish another article in which he makes casual note of a military commander's arrival at a military conference in a shiny new Chrysler. And when he reports Bung Karno's departure by air with a big entourage on another round of gala visits to the provinces, he will also insert an article about new curtailment of Garuda's domestic flight schedule because of withdrawal of planes from ordinary service.

To a very great extent, however, the zest and the flamboyance have gone out of the Indonesian newspaper world since the inadvertent withdrawal of Mochtar Lubis. The papers can now pick up and enlarge upon the case of an urchin in Palembang who was sentenced to six months in jail for theft of one banana. They can make quite a lot of copy about a phony Sumatran "radja" and his consort who imposed upon Central Javanese officialdom for a series of expensive entertainments. They can feature a self-styled Prof. Djokosumito, M.A., President of Madjapahit University, who during his trial for issuing fraudulent correspondence school diplomas admitted in court that his own education had progressed little beyond elementary school, that he had awarded himself his own degree, and that his take from trusting students had run as high as Rp. 70,000 monthly. They can make oblique references to a "Tandjung Priok Barter Scandal," in which high military officers engaged in illegal trade presumably for Army profit. They can refer also to the reinstatement of the cadets of the Naval Air Wing, without, however, mentioning the fact that the cadets were suspended and jailed in the first place for refusing to accept as their commanding officer a man whose qualifications they rejected. But much of this has come out either because it was trivial or because it was already public knowledge anyway--and the press has openly exposed a very great deal less than much of the public already knows. It takes a Mochtar Lubis to discover and break the really dramatic news and all the details of the news, complete with photostats and secret police records and sworn testimonies.

The situation in Indonesia today, perhaps, is much too tense for anyone to risk any campaign that would topple the Government as Mochtar Lubis virtually shook one down in 1957. And Mochtar Lubis personally, perhaps, is safest exactly where he is--under guarded house arrest. But the principles of justice to the individual and of freedom of the press--to both of which Indonesia officially subscribes--seem to be denied the more categorically each additional day that Mochtar Lubis remains under detention for an unspecified offense.

NOTE: For other references to Mochtar Lubis and/or the Indonesian press see the following AUFS publications: Djakarta Merry-Go-Round (WAH-9-'56); "Eternal" at Five and One-half: The Biography of a Newspaper (WAH-12-'56); and Coups, "Smuggles," Demonstrations and Korupsi (WAH-1-'57).

SOUTHEAST ASIA SERIES
Vol. VII   No. 34
(Indonesia)

American Universities Field Staff   REPORTS SERVICE

BUNG KARNO'S INDONESIA

Part XIX: Politik Bebas--
Independent Policy or Politics Unlimited?

by Willard A. Hanna

November 28, 1959

This publication is one of a continuing series on current developments in world affairs written by associates of the American Universities Field Staff. It is distributed by the AUFS as a useful addition to the American fund of information on foreign affairs.

AUFS Associates have been chosen for their skill in collecting, reporting, and evaluating data. Each has combined long personal observation and experience in his foreign area with advanced studies relating to it.

WILLARD A. HANNA, the author of this report, is based in Kuala Lumpur to write about Southeast Asian affairs. Before joining the AUFS in 1954, Dr. Hanna had spent a total of more than ten years in East and Southeast Asia as a teacher, administrator, and writer.

Publications under the imprint of the American Universities Field Staff are not selected to accord with an editorial policy and do not represent the views of its membership. Responsibility for accuracy of facts and for opinions expressed in the letters and reports rests solely with the individual writers.

Politik bebas, as any Indonesian newspaper reader can tell you, means "independent policy." It means, even more specifically, the government's "independent and active policy" in foreign affairs. It is a policy designed "to avoid entanglement with any power bloc," "to end colonial exploitation," "to advance the cause of nationalism" with special emphasis upon Indonesia's acquisition of Western New Guinea, "to develop friendly relations with all nations" of whatever political complexion, "to oppose military pacts," "to resist foreign interference in Indonesian affairs," "to promote world peace by easing world tensions," particularly within the framework of the United Nations and in conjunction with the Asia-Africa powers in neutralizing or bridging the gap between the two power blocs. In all, its intent is to make Indonesia a nation to be reckoned with by the world powers and to preserve for it freedom of decision, freedom of action, and, for that matter, foreign critics not infrequently complain, freedom of inaction and of unilateral reconsideration of agreements.

Politik bebas, it seems to many Westerners, is a policy of "neutralism," one that implies "naive acceptance of Communist-line doctrines," "pathological suspiciousness toward the Western world," a passion for noncommitment and reinterpretation of semicommitment, a "suicidal tendency" to risk

[WAH-30-'59]

collapse in order to achieve extremist demands. It seems a policy of indecision rather than of decision, of playing off the West against the East, and of inevitable drift toward Communist domination.

To anyone who cares to study word usage, politik bebas has further significance. Politik means either "policy" or "politics," as it does in the Dutch from which it derives. It has further overtones of "cunning," "trickery," and "deceit"; bebas has connotations not only of "independence" but of "release from all restraints." Politik bebas, accordingly, has not merely the officially interpreted and translational implications of "an independent policy," but also some of the additional implications of "politics and politicking unlimited."

Indonesia's foreign policy, like that of any other nation, must be considered not only in terms of the high moral principles in which it is enveloped but of the human motivation which underlies it. The very ambiguity of the term itself indicates that politik bebas is in actual practice not exclusively the perfectionistic striving for peace and justice which official spokesmen piously proclaim, nor the weak and dangerous playing off of international forces against one another which its foreign critics aver, nor the irresponsible trifling in international affairs as a personal political hobby which many of its local critics charge. Rather, it is a combination of all three, in different proportions at different times by different practitioners. The emerging blend can best be described by consideration of when, how, why, and by whom the policy was formulated and applied.

Phase one of politik bebas corresponded roughly with the year 1950, year one of full independence and that of the Masjumi-dominated cabinets of Hatta and Natsir. (Hatta Cabinet: December 19, 1949-September 6, 1950; Natsir Cabinet: September 6, 1950-April 26, 1951.) The Republic of Indonesia had just emerged into the international world after 340 years of colonialism and 10 years of war and revolution. It was a government in name only, one which had still to develop any really coherent national organization or administrative system or, for that matter, any experienced administrators, let alone a tested policy. It was afflicted almost from the moment of birth by a series of widespread regional insurrections, provincial rivalries and disputes, and rancorous conflict among its small clique of top leaders. It was practically overwhelmed, first, by importunate offers of advice and assistance from the Netherlands and the United States, then by invitations to establish close relations and co-operation with most of the established nations of Europe and of the emerging nations of Southeast Asia, the Middle East, and Africa. The year 1950 was also the first of the new China of Mao Tse-tung and Chou En-lai. It was a year of crisis in the cold war--one marked by the outbreak of fighting in Korea, of American decision to shield Taiwan with the Seventh Fleet, of intensification of the Communist terrorist emergency in Malaya, and of conflict between the French and the various local factions in Indochina. It was a year also of maneuver toward postwar settlements in Germany and Japan. In other words, 1950 was a year when major foreign policy decisions were demanding to be made, and the inexperienced, insecure, ineffectively organized Indonesian Government was in no position to be making any.

Hatta and Natsir, two of the most moderate, cautious, and circumspect of Indonesia's top political figures, are intellectually committed to the liberal democratic-socialist system, but fully cognizant of the powerful counterpressures of ultranationalism and quasi-Marxism. Both individually and jointly, they applied a politik bebas which was generally described as "neutral" and came to be attacked within Indonesia as a sort of timid neutralism which favored the status quo and strong ties with the Western world, including the Netherlands.

The two cabinets, accordingly, adopted many tentative, noncommittal, wait-and-see policies. They accepted established relations with the West, but were determined to stall off any dealings with the Communist nations. Hatta despatched a reconnaissance mission to Moscow in the spring of 1950, then guided follow-up measures into a circuitous blind alley. Both cabinets compromised on the issue of the Chinese. Hatta actually invited, then accepted recognition by Communist China in the spring of 1950; he accepted a Chinese People's Republic Ambassador to Indonesia that summer; but neither he nor Natsir sent an Indonesian Ambassador to Peking. Both watched the Communist Chinese Embassy's moves in Indonesia with great suspicion, and at the same time both tolerated continued activities of the Chinese Nationalists. Hatta and Natsir endeavored to arrest mounting Indonesian emotionalism on the Indochina problem, Natsir himself being responsible for blocking a move in Parliament to recognize Ho Chi-minh, and for substituting a new resolution (passed on June 3, 1950) recommending further investigation and cautious action. They served notice on the Philippines, via the Indonesian delegation to the Baguio Conference in late 1950, that they would not be party to any regional pro-Western, anti-Communist bloc. They ventured to accept insistent American offers of aid--first a $100 million Export-Import Bank loan in early 1950, then an American economic and technical assistance program (agreement of October 16, 1950); but they did not draw heavily upon the loan, they did not exhibit any particular eagerness to implement the assistance program, and they would not even talk with an American mission proposing military aid. They delayed until September 1950 in accepting Western sponsorship for admission to the United Nations, the outbreak in June of the Korean War having served to point up the difficulty of decision-making when and if Indonesia joined.

For the most part, by exercise of tactics of delay, caution, compromise, and restraint, Hatta and Natsir managed, just as they avoided policy decisions, to avoid any serious foreign policy disputes. They ran into strong criticism in early 1951, however, for two moves which were interpreted as signs of weakness and susceptibility to American and Western pressures. In the first important test case after joining the United Nations, Indonesia abstained on the resolution branding Communist China the aggressor in Korea, thus offend-

ing a powerful group of Indonesian politicians who demanded a vote against
the resolution. After failing in the course of the year 1950 to achieve any
satisfaction from the Netherlands on the subject of Western New Guinea--a
problem which the Round Table Conference Agreements had stipulated should
be settled within the year--Hatta and Natsir worked successfully for defeat of
a parliamentary resolution to denounce the Dutch and dissolve the Indonesian-
Dutch Union. The foreign policy of the Hatta and the Natsir cabinets had been
a failure, said its Indonesian critics, the most powerful and articulate of whom
were the leaders of the PNI (Nationalist Party); they had promoted neither
Indonesia's national interests nor its international prestige.

Phase two of politik bebas covered roughly the years 1951, 1952, and
early 1953, the period of the two Masjumi-PNI coalition cabinets. (Sukiman
Cabinet: April 26, 1951-April 1952; Wilopo Cabinet: April 1952-July 30, 1953.)[1]
During phase two, when first Masjumi, then PNI influences predominated,
politik bebas became redefined as both "independent and active." Both Sukiman
(Masjumi) and Wilopo (PNI) were political moderates and men of quiet, non-
flamboyant tastes and policies. While each of them was personally well disposed toward the liberal democratic system, they were more strongly nationalistic in their views than either Hatta or Natsir, and were surrounded by
associates much more strongly nationalistic than themselves. They attempted
sporadically to demonstrate that they were applying a foreign policy that was
really "active," thus to avoid the stigma of "negativism" which had attached
to the policies of their precedessors. Internal conflict within the cabinets was
so great, however, that policy decisions, when and if taken, tended either to
cancel each other out, or to lead to prolonged and bitter disputes. In the first
category came decisions relating to the Communist bloc; in the second, those
relating to the West. On the over-all, the record of the Sukiman and Wilopo
cabinets showed a disposition on the part of the Prime Ministers and a few of
their associates to strengthen relations with the West, and determination on
the part of many of their associates, primarily the PNI, to shift policy emphasis away from the West, with dramatic victories of the latter over the former
group.

With regard to such key issues as relations with the USSR, China, and
the new nations of Asia and Africa, the two cabinets engendered much dispute
but few decisions and little over-all change. Both cabinets contrived further
delays in exchange of diplomatic missions with the USSR, with the result that
in early 1953 an indignant Parliament passed a motion calling for exchange
of embassies within the year. Cabinet members--mainly the Masjumi mem-
bers--kept pointing out that there were great difficulties to be overcome on
both sides in merely supplying accommodations and logistical support to such
remote missions. They pointed out, also, with slightly more telling effect,
that establishment of a Soviet mission in Djakarta would mean establishment

_____

1 In official chronology there is no record of the exact date of the Sukiman
Cabinet's fall and the Wilopo Cabinet's assumption of power.

of an espionage center. Parliamentary debate was heated, but government action was imperceptible. As for Communist China, the Sukiman Cabinet in mid-1951 took a number of bold but nevertheless inconclusive steps. It barred 16 Chinese Embassy officers who sought to enter Indonesia without advance acceptance by the Foreign Ministry; it let word leak out that the Chinese Ambassador had published derogatory comments on President Sukarno and Vice President Hatta, and further that he had behaved in a manner unbecoming to a diplomat in publicly attacking American policy. The Ambassador was presently withdrawn. The Government appointed an Indonesian representative to Peking, but a young chargé d'affaires rather than an ambassador. It announced presently that he was both slighted in his official contacts and obstructed in his official travels, and that Chinese Embassy personnel in Indonesia, whose activities smacked of political interferences it was hinted, would experience retaliatory restrictions. Such measures served, of course, to stir up Indonesian press and public protest in two ways: against China for "arrogance and discrimination," but against the Indonesian Government also for laying itself open to such treatment by its own refusal to pay "proper attention" to a world power.

It was not Indonesia's direct relations with China, however, which were really central at the time to Indonesia's China policy. It was the exclusion of China from the United Nations, denial to it of Taiwan, condemnation of it for the Korean War--on all of these issues Indonesian opinion tended very clearly to favor China over the Western nations. Most specifically, it was the one international issue regarding China on which the Government really did assume a policy--the application of the United Nations' embargo on export of strategic materials. The Sukiman Government, although it had abstained in early 1951 on the United Nations' resolution calling for the embargo, abided by it nevertheless, as did the Wilopo Cabinet and the First Ali Cabinet as well. The embargo hit Indonesian exports of rubber and was widely interpreted as a malevolent American maneuver to depress prices on raw materials for which the United States was the major purchaser. The Government, subject to attack from many sides for apparent pro-American policy, offset attacks to a degree by asserting and reasserting support for Communist China's membership in the United Nations and its claim to Taiwan. It gave further indication of an "independent" stand on crucial area problems by consistently condemning the French and their Western allies in Indochina, by remaining aloof from Japanese overtures, by viewing with alarm continuation of British colonialism in Malaya, and by calling repeatedly to the attention of the Philippines the fact that Indonesia did not propose to be decoyed by the Philippines into any pro-Western alliance. It ventured afield from Far Eastern affairs to express support of the French North African colonies. It permitted the establishment in Indonesia of a Tunisian office and it admitted various other propaganda agents, including those of the Vietminh, North Africa, and Malaya.

The crucial foreign policy controversy of the period arose over the alleged susceptibility of the Sukiman Government to American influence. This

conflict brought about the collapse of the Sukiman Cabinet and resulted in a
greatly increased wariness toward commitments on the part of the Wilopo
Cabinet and its successors. The real trouble started with Indonesia's accept-
ance--at the last possible moment--of an invitation to attend the San Francisco
Peace Conference; its signing--again at the last possible moment--of the
peace treaty; and its negotiation in late December 1951 and early January 1952
of an interim agreement in which it conceded that reparations should be scaled
to Japan's ability to pay. Opposition to this "American-dictated" policy toward
Japan was already an extreme embarrassment to the Government when in
early February of 1952 the news leaked out that Foreign Minister Subardjo
had made commitments to the United States, in accordance with the recent Mutual Security Act requiring certain assurances in return for aid. The Indonesian assurances had been forthcoming at the last possible moment before the
deadline prescribed by the Act, they had amounted to a commitment to contribute "to the defensive strength of the free world," although they had been subsequently and retroactively paraphrased and weakened. Undeniably, however,
they constituted a commitment, and what was more, had been kept secret, the
Government very accurately gauging the degree of press, public, and parliamentary outrage which they would arouse if the facts became known, as it was
somehow hoped that they would not. So great was the furor that the Cabinet
collapsed within less than three weeks. Its fate was a lesson which no subsequent Cabinet has even momentarily overlooked in its relations with the Western world.

Consequently, in April 1952 the Wilopo Cabinet inherited the "MSA
mess" from its predecessor. It inherited also a formidable assortment of
domestic problems. It experienced within its own ranks even greater dissen-
sion and even greater influence of the PNI which was now making common
cause on many issues with the Communists. It was understandably handicapped, therefore, in making its "independent and active" foreign policy seem as
active as it was independent. It managed to sidestep a move in Parliament to
achieve solution of the increasingly explosive Irian Barat problem by resort
to force--just how force was to be applied was not clear. In late December
1952, it gained acceptance by Parliament of a new agreement with the United
States whereby aid would be continued without return commitments. It also
managed to negotiate the withdrawal of a Dutch military advisory mission
which had been widely regarded as an infringement of Indonesian independence
of action and judgment. These achievements, to be sure, seemed to most
observers of whatever political tendency more negative than positive. The
successor Government, the First Ali Sastroamidjojo Cabinet (basically PNI,
with no Masjumi participation) came into office to the accompaniment of what
seemed at first like extravagant promises of swift, decisive, "independent
and active" but also "positive" accomplishment in the field of foreign affairs.

Phase three of politik bebas was that of the two Ali Sastroamidjojo
Cabinets (July 30, 1953-August 11, 1955; and March 20, 1956-April 9, 1957),
and the brief interim of the predominantly Masjumi-Socialist Harahap Cabinet

(August 11, 1955-March 20, 1956). The period of the First Ali Cabinet was
one of rapid deterioration in the domestic situation, with inefficiency, inflation,
corruption, and political bickering reaching new highs. All the same, it was
also a period of striking enhancement of Indonesia's international influence,
achieved, declare its critics, at the cost of domestic progress, at the risk of
Communist take-over, and to the great prejudice of Indonesia's relations with
the Western democratic world. The itemization of the Cabinet's foreign policy
measures reads almost like a check list of its promises. It affords an insight
into the personality of the Prime Minister, a man of extraordinary ability and
ambition, ardently nationalistic, with both a fascination and a flair for international wheeling and dealing.

The First Ali Cabinet, in the course of the year 1954, "regularized"
Indonesia's relations with the USSR and with Communist China; it arranged
an exchange of embassies with Moscow, and at long last sent an ambassador
and full staff to Peking; it devoted itself further to the development of economic and cultural relations with both countries, with a consequent pick-up
in statistics on trade and travel. Dr. Ali master-minded the Bandung Asia-
Africa Conference of April 1955 and the formation of an Asia-Africa bloc
which began to exhibit a remarkable degree of solidarity on such issues as
the French African colonies, NATO and SEATO, Indochina, and later the Suez
and other Middle Eastern crises, on all of which, needless to say, the Asia-
Africa views accorded much better with those of the Communist than the anti-
Communist bloc. The Cabinet stepped up the campaign for acquisition of
Western New Guinea, submitting the issue repeatedly to the United Nations,
debating vigorously on behalf of Indonesia's claims, and undertaking pro-
grams also to stir up mass sentiment within Indonesia in support of the "na-
tional claims" against the Dutch. It reiterated frequently and vigorously
Indonesia's determination to remain clear of anti-Communist entanglements,
and in consequence gave very chilly reception to advances from the United
States, Great Britain, and France, also from the Philippines, Thailand, and
Japan. It deplored the very existence of separate governments in Taiwan,
South Vietnam, and South Korea.

The brief interlude of the Harahap Cabinet was a period of warming
of relations with the West and of cooling toward the Communist bloc. But the
only major foreign policy program, that relating to negotiations with the Dutch
for acquisition of New Guinea--negotiations which ended in failure that, together with revival of PNI strength and opposition, precipitated the fall of
the Cabinet.

The Second Ali Cabinet brought a return to the policies of the first,
with few new departures but many reinforced trends. It repudiated the Dutch-
Indonesian Union (as the Harahap Cabinet had done before it--"illegally,"
according to the opposition); it repudiated huge Indonesian debts to the Netherlands; it reintensified efforts inside and outside the United Nations to gain
Western New Guinea. It negotiated a $100 million loan from the USSR and

opened loan negotiations with China. It reacted swiftly and vehemently to the English-French invasion of the Suez area, but exhibited great reticence in judging Russian action in Hungary. Then, after its first year, it became so engrossed in a nearly catastrophic series of troubles at home that it began of necessity to de-emphasize foreign policy. Even before the protracted period of its collapse on issues of domestic policy, it had passed foreign policy over into the hands which still retain it--the ready hands of President Sukarno.

Phase four of politik bebas overlapped phase three and extends through the First Djuanda Cabinet (April 9, 1957-July 13, 1959) and the current, Second Djuanda Cabinet (July 13, 1959-) into the present. Phase four is a period in which the Ali professionalized emphasis upon foreign policy to the exclusion of much else was supplemented, then superseded by the Bung Karno personal touch and personality cult. In the spring of 1956 Bung Karno, who had previously traveled abroad to Japan in 1943, to Indochina in 1945, to India, Pakistan, and Burma in 1950, to the Philippines in 1951, and to the Near East in 1955, launched himself upon the international world, East, West, and inside the iron and bamboo curtains. He turned in a series of dazzling demonstrations of what a gifted, handsome, eloquent, and peripatetic national leader can accomplish in people-to-people diplomacy and in person-to-person contacts with international leaders. Since 1956 Bung Karno has whirled repeatedly about the world paying one, two, or three visits to major countries of the Far and Middle East, Europe, and North and South America. Everywhere he has preached the doctrine of Asian nationalism in its "inevitable victory" over colonialism, imperialism, and capitalism. Wherever possible, he has elicited endorsement of Indonesia's policy and action regarding Western New Guinea and fulsome declarations of undying affection and mutuality of ideals. He has missed no opportunity for mass audiences, fraternizing with the onlookers, television shows, press conferences, and the news cameras. He has enjoyed his greatest triumphs and garnered his most ringing endorsements in China, the USSR, Yugoslavia, Egypt, and North Vietnam, in approximately that order. The return visits to Indonesia of Voroshilov, Tito, and Ho Chi-minh have been corresponding triumphs of mass welcome, whether contrived or spontaneous, various observers judge variously. Indonesia's prestige within the Communist bloc has risen, and also within the Asia-Africa bloc.

President Sukarno has been emboldened to take the really dramatic new actions which seem to many observers to be the culmination, and either the vindication or the destruction of politik bebas. In late 1957 and early 1958 he expelled Dutch residents and in effect nationalized their properties, to the shock of the Western world. He followed up with economic measures against the Nationalist Chinese; he is following up now with measures against practically all Chinese in Indonesia--including the Communists--with consequences to Indonesian-Communist Chinese relations which are impossible to predict.

The current era of Indonesian foreign policy, in which politik bebas becomes even more unpredictable than before, particularly in relation to the interests of the various power blocs, is the era of Bung Karno's personal decision-making. Politik bebas retains all of its original features: it reflects intensified determination to counterbalance Western with Eastern influence; to assert Indonesia's independence of influences from either bloc or from any other quarter, while at the same time reacting to those influences, in a manner, most Western observers feel, more to the interests of the Communist than the anti-Communist powers. It is being complicated today by reason of Indonesian discrimination against Communist Chinese domiciled in Indonesia and Peking's angry reaction to that discrimination. This circumstance may quite possibly start the balance swinging back again toward greater cordiality with the West. On the other hand, it could just as well result in even closer rapport with the Soviet Union. Always, Bung Karno professes the motive of eliminating imperialism, colonialism, and capitalism, and whether he is acting against the local Chinese, or the Dutch, or the Indonesian insurrectionist movements, he keeps admonishing the West:

". . .It seems that the Western world, or, more precisely, colonialist-imperialist elements of the Western world like to play the Juggernaut of History. They oppose, or at least slight anything that appears to be seeking realization in Asia and Africa. They interfere with growth in Egypt, and they resist growth in other Arab States. Cannot they realize that history is against them?. . .

"How good it would be if the Western world would but understand that Asian nationalism is a historical certainty, a historical phenomenon, and that Asian nationalism certainly has at least two faces. We are not asking for assistance, we only ask to be understood and to be left alone. Let us look for our own personality ourselves. Leave us to develop according to our own destiny.

"But what have we experienced? We are constantly being disturbed, we are constantly being opposed, we are constantly being hindered. Apparently the Western world thinks it their duty to model us after them. Consequently, there are continuous conflicts and tensions between the West and Asia. . . .

"The cause is the little understanding of the West about the essence of nationalism in Asia and Africa. Everyone knows that we have always proposed coexistence between the communist and anti-communist blocs, and indeed we refuse to enter either of the two blocs. Our policy is a policy of nonalignment. Our policy is a policy of forming our own personality. Leave us to implement that policy! But again, what have we experienced? We are not left alone, we are not understood, but constantly bothered, continuously slighted, often undermined and sometimes attacked openly.

"Bluntly I say that at the end we will not be the loser, but you will! . . .

"It would be better if we just do not disturb each other!" [2]

If Indonesia's foreign policy today were to be summarized into a bluntly worded set of rule-of-thumb precepts, such as foreign policy makers of any nation dislike to think they are guided by, it would seem reasonably fair to state them as follows:

(1) Fend off the United States, but don't jeopardize the possibility of continuing support and aid.

(2) Play up to the USSR, but don't trust its intentions.

(3) Beware of Communist China, but don't risk massive Chinese retaliation for intolerably stringent measures against Indonesian Chinese.

(4) Head up the Asia-Africa bloc, but don't openly compete with India, China, or Egypt, and don't startle Malaya, Burma, and Pakistan unnecessarily.

(5) Make use of the Japanese, but don't let the Japanese get an economic grip on Indonesia.

(6) Drive out the remaining Dutch, but don't scare off other Western capitalists altogether--or at least not yet.

Thus crudely put, politik bebas reveals both its strength and its weakness. It is at least as inconsistent and as difficult to implement effectually as any other nation's foreign policy, and as subject to improvisation and adaptation. But it has already passed what is after all the basic test: it has made Indonesia a nation to which other nations pay increasingly keen attention in formulating their own foreign policies.

The great international foreign policy question of the mid-20th century may be whether it is more difficult to restrain the major powers from blowing themselves up, or to restrain the lesser powers from pulling themselves down. In the one case, the most frightening threat seems to be the very increase in material power and productivity, and the possible disposition to panic in beating others to warlike application of them; in the other, it seems to be material weakness and human inertia, combined with a predilection for demanding rather than developing, and a reckless willingness to go under rather than to adjust idealism to reality. If the United States and the Soviet Union typify the fallacy of relying upon strength, then India and Indonesia typify that of capitalizing upon weakness. To prevent the two groups from disastrous collusion or collision requires a renaissance of statesmanship in

---

2 A Year of Challenge. Speech by H.E. the President of the Republic of Indonesia in commemoration of Independence Day, 17th August, 1958. (Ministry of Information. Republic of Indonesia. Special Issue 18. 39 pp.) Pp. 28-30.

not just one but several quarters. From the American point of view, perhaps the most disconcerting factor of all is that in their relations with nations like Indonesia, the Communist bloc nations generally find it both easy and advantageous to give immediate and resounding endorsement to most of the key manifestations of a politik bebas, while the United States and the Western bloc frequently can express only mild and belated reassurances that their own apprehensions are perhaps not altogether well founded. Indonesia's reaction in each case is what might be expected.

In the remaining reports in this series, it is my intention to move from the general historic background to the crowded immediate foreground and to examine how some of the leading Communist, non-Communist, and anti-Communist nations are now reacting to Indonesia's politik bebas, and how Indonesia in turn is reacting to them.

SOUTHEAST ASIA SERIES
Vol. VII   No. 35
(Indonesia)

American Universities Field Staff REPORTS SERVICE

BUNG KARNO'S INDONESIA
Part XX: The Dutch Cut Their Losses

by Willard A. Hanna

November 30, 1959

This publication is one of a continuing series on current developments in world affairs written by associates of the American Universities Field Staff. It is distributed by the AUFS as a useful addition to the American fund of information on foreign affairs.

AUFS Associates have been chosen for their skill in collecting, reporting, and evaluating data. Each has combined long personal observation and experience in his foreign area with advanced studies relating to it.

WILLARD A. HANNA, the author of this report, is based in Kuala Lumpur to write about Southeast Asian affairs. Before joining the AUFS in 1954, Dr. Hanna had spent a total of more than ten years in East and Southeast Asia as a teacher, administrator, and writer.

Publications under the imprint of the American Universities Field Staff are not selected to accord with an editorial policy and do not represent the views of its membership. Responsibility for accuracy of facts and for opinions expressed in the letters and reports rests solely with the individual writers.

"We've nothing more to lose, and nothing more to gain in Indonesia," a Dutch official told me in The Hague last year. "We foresaw what was coming; we transferred what we could and amortized the rest. We took steps to develop our economy at home and diversify our interests abroad. Naturally, individuals have suffered crippling losses. But the nation is more prosperous than ever before, our economy is more soundly based, and now that the Indonesians themselves have closed the door to negotiations on New Guinea, our internal political differences are less serious. We would have preferred, of course, to work out some reasonable compromise with the Indonesians, but they wouldn't have it that way and no unilateral concessions we might have made would in the long run have made the slightest difference. The Indonesians decided to 'bring us to our knees,' as they put it, and look what's happened: it's boom for us and bust for Indonesia."

"We have nothing against the vast majority of the Dutch as individuals," an Indonesian official told me recently in Djakarta, "but Dutch obstinacy over West Irian and Dutch avarice in exploiting Indonesia even after our independence left us no alternative except to take strong action. We gave plenty of warning and we offered plenty of chances for negotiation, but the Dutch didn't believe we meant what we said. Now they've lost their holdings

[WAH-31-'59]

in Indonesia. We are willing to discuss compensation once they agree to give back Irian Barat, but we will never discuss return of onetime Dutch enterprises to Dutch control. In three and a half centuries the Dutch took fabulous wealth from Indonesia, so they have no just cause for complaint if they lose heavily now. It's our turn to enjoy our own wealth. With it, we can develop Irian Barat, for we'll have that too in the end."

"Djakarta's politicians have grabbed the Dutch properties to enrich only themselves," a non-Indonesian, non-Chinese Southeast Asian observer told me, "and now the Chinese are getting the same treatment. You Americans will be next. Then, when they've run through all the easy money, plus all the aid you are willing to pour in, they'll turn Communist. But only after they've tried to make suckers of the Communists too and find that that doesn't work out as they expect."

"There would be no real problem of developing Indonesia into a modern nation," said a British official, now in the service of the independent Federation of Malaya, "if only the Dutch had been wise enough to adjust to the times or if the Indonesians had been tolerant enough to accept Dutch cooperation. Indonesia affords so much wealth and opportunity that it wouldn't notice what it cost to hold onto 100,000 Dutchmen--administrators, bankers, executives, engineers, teachers--exactly the qualified manpower Indonesia still lacks. And now Indonesia can't get the amount or the quality of assistance it now needs from anywhere else at any price. What puzzles me is how you Americans think you can possibly take over the role the Dutch might have performed when you don't have the experience, the language, or the patience. Indonesia's one chance was for the Dutch to stay on, and I fear that was doomed from the start. Other Western efforts will almost certainly turn out in the end to be a waste of men and money."

There can be no dispute that the record of Dutch-Indonesian cooperation since 1950 has been one of dismal failure and that the omens for other Western efforts are not encouraging. On both sides, there were people of competence and good will, and on both sides the political obstacles proved too great. The epilogue to that effort is being written in Djakarta today, and it is in its way almost as sad as the prologue, the armed conflict of 1945-49 which, in combination with 340 years of colonialism and half a century of nationalism, resulted in the mutual suspicion on the part of the many which no amount of mutual effort on the part of the few could ever dispel.

The major and tragic events of Dutch-Indonesian relations in late 1957 and early 1958 can be briefly recapitulated. The Dutch failed to make any acceptable concession on the subject of Western New Guinea--not the real issue, anyway, said the Dutch, but only a pretext for Indonesia to harass the Dutch. Beginning on December 1, 1957, the Indonesian Government mounted its anti-Dutch campaign which resulted in a few weeks' time in the expulsion of a major part of the Dutch population; the nationalization, in effect, of Dutch holdings; and the transfer to Indonesian hands of a vital sector of the national economy which began promptly, for lack of sufficient competent, experienced management, to deteriorate. For instance, the Indonesian Government seized 38 out of 88 ships of the KPM fleet (all that were in Indonesian ports at the time or could be taken over at sea). These ships, which had maintained vital inter-island freight and passenger services, were held in port and returned to the Dutch owners about four months later, only when Lloyds' of London threatened to suspend insurance for shipping entering Indonesian waters. Indonesia then shopped the international shipping world--Japan, Poland, Russia, Singapore, Finland, Italy, and even Holland--for replacements which proved in most cases expensive, unsuitable, or long delayed in building or delivery or putting into service. Consequently, inter-island shipping services have been badly disrupted and probably will remain inadequate for years to come. The Government also denied continued landing rights to KLM, thus reducing international air services to Indonesia; it cancelled its contract with KLM for pilots, crews, and servicing facilities for Garuda Indonesian Airways, thus disrupting local services. It seized, among other Dutch concerns, the so-called Big Five which performed a major part of Indonesia's export-import, banking, and estate management. It seized also many hundreds of smaller concerns, such as sugar mills, public utilities, retail business establishments, and rubber, tea, coffee, tobacco, and other estates. It just barely managed to prevent many of these concerns from falling into the hands of "youth," "labor," and "veterans" organizations of no commercial experience whatever, by placing them under the supervision of Army officers, many of whom had just slightly more impressive credentials. The operating efficiency of many of the enterprises fell off swiftly and alarmingly and despite reports of improvement of late, the medium-range prospects appear from bad to poor. The Government first obstructed then expedited the departure of some 40,000 Dutch nationals who were permitted to take with them such personal belongings as clothing and some household effects, but who left behind houses, automobiles, household equipment, and everything that was too bulky or expensive to ship out immediately by the limited available transportation.

In the course of 1958 and 1959, the Dutch population of Indonesia fell from approximately 50,000 to approximately 6,000, and the exodus continues. Of the Dutch who remain, about 2,000 are connected with the oil industry, principally the Shell Oil Company which is endeavoring to replace Dutch with British or other employees as rapidly as possible. About 1,400 are Roman Catholic priests who, on instructions from Rome, are seeking to become Indonesian citizens. At least 1,000 others are aged and indigent persons who will require nearly total assistance to arrange transportation and resettlement in the Netherlands. Only about 200 are businessmen, at least three fourths of them attached to the Big Five and remaining temporarily with the companies on orders of the head offices in the Netherlands in the hope that something may yet be salvaged from the wreckage. A scattered few are with the rubber, coffee, tea, and tobacco plantations, mostly with plantations which are owned by non-Dutch European concerns and themselves face a highly uncertain future.

Some of the British estates, for instance, have already been half taken over by the Indonesian Army.

Of the Dutchmen who have left Indonesia, many have found other employment in Holland, although generally in less responsible, less lucrative jobs; a considerable number of the younger or more prominent have gone to Africa or various other countries of Asia, and a few to the United States; a great many are retired or semiretired in the Netherlands, living on accumulated savings or on the expectation that some day some sort of compensation may be paid. At present, the only visible compensation is a minute rental being paid into frozen accounts in Indonesia for Dutch-owned private houses-- a rental that amounts in U.S. dollar equivalent to about $4-5 per month for a house worth $50,000, of which there are many. The invisible compensation is a vague Indonesian Government promise to pay, but not, it is reiterated, until Western New Guinea is handed over, and not on any scale calculated to work hardship on the Indonesian economy.

The Dutch seem, indeed, to have written off Indonesia and all of their holdings there; and yet there are many Dutchmen who would like to return. The huge, rich, tropical archipelago exercises an almost irresistible attraction upon the Dutch who feel, with reason, that their small homeland scarcely offers scope for their needs or their abilities. Despite all of the bitterness of the Dutch-Indonesian conflict of the last few years, there exists amazingly little person-to-person bitterness on the part of the Dutch, many of whom continue in Holland to maintain friendly associations with the rather sizeable Indonesian expatriate community, to give prominent place in their homes to objects collected in Indonesia, and to patronize the Indonesian and Chinese-Indonesian restaurants which are the culinary landmarks of The Hague and other Dutch cities. The Dutch, one feels, given very moderate encouragement, would try again in Indonesia and on the basis of having already twice gone through the prolonged and painful cure for addiction to colonialism of whatever type.

In Indonesia, as in the Netherlands, there is relatively little person-to-person hostility. There exists, nevertheless, so profound and so bitter, though impersonal, a resentment of what is judged to be Dutch exploitation and Dutch perfidity that there seems very little likelihood that the Indonesians will give the Dutch another chance for at least another generation. But by that time, the Dutch will have lost many of their personal ties with Indonesia, and the Indonesians in turn, if they carry out the exhortations of Bung Karno and their other leaders, will have "cured" themselves of "Dutch-mindedness." This trait by extension includes command of the Dutch language, familiarity with Dutch history, literature, and culture, personal affection for Dutch friends, and nostalgia for Dutch places--Leiden University, for instance, where many of the present Indonesian leaders gained both a professional and a cosmopolitan education. Even before the punitive campaign against the Dutch started in late 1957, the Indonesian Government had begun to divert its students in the Netherlands to other countries. After the campaign began, it transferred virtually all government-supported students in Dutch universities to universities elsewhere--to East and West Germany, Switzerland, and Central Europe. The campaign to eliminate "Dutch-mindedness" which is being waged among Indonesian students at home and abroad, and among other social groups as well, may serve to "correct" the tendency toward rigidity and emphasis on theory which the Dutch themselves frequently admit to as a national characteristic. It will serve also to eliminate one very strong and at times emotional tie between Indonesia and the Western world.

The explusion of the Dutch from Indonesia has neither solved any of Indonesia's immediate problems nor resulted in a slacking-off of anti-Dutch agitation. Relations seem likely to remain for some little time at what Dutch officials call the "all-time low." Indonesia has not acquired Western New Guinea, but rather saddled itself with an increasingly disruptive political cause; it has not found a panacea to its economic problems, but rather prejudiced its own economic well-being; and with these two most rancorous disputes of the past still unresolved, new disputes keep cropping up. For instance, the Indonesian Government accuses the Dutch of deliberate and malicious sabotage of Indonesia's efforts to reorganize its badly disorganized import-export system. Indonesia is attempting to build up a tobacco market in West Germany to replace the former market in Holland. Dutch tobacco concerns managed throughout most of 1959 to tie up a large part of Indonesia's export tobacco crop by entering suit in Bremen to establish their own claims as "legal owners." The case has been decided in Indonesia's favor, but while Indonesian Government spokesmen announce "jubilation" at the decision, Dutch company spokesmen point out that many months' legal delay most certainly did not enhance the value of a highly perishable crop which was not properly cured, packed, shipped, or stored, for lack of expert supervision.

It is the continued and galling demonstration of the need for Dutch co-operation and the unhappy consequences of its enforced withdrawal which serves to make anti-Dutch feeling in Indonesia today perhaps even more bitter than when the Dutch were physically present, and to make it seem that the bitterness will attach to all who wish to be friends both with the Dutch and the Indonesians.

Willard A Hanna

SOUTHEAST ASIA SERIES
Vol. VII   No. 36
(Indonesia)

American Universities Field Staff   **REPORTS SERVICE**

BUNG KARNO'S INDONESIA

Part XXI: The Japanese Pay Up

by Willard A. Hanna

December 1, 1959

This publication is one of a continuing series on current developments in world affairs written by associates of the American Universities Field Staff. It is distributed by the AUFS as a useful addition to the American fund of information on foreign affairs.

AUFS Associates have been chosen for their skill in collecting, reporting, and evaluating data. Each has combined long personal observation and experience in his foreign area with advanced studies relating to it.

WILLARD A. HANNA, the author of this report, is based in Kuala Lumpur to write about Southeast Asian affairs. Before joining the AUFS in 1954, Dr. Hanna had spent a total of more than ten years in East and Southeast Asia as a teacher, administrator, and writer.

Publications under the imprint of the American Universities Field Staff are not selected to accord with an editorial policy and do not represent the views of its membership. Responsibility for accuracy of facts and for opinions expressed in the letters and reports rests solely with the individual writers.

Japan's relations with Indonesia, from the Indonesian point of view, can be summed up in one word: reparations. For the Japanese, the matter is rather more complicated. The main question is how to make reparations serve as an instrument for reintroducing Japan into the Indonesian political, economic, and social scheme, this time not as a would-be dominator but as a co-operating partner.

So far, neither the Indonesian nor the Japanese government has been particularly happy about the achievement of its objectives. The Indonesian Government held out for almost eight years for impossibly high reparations payments (at first, a total of US$18 billion) and impossibly difficult terms.[1] Finally, in November 1957, when its mounting domestic crisis dictated a more realistic attitude, it began negotiating in earnest. In March 1958 the Parliament agreed to a settlement that was relatively modest in comparison with earlier demands: US$223 million, payable in goods over a 12-year period; plus $400 million in private economic co-operation projects encouraged by the two governments; plus cancellation of $177 million in

---

[1] See Problems of Japanese-Indonesian Relations (WAH-3-'55), and Japan Begins to Pay Reparations (WAH-4-'55), AUFS publications.

[WAH-32-'59]

outstanding debts to Japan for consumer goods long since delivered, consumed, and, as far as the Indonesians were concerned, all but forgotten.

The settlement involved for the Indonesian Government not only a drastic reduction of its already scaled-down demands for an outright $800 million settlement, but criticism that it was laying itself open, via economic co-operation projects, to unwanted Japanese economic penetration. The settlement involved for Japan a sharp increase of its earlier offers, reluctant acknowledgement that the $177 million trade debt was unreclaimable, and reopening of negotiations with Burma for re-scaling upward of reparations payments to bring them into line with payments to Indonesia. It involved also criticism that Indonesian demands for consumer goods under the reparations plan would cut very seriously into Japan's normal trade with Indonesia at exactly the time when Communist China was making major inroads into Japan's Indonesian market. Nevertheless, despite all its inevitable imperfections, the reparations agreement brought a solution to a rancorous problem which had made normal relations between the two nations impossible.

The Indonesian and the Japanese governments have now raised their special missions in Tokyo and Djakarta to embassy status; they have exchanged reparations representatives; and they have undertaken the difficult job of planning and implementing reparations schedules. In 1958, the first partial year of reparations payments, the program got under way on a strictly ad hoc basis, with Japan agreeing to provide $20 million worth of goods, and Indonesia presenting a series of special requests for items totaling approximately that amount. The Japanese endeavored, without success, to elicit a firm list of items to be supplied; the Indonesians endeavored, without success, to gain advance and informal commitments for a great deal more, especially ships, than the first $20 million provided for. The first firm commitment, as of June 1958, was for nine ships of about 2,500 tons each, five new and four remodeled, priced at $7.2 million in all. Indonesia desperately needed these vessels to help replace the Dutch KPM fleet which had been forced to withdraw from the Indonesian service as of December 1957. Ever since then, ships have featured conspicuously on reparations lists, but there has been a series of minor misunderstandings and disagreements. The Japanese have complained that they frequently cannot discover just who they are dealing with-- which of the shipping lines and which of the Government ministries are actually authorized to approach Japanese companies. The Indonesians have complained that Japanese shipbuilders have overpriced their product and have refused to accept payment in rupiahs for any difference between selling price and available reparations funds.

Other items and projects which loom large either on the 1958 $20 million program or on the 1959 $35 million program or both are the following:

(1) 17 small coastal vessels valued at $10 million, some of them already delivered.

(2) Textiles valued at $6 million, one half of them already delivered and the rest scheduled for delivery soon.

(3) Two paper factories, one for Kalimantan (Borneo), one for Sumatra, each to cost about $1.5 million, with construction soon to start under the supervision of Japanese engineers who are already on hand.

(4) Cotton spinning machinery, a chemical plant, a fertilizer plant, railroad equipment, road building equipment, and machinery for use in clearing land for experimentation with mechanized agriculture in transmigration areas.

(5) Materials and technical assistance for the construction of the new $8 million hotel in Djakarta.

(6) Participation in the newly developing Kalimantan lumber industry.

(7) Participation in the Sumatran oil industry upon terms, now under negotiation, which would require Japan to supply equipment and technical assistance and enable it to buy a large share of the output below world-market prices.

Several of the items above warrant comment. The oil project has been on-again-off-again for many months. Confident Japanese announcements that agreement has been reached or is about to be reached have been followed up by Indonesian announcements that bids from other countries are also under consideration. The hotel project was undertaken as a result of a virtual ultimatum from Bung Karno that the Japanese had better get interested in this long-languishing, economically unattractive proposition if they expected to elicit favorable Indonesian response to other proposals. The cotton textiles, which Japan agreed most reluctantly to provide as a result of Indonesian Government insistence that it must have copious supplies of cheap textiles for sale last spring, did nothing to enhance Japanese manufacturers' reputation for producing quality merchandise or the Indonesian Government's reputation for impartial and efficient distribution. The Japanese ships form part of an astoundingly polyglot fleet which Indonesia is assembling from Japan, Poland, the USSR, Italy, Finland, and other countries, a fleet which has been subject to the criticism that it is expensive to operate, unsuitable to Indonesian waters, and difficult to maintain and repair. Installation of Japanese factories and factory equipment can lead to acrimonious exchanges such as have occurred with regard to a Japanese caustic soda factory in Surabaya. Soon after this factory got into production about three years ago, the main boiler blew up--as a result, said the Indonesians, of inferior Japanese materials; as a result, said the Japanese, of careless Indonesian operation. After the plant was put back into operation its output had to be sharply curtailed because no provision had been made for disposal of poisonous by-products.

All in all, however, the reparations program appears to be working out more to the advantage of both Indonesia and Japan than might have been predicted on the basis of earlier indications. Indonesia has not attempted to concentrate primarily on consumer goods, which would ruin Japan's normal Indonesian market. (In 1958, Chinese competition was a more serious factor than reparations goods, accounting for a 30 per cent decline in textile exports to Indonesia.) Japan has been able, by reason of supplying capital goods, to get itself into a position where it may be able to supply considerably more maintenance and replacement goods outside the reparations agreement itself. Furthermore, the Japanese have achieved a somewhat more favorable position merely as temporary residents and short-term visitors to Indonesia. Visas are now granted for three to six month periods, after protracted delay to be sure, but with reasonable chance for extension on reapplication from abroad. A total of about 30 Japanese companies now maintain representatives in Djakarta, and a joint-capital Japanese-Indonesian bank has been opened to expedite commercial transactions. Japanese steamships, both regular and tramp, are calling with increasing frequency at Indonesian ports and are subject to somewhat less suspicious scrutiny and restrictive regulations than before. A dozen or so technicians, some of them under Colombo Plan auspices, have performed useful services in various fields, including chinaware production, fisheries, and geological exploration. A Japanese-Indonesian Friendship Association has been formed, with Djakarta's 120 Japanese residents its more enthusiastic supporters. Prominent Japanese, including Vice Admiral Maeda, onetime Chief of the Japanese Naval Liaison Office in Indonesia and a sympathizer, in the main, with the Indonesian Revolution, have been cordially received and entertained. Even tourism is beginning to get under way on a very modest scale. Many of the hundred or so Japanese businessmen-visitors each month take advantage of the chance to see Bandung, the Borobudur, and Bali. Increasing numbers of Indonesians, some of them mysteriously provided with foreign exchange about which there are recurrent rumors of bribery, make tours of Japan at cherry blossom time and other seasons of the year as well.

It is much too soon to say that Indonesian suspicions of Japan's political, economic, and military intentions have as yet been dispelled, or that Japanese distrust of Indonesian semicommitments has been diminished, but a beginning is being made in a process by which improved relations may ultimately be achieved.

Willard A. Hanna

SOUTHEAST ASIA SERIES
Vol. VII   No. 37
(Indonesia)

American Universities Field Staff

REPORTS SERVICE

BUNG KARNO'S INDONESIA

Part XXII: The Chinese Take a Second Look

by Willard A. Hanna

December 3, 1959

This publication is one of a continuing series on current developments in world affairs written by associates of the American Universities Field Staff. It is distributed by the AUFS as a useful addition to the American fund of information on foreign affairs.

AUFS Associates have been chosen for their skill in collecting, reporting, and evaluating data. Each has combined long personal observation and experience in his foreign area with advanced studies relating to it.

WILLARD A. HANNA, the author of this report, is based in Kuala Lumpur to write about Southeast Asian affairs. Before joining the AUFS in 1954, Dr. Hanna had spent a total of more than ten years in East and Southeast Asia as a teacher, administrator, and writer.

Publications under the imprint of the American Universities Field Staff are not selected to accord with an editorial policy and do not represent the views of its membership. Responsibility for accuracy of facts and for opinions expressed in the letters and reports rests solely with the individual writers.

Official relations between the Republic of Indonesia and the People's Republic of China, during the last few years have been marked by frequent reciprocal declarations of amity, admiration, and co-operation. However, of recent weeks they have been marked by repeated exchanges of warning, accusation, and contradiction. The abrupt change of tone has been occasioned by a series of belated discoveries on both sides. It may well be indicative of a sharp change of tack on the part of both China and Indonesia and of a readjustment of relations with each other and with other interested nations.

The discoveries on the Indonesian side have been the following: 1) That Communist China, whose dramatically swift achievement of national unity and material progress was formerly regarded by many important Indonesians as an inspiration and perhaps even a model, may constitute in fact a menace, if not directly to Indonesia at the moment, then in the not too distant future; 2) That Communist China, for all its pious approbation of Indonesia's "total independence" of policy and action, does not extend that endorsement to Indonesian policy and action discriminating against Chinese citizens domiciled in Indonesia.

The discoveries on China's side have been the following: 1) That the Indonesian Government equates indigenous Chinese interests and Peking's

[WAH-33-'59]

protection of such interests with foreign exploitation and interference, no less odious for being Chinese rather than Dutch; 2) That the Indonesian Government fully intends to apply extremely severe restrictive measures against all Chinese in Indonesia, not merely against the Nationalist Chinese whose earlier debacle the Peking Government abetted.

In all this there are many elements of irony. The results may include exposure of Communist standards of international morality to the Southeast Asian world, and enlightenment of Indonesia in particular regarding some of the real differences between the "progressive people's democracies" and the "decadent liberal democracies of the West." But the situation also includes greater elements of tragedy, for those who stand to suffer most gravely as a result of present Indonesian and Chinese policies and conflicts of policy are the innocent bystanders. They are the thousands of politically neutral overseas Chinese who perform an important and indeed an essential function in Indonesia, and the millions of ordinary Indonesians whose welfare is dependent upon the smooth continuation of the services the Chinese now render and which no one else is likely to take over efficiently.

The present conflict, to reduce it to a blunt oversimplification which neither side would accept, centers upon the Indonesian Government's determination to put Chinese out of business in Indonesia, and the Chinese Government's determination to protect the interests of all who declare themselves loyal to Peking, or who are yet uncommitted, and thus to retain or gain their loyalty. One curious anomaly--as Indonesian officials point out--is that most of the Chinese whose interests Peking is espousing are either big or small-time capitalists, Communists of convenience and not of conviction. Another no less curious anomaly is that the program on which the Indonesian Government has embarked amounts to the sort of nationalization and socialization of which Peking is the most ardent proponent. A third is that neither Peking nor Djakarta seems to have foreseen how the other would react either to its policies or to its explanations of them, Djakarta obviously having assumed that Peking would not risk exacerbating its nationalist sentiments, Peking as obviously having assumed that Djakarta would not defy its power or jeopardize its trade and aid.

Within a matter of weeks the Indonesian-Chinese crisis has become so serious, so undisguised, and so much a matter of national prestige as well as of nationalistic interest, that each government may find it virtually impossible to retreat from its assumed position. Yet, if neither retreats, large-scale, wide-spread, and protracted conflict may prove impossible to avoid. The Peking-Djakarta conflict, particularly if it should lead to multinational involvement, may yet turn out to be that unpredictable development which could prove the salvation or the undoing of the shaky Djakarta regime, forcing it at last to take up a really decisive international stand. It is more likely, however, merely to intensify without clarifying Indonesia's interminable domestic crisis, and since it seems likely to be long continued, the antecedents warrant careful review.

Although in their eagerness to find common ideological cause both the Indonesian and the Chinese governments have deliberately obscured the fact, Indonesia's long-term relations with Communist China are conditioned by the presence in Indonesia of some 2,600,000 or more overseas Chinese. Relations are further conditioned by the fact that these Chinese--many of the families have lived in Indonesia for a dozen generations--control a major segment of the national economy, including both big enterprises like factories and estates, and small businesses like village general stores. Through these undertakings, it is estimated they earn 40 per cent of the national annual income.

With due allowance for a high percentage of Chinese multimillionaires and a low percentage of Chinese poor, Indonesia's overseas Chinese population in the past constituted the bulk of the prosperous business and professional middle-class layer between the Western officials and big businessmen and the Indonesian peasants and workers. With the sharp increase in recent years in the Indonesian middle and upper classes of professional men, businessmen, and officials, the conflict of interest between Chinese and Indonesians has been compounded. To the old conflict between Chinese tax collector and money lender on the one hand and Indonesian debtor on the other, has been added the newer conflict of competition within the same levels of society. Indonesians now have the advantage of political pull, but Chinese have the advantage of experience, organization, and adroitness in circumventing whatever restrictions are imposed upon them. Differences in economic resources and standards of living between either the ordinary or the exceptional Chinese and Indonesian, always a cause for mutual suspicion, have been leveled off to a degree in the upper social strata; but they have been increased to a more than offsetting degree among the lower classes, with a consequent general increase rather than a decrease of antagonisms.

The really opulent Chinese millionaire is no longer so conspicuous as in former days, but many of his kind remain and the memory of others is likely to persist. The Oie family of Semarang, for instance, until recent years one of the world's richest, no longer lives on quite the old scale, although it could probably still afford to. It used to center on a vast mansion in Semarang, complete with an ornate family temple (the Japanese vandalized the temple), French period furniture (the Japanese cut down the legs), and a huge garden inhabited by a menagerie of birds and beasts (the Japanese killed the tigers and ate the deer). But if the Oies are no longer so ostentatious, thousands of other Chinese, many of them newly rich, are responsible for many of the biggest, fanciest new houses in Indonesia; they drive some of the biggest, flashiest American cars; they also drive shrewd business deals--not necessarily legal--which net them millions of rupiahs; and when the currency is suddenly devalued they are the quickest to recoup their losses. Even the "little" Chinese, the wholesale and retail dealers who keep the Indonesian communities supplied with both daily necessities and luxuries, are likely to earn and to consume on the order of at least 100 to 1 as compared with their customers. Furthermore, they have for centuries lived more or less aloof from the

Indonesian community, maintaining their own language, customs, religion, and educational system, sometimes bringing Indonesian wives into their family circle but far less frequently marrying off sons or daughters into Indonesian families. The Chinese have long been an object of Indonesian resentment and suspicion, and in times of trouble they have served as scapegoats and have been subject to retaliation. Times are troubled in Indonesia today, and the big question in Chinese minds in recent years has been not whether new and worse troubles were to be expected, but merely what form these troubles would take, whether predominantly political, economic, or physical.

It has been primarily in the anticipation of trouble--although other considerations, including purely ideological ones, have weighed heavily, particularly with youth groups fired by the new China's "renaissance"--that overseas Chinese in Indonesia have adopted political affiliations which, according to their best calculations, would minimize the unfortunate consequences to themselves. One large and important group has endeavored to identify itself with Indonesia, convinced that by becoming Indonesian citizens they could best solve their problems. Another group, at least as large and important, has lined up with Communist China, reasoning that Peking would provide protection against Indonesian nationalistic discrimination. A much smaller, but formerly influential group continued to support Nationalist China, even after it became apparent that this course would lead only to confiscation of property and expulsion. Finally, another group of considerable size has either declined to take any stand at all, or has switched back and forth from one position to another, hoping to keep all entrances and exits open. In the absence of any authoritative estimates, a reasonable conjecture is that the ratios are about 40-30-10-20, in the order listed above, with due allowance for the fact that many persons allow their decisions to be made for them by business or family associates.

Whatever the position a Chinese may have adopted, he has encountered Indonesian mistrust as to his true intentions. He has been made aware of Indonesian determination that regardless of the choice the Chinese may make, the Indonesians must see to it that the Chinese are no longer in a position to "exploit" or dominate the Indonesian economy. The Indonesian Government has been confronting the Chinese community with a series of increasingly restrictive measures which add up over the last few years to about one major crisis per year. The record of accelerating anti-Chinese discriminatory measures seems to be coming to a climax just now; but it may, of course, be a mere preliminary to a bigger crisis to follow.

The current series of crises got under way at the time of the Asia-Africa Conference in Bandung in April 1955. At that time the Indonesian Government negotiated with Chou En-lai an agreement whereby the Peking Government renounced China's long-standing adherence to the principle of dual citizenship for overseas Chinese. The Indonesian Government undertook in return to present all Chinese in Indonesia with a choice of three alternatives: Communist Chinese citizenship, Indonesian citizenship, or stateless person status. For the People's Republic of China, this was an important concession, one which formed a precedent in its relations with other Southeast Asian countries; it was also, however, an important victory, for it meant the denial to the overseas Chinese in Indonesia of the right of continued overt affiliation with the Nationalist regime in Taiwan. For the Indonesian Government, the agreement represented a change from the "negative" or "passive" policy of the past to an "active and positive" policy, in line with the promises of the First Ali Cabinet which was then at its political peak. Previously, the Indonesian Government had permitted the Chinese, if they chose, to reject Indonesian citizenship. If they did not so opt, the assumption had been that they were Indonesian citizens, and the tacit understanding had been that if they cared to risk it, they might continue their relationship with Taipei. The new citizenship treaty was designed, reported highly placed Indonesians, to dislodge the local Chinese from their accustomed and favored posture of fence-sitting. It was better designed, declared its Indonesian critics, to force them into the Communist camp.

For three years the Indonesian Parliament held desultory debates on the treaty, then finally, in mid-1958, ratified it. The Chinese were given one year, until mid-1959, to declare themselves. But administrative procedures for declaration were not clarified until the interval had almost elapsed; application forms were not available; application fees were not clearly fixed; supporting documents were not clearly stipulated--all the familiar Indonesian bureaucratic snarl-up obtained. By mid-1959, however, a great majority of the Chinese had managed by a combination of ingenuity and bribery to provide themselves with one and in some cases two sets of citizenship papers. The statistics on Chinese citizenship options have not as yet been compiled or published. Meanwhile, the exchange of instruments of ratification between Peking and Djakarta has been indefinitely postponed, presumably because of recent differences of opinion on other matters.

The choice of citizenship problem was complicated on July 1, 1957, by promulgation of Emergency Act No. 15, levying a head tax on all alien residents in Indonesia. The tax amounted to Rp. 1,500 for each head of family or single adult, Rp. 750 for a wife, and Rp. 375 for every minor child. The total worked out to about Rp. 3,000 per Chinese family, well above the annual cash income at that time of the average Indonesian family. The official explanation was that Indonesians would collect some Rp. 900 million annually to offset "the present critical financial situation of the country."

"Indonesia is the property of the Indonesian people," one official Government statement read. "Foreigners in Indonesia are, in fact, getting a favor to settle in this country. . . .Further the foreigners coming to Indonesia or settling down in Indonesia are well-to-do persons. . . .And in many cases the foreigners are emerging as winners in the struggle for life because of their better education and also because of their perseverance. The conclusion can be drawn that it is only just that the aliens. . .should co-operate in lightening the state expenditures through payment of specific taxes. It cannot be denied that the foreigners also are already paying the necessary taxes like the Indonesians themselves (for instance, income tax, etc.) but those taxes are not specific taxes for foreigners."

On July 2, 1958, after one year's collection of alien head tax had yielded about 10 per cent of the expected revenue, the Indonesian Government converted the Emergency Act into a permanent law and started to tighten up on collection procedures. As the Indonesian economic crisis worsened, speculation began to be heard that the alien head tax would be increased. The tax bill and the anticipated increase in rate was beginning to help a great many Chinese to make up their minds to opt for Indonesian citizenship when presently there developed yet another prolonged crisis which made Indonesian citizenship look rather less advantageous.

On September 15, 1958, the Indonesian War Administration, using its emergency powers under a long-continued state of war, cracked down on Kuomintang sympathizers, and Taipei, it immediately became apparent, was powerless to intercede. Overseas Chinese in Indonesia, whether they had been leaning toward Nationalist, Communist, Indonesian, or indeterminate status, began to feel even more acutely than before the need for foreign protection. Only Peking, it appeared, was likely to provide it, only outright affiliation with Peking would gain it for them, and without that, sooner or later, they were likely to suffer the fate which now befell those who actually adhered to or were accused of adhering to the Taipei regime. The Indonesian Government seized banks, businesses, estates, factories, and theatres owned by alleged Kuomintang adherents; it closed schools, sports clubs, and other organizations; it arrested hundreds of suspected Kuomintang sympathizers, regardless of their citizenship status. Since it had required the immediate registration of all persons who had belonged to the party or had visited Taiwan at any time since 1950, it had a good basic working list of suspects, and it quickly added new names. Sympathy and assistance afforded to the insurrectionist movements by the Kuomintang Party in Taiwan--and accusations of involvement on the part of Kuomintang sympathizers in Indonesia--were given as the reasons for the clamp-down, also the necessity to bring Chinese commercial enterprise in general more closely under government control.

Chinese businessmen of all types and of all political affiliations had been having their serious troubles with the Government over a period of years. Even the Government moves in late 1957 and early 1958 to take over Dutch enterprises had hit a considerable number of Chinese who maintained Dutch citizenship. The moves of late 1958 were ostensibly directed against the Kuomintang Chinese, but they were also clearly related to a general and long-continued Government drive against Chinese businessmen per se, Communist as well as others.

Many Chinese had sought to avoid anti-Chinese discrimination by devising hastily and loosely contrived partnerships with ethnic Indonesian citizens. The ordinary pattern of such partnership was that an Indonesian sat in the front office, signed all the innumerable official forms and drew a good share of the profits, while the Chinese continued to run the business and, naturally, to pick up profits of his own. These "Ali Baba" firms--Ali being one of the commonest of Indonesian given names, Baba being slang for a locally-born Chinese--had about them a truly Arabian Nights quality of fancy and profit, and very fancy profit too. The 1958 move against the Kuomintang Chinese, then, which had begun by placing many of the really big Chinese business firms under Indonesian government control but, for lack of available replacements, leaving the Indonesian "owners" in managerial capacity, presaged a renewed and intensified drive against the Ali Baba firms, and that in turn a drive against all Chinese business enterprise.

The Government had just carried out its new measures against the Kuomintang Chinese, to the accompaniment of applause from Peking and the Indonesian Communist Party, when it published, on May 14, 1959, yet another decree. This time, it banned aliens--meaning mainly Chinese--from engaging in any business enterprise outside the provincial or regencial capitals; by December 31, 1959, all such aliens must cease commercial operations outside the few larger cities. According to recent interpretation of the decree, they must also, in many instances, give up residence outside the larger cities and, on moving into the cities--some of them, Djakarta and Bandung included, have been closed to these resettlers--they must live in certain restricted, economically and residentially unattractive areas to which have been quickly applied the term "ghetto."

Facts and statistics are difficult to assemble in Indonesia, but it was clear that the new regulations would affect perhaps 100,000 commercial enterprises, at least 300,000-500,000 individuals, and a minimal Rp. 60-70 billion annually in local trade. Furthermore, these 100,000 or more Chinese-owned enterprises are those which virtually monopolize in many of the rural areas the collection and marketing of produce and the distribution of daily necessities. Enforcement of the decree could obviously mean the very serious and perhaps disastrous disruption of the Indonesian rural economy. It would certainly involve extreme hardship to the individual Chinese. He would simultaneously be deprived of extremely valuable holdings and required to move to already overcongested urban areas, there to seek to establish new enterprises that would compete with already-established Chinese businesses, themselves often in difficulties.

The Chinese community of Indonesia was much agitated, naturally, by this new decree. But December 31, 1959, was distant, Indonesian government regulations were notoriously changeable or evadable, and almost anyone could see that actual enforcement of this one was an invitation not only to economic dislocation but to open racial and even international conflict. The regulation, it was widely felt, might be selectively enforced in certain areas, ignored in others; it was probably designed not actually to squeeze out but only to put more of a squeeze upon the Chinese businessman who was already quite accustomed to budgeting a good part of his profit for pay-offs. And besides, there was always Peking to consider.

By mid-1959, however, the situation began to look both urgent and critical. The Indonesian Government began repeatedly to declare its intention of actually enforcing the decree, and the various regional military commands began to announce complicated and by no means consistent interpretations, regulations, and schedules. Prior to September 1, 1959, according to the one uniform announcement, all alien Chinese who maintained businesses or residence outside the larger cities were to declare themselves and register their intentions--whether they proposed to close down altogether, to sell out, or to transfer ownership and management to an Indonesian citizen. Chinese organizations made repeated representations to the Government, pointing out the very serious consequences not only to the Chinese but to Indonesians as well.

The Indonesian officials remained adamant. Chinese owners began to make panicky last-minute arrangements. Even those who had opted for Indonesian citizenship felt themselves threatened. They could not be sure their option was valid until the exchange of the ratification instruments. They could not be sure, even then, that it would afford them a very long reprieve. Chinese owners attempted generally either to transfer properties to relatives and friends who had enough pull with local authorities that they might hope to retain them or to set up "Ali Baba" partnerships. And then the Government announced a new alternative which virtually closed the door on the others: transfer of ownership and management to an Indonesian co-operative, with the possibility that in some instances the original Chinese owner might be retained as a salaried employee. This device, high government spokesmen declared, would achieve the "socialization" of the Indonesian economy; it would also, it was obvious, provide an argument for use with the Peking Government which was at last beginning to exhibit open concern about developments.

Meanwhile, as of August 25, 1959, the Government had adopted its drastic new "financial reform" and currency devaluation measures. The burden of this measure, it announced, would fall upon those who had great hoards of "hot money," specifically, the "corruptors," the "black marketeers," the "tax-dodgers," and the "wealthy classes"--all of these euphemisms for the Chinese, but involving by extension their partners in the Ali Baba firms and a great many get-rich-quick Indonesians. Much of the burden did indeed fall upon the Chinese, but it also fell, quite unexpectedly so far as the Government was concerned, upon practically everybody else. It fell even upon the Indonesian peddler and farmer for whom inflation had made the devalued Rp. 500 and 1,000 notes not a symbol of wealth but merely of convenience. Of all those who suffered from the measures, the Chinese were the best equipped to recoup their losses. The spectacle of Chinese quickly beginning to amass new fortunes seemed to irritate high Indonesian government officials. It reinforced their resolution to carry out the restrictions on Chinese businesses on schedule, come what might, including what now did come and worsened matters all around: open protest and "intervention" by representatives of the Peking Government.

Djakarta-Peking relations began quickly to turn sour. The Djakarta Government had thought up two rationalizations of its policy, one for Peking's consumption, one for that of the West, and both served to create mistrust on all sides. To Peking the Djakarta Government explained that the measures were directed not against Chinese as such, and certainly not against Communist Chinese, but merely against capitalists, exploiters, and colonialists, who just happened in this case to be Chinese. It was seeking to "socialize" the Indonesian economy and to substitute co-operative effort for private enterprise. For private Western consumption, the explanation was that the measures were designed to eliminate cells of Communist infiltration and to preclude the possibility that the People's Republic of China, now swiftly increasing in material power and demonstrably exhibiting territorial ambitions (in India, for instance), would be able at some future date to use Chinese Communists in Indonesia as its fifth column.

The pattern of take-over was that already applied to Dutch and to Kuomintang enterprises. It was clearly applicable in the future to all Chinese, and, for that matter to Western enterprises not as yet directly affected. Foreign Minister Subandrio was roused--in the mood and manner of his fulminations against the Dutch--to declare in a press conference (September 22, 1959) that no "self-respecting nation" could "tolerate" the sort of economic domination which Indonesia was experiencing, especially since the businessmen in question constituted a "cartel" which "represented a solid front for collecting the biggest possible profit without taking the interests of the country and her people in mind."

Soon after the press conference, Foreign Minister Subandrio visited Peking (October 7-11) to make his explanations there. He did so to the accompaniment of outspoken criticisms at home that rather than the Indonesian Foreign Minister going to Peking, the Chinese Foreign Minister should come to Djakarta, if, indeed, the matter was to be discussed at all. After four days in Peking, Dr. Subandrio and Vice Premier and Foreign Minister Chen Yi issued a joint communique declaring that "both Foreign Ministers take cognizance of the fact that in progress toward economic development and stability in Indonesia the economic position of Chinese nationals might be affected in some ways" and that "an appropriate way should be sought respecting their proper rights and interests." The communique was variously interpreted in Indonesia as a Subandrio victory over Chen Yi, and as a Chen Yi victory over Subandrio, but in neither case as a very explicit understanding.

In mid-November there came a series of swift and overlapping revelations in Djakarta. Of the 100,000 or so Chinese traders affected by the new regulations, 83 per cent had declined to make any statement of their intentions of disposing of their property. Chinese Embassy officials from Djakarta had been discovered advising the Chinese of West Java both to disregard the government regulations and to defy explicit Army orders to move out. Already there had occurred a couple of instances of violence about which few details were available.

Chinese Ambassador Huang Chen met with Foreign Minister Subandrio and then with President Sukarno himself. Sukarno and Subandrio announced that all was well, that amicable relations prevailed, and that a mutually satisfactory understanding was being reached. Dr. Subandrio even announced that the Chinese Ambassador had undertaken to assist in the orderly implementation of the Indonesian Government's orders. Ambassador Huang promptly and flatly announced that he had given no such assurance. Subandrio expressed shock and dismay at such undiplomatic conduct. Then came the really dramatic admission, one about which unconfirmed rumors had been circulating in Djakarta for weeks: Foreign Minister Subandrio, on his visit to Peking, had been subjected to outrageous treatment. He had been scolded, abused, and threatened. He had been roused from bed at 1:00 a.m. on the morning of his scheduled departure; he had been summoned into conference with high Chinese officials who pressured him for approval of draft after draft of a joint communique; and only on the fourteenth try had there been reluctant agreement on the final version as published. This, Indonesian official, press, and public spokesmen declared, with varying degrees of diplomatic restraint, was no way to conduct international negotiations and no way to maintain friendly relations; the Indonesian Government was fully justified in going ahead with its plan, and the Chinese Government stood condemned for intimidation and interference.

The December 31 deadline is drawing near, and the enforced moving of Chinese families has begun. If the Indonesian Government wavers in its resolution, it will be betraying signs of weakness in the face of pressures from Peking. If it persists in enforcing its regulations, it will be recklessly sabotaging its own economy and inviting racial disorders, to add to all the other disorders with which it is beset. The dilemma is one for which the Indonesian Government has only itself to blame, a circumstance which seems unlikely to improve official tempers or to encourage rational counsels.

SOUTHEAST ASIA SERIES
Vol. VII   No. 38
(Indonesia)

American Universities Field Staff

REPORTS SERVICE

This publication is one of a continuing series on current developments in world affairs written by associates of the American Universities Field Staff. It is distributed by the AUFS as a useful addition to the American fund of information on foreign affairs.

AUFS Associates have been chosen for their skill in collecting, reporting, and evaluating data. Each has combined long personal observation and experience in his foreign area with advanced studies relating to it.

WILLARD A. HANNA, the author of this report, is based in Kuala Lumpur to write about Southeast Asian affairs. Before joining the AUFS in 1954, Dr. Hanna had spent a total of more than ten years in East and Southeast Asia as a teacher, administrator, and writer.

Publications under the imprint of the American Universities Field Staff are not selected to accord with an editorial policy and do not represent the views of its membership. Responsibility for accuracy of facts and for opinions expressed in the letters and reports rests solely with the individual writers.

BUNG KARNO'S INDONESIA

Part XXIII: The Russians Are Willing

by Willard A. Hanna

December 14, 1959

The USSR has been in the happy position in the past of having virtually no open conflict of interests with the independent Republic of Indonesia. To be sure, until very recent years, Russia also had virtually no direct contact with Indonesia, no trade relations, no resident Russian citizens, and not even much intellectual curiosity. An occasional Czarist traveler or scientist visited Batavia in Dutch colonial days; and after 1917 a very few White Russians ended up there--just about the end of the line so far as Russian emigrés were concerned. A few Indonesian political refugees, members of the Dutch-sponsored Communist Party for the most part, found asylum in Moscow during the 1920's and 1930's. Their stay, however, was relatively uneventful; their services were little exploited; their reward was to be sent off on missions of subversion throughout Southeast Asia and then, after the war, to be sent back to Indonesia to foment a counterrevolution in which some of the most important of them died.[1] A Russian Tass correspondent, who later returned as a Russian Embassy official, and a couple of Russian bar girls, brightened the lives of Dutch counterintelligence agents in Batavia in the grim years of the late 1940's. Counterintelligence was then mainly counter-Indonesian Revolution, and counter-Russian intelligence offered diversity and diversion.

[1] See From Jail to Jail: The Saga of Tan Malaka (WAH-1-'59), an AUFS publication.

[WAH-34-'59]

Indonesian-USSR relations began to give rise to national and international excitement only with the following series of events: premature Russian semirecognition of the Indonesian revolutionary government, on May 26, 1948; Russian instigation of the Communist uprising at Madiun (late 1948); and belated recognition by the USSR of the new Republic, on January 25, 1950.[2] On all of these matters, however, memory became quickly and curiously clouded both in Djakarta and Moscow. When Moscow and Djakarta finally exchanged diplomatic missions in 1955, to the accompaniment of crises over accommodations and personnel at both ends, there came the real beginning of really close contacts. Indonesian personnel presently adjusted to the cold and the discomfort of life in Moscow and began to study--some of them to master-- the language; the Russians, after some preliminary stir over inadequate housing, settled into an imposing Embassy and a modest and almost transparently innocent "Little Moscow" in Djakarta's new residential suburb of Kebajoran, some of them already speaking remarkably fluent Indonesian upon arrival. Trade relations between the two countries gradually became perceptible on the import-export tables. The exchange of athletic, cultural, commercial, youth, labor, and other missions which had begun a little earlier, began to pick up rapidly as more and more visitors sped each way through the Iron Curtain, with one government or the other picking up the check.

In 1956-57 came the real Russian-Indonesian rapprochement, when "Tovarich" Sukarno[3] and "Bung" Voroshilov exchanged state visits to the accompaniment of monster public demonstrations of welcome, and effusive reciprocal declarations of undying affection and unwavering support for each other's policy objectives. The year 1956 brought also preliminary agreement on a Russian $100 million loan. Actual implementation of the loan, however, was slowed down for almost a year and a half while the Indonesian press, public, and Parliament eyed it with suspicion. Parliament finally accepted it unanimously in February 1958, just as Indonesia's economic, military, and political crisis was rising to an all-time high. Informal binational commitments prior to Parliamentary approval of the loan resulted in a beginning of delivery of jeeps, tractors, bulldozers, ships, and jet planes, either shortly before or (in the case of the ships and jets, the first few of which came from Czechoslovakia) shortly after the loan agreement was ratified.

Since early 1958, the emphasis in Indonesian-USSR relations has been upon increase of cultural exchange, trade, and aid--all of which, as noted, had got under way prior to 1958. In the area of cultural exchange, it is difficult to produce statistical evidence of the recent speed-up, but some of the more conspicuous results are worth mentioning. Russian cultural good will

---

[2] See An Indonesian Excursion Behind the Iron Curtain--and Its Sequel (WAH-10-'56), an AUFS publication.

[3] See Moscow Comes to Bung Karno--and So Does Peking (WAH-20-'56), an AUFS publication.

missions to Indonesia are now a common occurrence, and in the course of my
own recent visit to Indonesia, for instance, I kept crossing and recrossing the
trail of a group of distinguished professors and a composer who were seeing
the country and its prominent citizens. A Russian professor of Russian language has been accepted by the University of Indonesia; Russian reference
and text books have been presented to the University library; and large quantities of cheaply priced books from the USSR's Foreign Languages Press (both
in Russian and English)--classics, dictionaries, textbooks, technical works,
as well as straight political propaganda--are now conspicuously displayed in
many of the bookstores. The Moscow Publishers of Foreign Literature have
already brought out Russian translations of significant Indonesian books, including one by President Sukarno, and are reported to be making a great point
of adding to the list of titles.

In trade relations, the USSR is by no means an important rival as yet
to Indonesia's traditional trading partners. Nevertheless, direct trade with
Indonesia is increasing, and Russian-encouraged Communist bloc trade is becoming a significant factor in Indonesia's economy. Indonesia's own announced
intention is to seek diversified markets to supplement and--in the case of the
Netherlands--to supplant its already established markets. The policy seems
to be leading to the beginnings of a shift in Indonesia's trade from Western to
Eastern Europe. Recent or exact statistical evidence, however, is difficult to
obtain--my own experience with the Bureau of Statistics being that I could get
import figures for January through March, 1959; export figures for January
through November, 1958; but no sets of import-export figures for parallel or
comparative periods. One very rough index to the growth of Indonesia's trade
with the Communist bloc countries is that total Indonesian exports to the Soviet Union amounted to Rp. 107,123 in value in 1955, and Rp. 8,619,657 in the
first quarter of 1959. Indonesian imports from the USSR amounted to
Rp. 2,317,734 in value in 1955, as compared with Rp. 15,994,940 in January-
November,1958. The principal imports from the USSR--apart from the jeeps,
bulldozers, ships, jets, and such, as yet a group of important omissions from
the statistical tables--have been textiles (Rp. 10,000,000 in the 1958 period)
and cement (Rp. 2,000,000). Indonesia's exports to the Soviet Union consist
almost exclusively of rubber, the agreed purchases for 1959 coming to 14,000
tons--less than 2 per cent of Indonesia's total rubber export, but still 14,000
tons more than the USSR purchased from Indonesia a very few years ago.

Indonesia's direct trade with the satellite countries of Poland, Hungary,
and Czechoslovakia is growing, but in no case does it reach the same proportions as its trade with the USSR. The major significance of this trade, like
that with the USSR itself, is not its amount or its percentage component in
Indonesia's over-all total, but the disproportionate political effect and also
the disadvantageous terms--as it seems to a Western observer--for Indonesia itself. The trade is conducted under special agreements and arrangements to which are given many different names--"parallel transactions,"
"compensation transactions," and the like: in other words, barter. The chief

product which the Communist nations seek from Indonesia is rubber, but not the low-grade rubber which Indonesia has difficulty disposing of elsewhere and had hoped to sell to them; and while they sometimes offer prices above world market averages for high-grade rubber--and for a few other products like tobacco, coffee, and tea--they are reported to dispose of a good part of their purchases on the Western European market below cost, a practice which results, naturally, in depressing prices on goods which Indonesia itself is seeking to dispose of advantageously. In return for its exports, Indonesia receives credits in nonconvertible currencies, and is forced either to let the credits lie idle or to use them for purchase of Eastern European manufactures which tend to be both overpriced and unsuitable for the Indonesian home market. To be sure, with the implementation of recent loan agreements between Indonesia and the Eastern European countries, the terms of trade may come to appear more advantageous to Indonesia, or at least the disadvantages may be glossed over and the accounting postponed. Then again, a truly healthy reciprocal trade may grow up, just as Indonesian government planners think it may.

Despite long-term Indonesian insistence that what it wants of the outside world is trade, not aid, the developing pattern of economic relations with the Communist-bloc nations is based, to a far greater extent than has ever been the case in relation to the West, upon aid, not trade. In the last two to three years, beginning with the $100 million loan from the USSR on which swift, preliminary negotiations were conducted by President Sukarno himself during his first visit to Moscow, Indonesia has accumulated a total of approximately $260 million in actual or prospective loans from the Communist countries, including $36.4 million from Communist China. The exact amounts of the loans, the exact terms, and their current status--whether only proposed, or agreed upon "in principle" at high official levels, or ratified by the Indonesian Parliament, or scheduled for implementation--are exceedingly difficult to ascertain and, indeed, seem to be subject to change without notice as subsequent negotiations revise the terms of earlier ones. Some of the most significant items included in the loan agreements--fleets of MIG 15s and 17s, Ilyushin cargo planes and bombers, warships, submarines, rocket launchers, and other military equipment--are not included in the following itemization; and while the actual amounts and valuations indicated are open to dispute, the list is at least illustrative:

Aid from the USSR	Estimated Cost (in US$ millions)
Two iron and steel plants, each of 50,000 tons annual output; and roadbuilding equipment.	51.0
Building of 622 km. of roads in Kalimantan (Borneo)	11.5
Textiles	10.0
Ten freighters	9.0

	Estimated Cost (in US$ millions)
Aid from the USSR (cont.)	
4,000 jeeps	8.0
Fertilizer plant of 100,000 ton annual output	7.0
Development of mechanized rice farming on two project sites of 10,000 hectares each in Kalimantan	6.5
Two tankers	3.3
Glass factory	2.5
Diesel generators	0.8
Stadium for 1962 Asian Games, seating capacity 100,000; plus auxiliary sports centers.	12.5
Technical Faculty for University of Ambon, to be built, equipped, and staffed by the USSR for study of oceanography and shipbuilding.	5.0
	Sub-total: 127.1
Aid from Poland	
24 ships	39.2
Shipbuilding materials and equipment	5.0
	Sub-total: 44.2
Aid from East Germany	
Sugar factory in Jogjakarta	8.6
	Sub-total: 8.6
Aid from Czechoslovakia	
Diesel electrification equipment	25.0
Tractors and farm equipment (1,800 machines in 3 years, 1959-61)	10.4
Hydroelectric plants (34 small plants of up to 3,000 kw capacity)	5.0
Tire factory	1.6
	Sub-total: 42.0
Aid from Hungary	
20 diesel buses, spare parts and workshop	0.9
	Sub-total: 0.9

Aid from Communist China	Estimated Cost (in US$ millions)
Rice	5.2
Textiles	11.2
Textile factory and equipment	20.0
Sub-total:	36.4

GRAND TOTAL: US$259.2 million

The margin for error in the figures reported above is about 10-20 per cent. The ordinary terms of loan call for repayment over a 6 to 15 year period, after the beginning of the project, with an interest rate generally of 2.5 per cent, sometimes less. The ratio of loans in a relatively firm stage of negotiation and ratification as against those proposed or under preliminary negotiation is about 70-30. Of the loan sums already available, about 40 per cent of their total has been drawn upon. The most significant projects already completed or nearing completion are: the East German sugar factory; the Chinese rice and textile deliveries; and the Russian jeep, roadbuilding equipment, and ship deliveries, plus, of course, the MIGs which every air traveler to Djakarta sees parked all about the airfield.

Communist bloc aid programs, which total just under $260 million at present, as compared with a United States aid total of $567.35 million since 1945, are running into their share of snarl-ups, just as American and other aid programs have before them. The sugar factory project, for instance, was a prolonged near-fiasco of mismanagement--on the part of both Germans and Indonesians, it seems--before it finally went into successful production last year. The Czech tire factory shares the difficulties of the whole Indonesian rubber manufacturing industry: it has rubber, but because of incredibly whimsical bureaucratic import controls, it is short of the essential chemicals for processing it, and shortage of even one small ingredient can stall production. The first big consignment of Russian jeeps, it is widely reported, arrived without adequate spare parts, and many vehicles had to be cannibalized to keep the rest of the fleet in motion. The Hungarian diesel buses have not yet arrived, but cynics predict for them the fate of earlier Australian buses, Colombo Plan gifts, which were so badly operated and maintained that at least half of them were retired a year or two after arrival. The Chinese textiles--which, incidentally, have been priced well below competing Japanese products and have given Japanese manufacturers an extremely rough time not only in Indonesia but elsewhere in Southeast Asia--sold originally at the officially fixed price, but quickly drifted into the black market at a mark-up which made few friends for China.

Aid projects, accordingly, have developed their headaches. Trade has been far from smooth. The Czech trade counsellor in Djakarta has complained publicly and officially that Indonesia overprices her products and then surrounds both export and import with unnecessarily complicated controls. The Indonesian Government for its part, has spoken sharply to the USSR about the unexpected appearance on international markets last year of Russian tin, which tended, of course, to depress the price of the Indonesian product. And as aid and trade generate problems, so too at times does cultural exchange, but nothing of late to compare with the series of furors over a Russian acrobatic circus tour back in 1957. The troupe got into a nonstop sequence of troubles when, for instance, its "plastic lady" contortionist was judged obscene in costume (Bikini) and posture, and was either banned outright in some towns or allowed to appear only when draped in Arabian Nights-like pants and blouse; irate male acrobats and schoolboys threw chairs and pop bottles at one another in an overpacked hall during a special children's matinee; and its managers cancelled performances without notice and demanded accommodations such as are generally unobtainable in Indonesia.

The USSR and other Communist bloc countries, in other words, are beginning, as they develop closer relations with Indonesia, to experience conflict of interest and conflict of personalities as well. Two new sources of friction may very soon develop, as big-scale aid programs get under way: first, importunate requests on the part of Russian technicians for Indonesian attention and assistance in getting paper plans for co-operative projects actually converted into co-operation; and second, the quite human expectation on the part of the Russians that for their aid they will receive some measurable returns. If such conflicts do not develop, then the Russians will indeed demonstrate that they have a special technique for good international relations which the Western nations would do well to study.

SOUTHEAST ASIA SERIES
Vol. VII   No. 39
(Indonesia)

American Universities Field Staff **REPORTS SERVICE**

BUNG KARNO'S INDONESIA

Part XXIV: The United States Is Perplexed

by Willard A. Hanna

December 16, 1959

This publication is one of a continuing series on current developments in world affairs written by associates of the American Universities Field Staff. It is distributed by the AUFS as a useful addition to the American fund of information on foreign affairs.

AUFS Associates have been chosen for their skill in collecting, reporting, and evaluating data. Each has combined long personal observation and experience in his foreign area with advanced studies relating to it.

WILLARD A. HANNA, the author of this report, is based in Kuala Lumpur to write about Southeast Asian affairs. Before joining the AUFS in 1954, Dr. Hanna had spent a total of more than ten years in East and Southeast Asia as a teacher, administrator, and writer.

Publications under the imprint of the American Universities Field Staff are not selected to accord with an editorial policy and do not represent the views of its membership. Responsibility for accuracy of facts and for opinions expressed in the letters and reports rests solely with the individual writers.

Here, in case anyone should wish to have it, is the formula for swiftly winning the approbation of the present Indonesian Government for American policy: (1) Endorse Indonesia's claim to Irian Barat and offer to co-operate in any program Indonesia proposes for its speedy acquisition. (2) Set up a $1 billion no-strings-attached Indonesian development fund, expendable at will and without accountability by the Indonesian Government, making it clear that there is more where that came from and that whatever the ultimate total, it is not charity but simple justice, in view of past American profit-taking from the Indonesian market. (3) Buy up Stanvac, Goodyear, Proctor and Gamble, National Carbon, and any other incidental American capital interests in Indonesia, turn them over to the Indonesian Government to run, retaining American technicians paid by the United States Government just long enough to train Indonesian replacements. (4) Dissolve NATO and SEATO; cease to support the build-up of Japan's armed forces; propose Communist China as a member of the United Nations and take steps to defrock Taiwan, withdrawing all support from the latter. (5) Apply embargoes on all trade with colonial or semicolonial areas in Asia and Africa; recognize Ho Chi-minh's Government as the rightful one for all of what was once French Indochina; restrain the Philippines from assisting the Indonesian rebels. (6) Adopt stern measures against any American newspaper or magazine

[WAH-35-'59]

writers who "misrepresent" the situation in Indonesia, especially any who detect pro-Communist tendencies among the present leaders, or demagogic traits in Bung Karno. (7) Purchase Indonesian rubber and tin at prices to be specified by Indonesia and accept payment in rupiahs at the official rate, payable into blocked accounts, for any list of proposed Indonesian imports from the United States. (8) Renounce experimentation in or reliance upon atomic weapons.

Sufficiently drastic change of American foreign policy to satisfy its Indonesian critics does not seem imminent. The American approach to Indonesia over the last few years has been to avoid the large areas of dispute, to reiterate the customary platitudes regarding mutual aspiration toward world peace and friendship, and to concentrate upon practical demonstration that the United States is indeed eager to assist Indonesia in becoming a stable and prosperous nation. The last mentioned, of course, means aid, and American aid of various types has amounted to approximately $550 million since 1945, about $400 million of it since Indonesia achieved independence at the end of 1949.

American aid in itself, however, has always been an extremely delicate subject in Indonesia. It has led to the three major crises and dilemmas in United States-Indonesian policy, past, present, and (predictably) future. The first was that of 1952, when Indonesia all but renounced American aid and only reluctantly agreed to its continuation. The second occurred in 1958, when a great part of Djakarta's officialdom and press accused the United States of withholding military aid from the central Government and at the same time providing it to the anti-Djakarta insurrectionists. The third is a contest, now apparently getting well under way between the Communist and anti-Communist blocs, to see who can provide the most aid on the easiest terms with the greatest and most favorable impact upon Indonesian public opinion, a contest which the Djakarta Government seems prepared to promote, with the Russians taking up the position of challenger.

The 1952 crisis is a matter of still imprecise and disputed historical record. In brief, it was a year-long debate waged furiously throughout Indonesia as to exactly what commitment the Indonesian Government had made to the United States in return for aid; whether any commitment at all was actually necessary within the context of American aid legislation; whether any commitment of any sort would not be dangerously prejudicial to Indonesia's politik bebas[1]; whether the Indonesian Government had not been duped by the United States; and whether American aid was either necessary or desirable in any event. The crisis finally blew over, but the aid program, which had continued under a cloud in the interval, has been carried on ever since under a psychological handicap. It has required a high degree of dedication on the part of both the Americans and the Indonesians implementing it to make the program a reasonable success.

---

[1] Independent policy. For further explanation of this term see Bung Karno's Indonesia, Part XIX.

The 1950-59 aid program has included Marshall Plan assistance ($40 million) for purchase of basic commodities; Export-Import Bank loans totaling $114 million for economic development projects; provision of surplus agricultural commodities ($96.6 million prior to 1959, and an additional $40.3 million this year); and economic and technical assistance ($78 million) under the present International Cooperation Administration and its predecessor programs. A good case might be made that the provision of commodities, whether through the Marshall Plan, or surplus commodities programs, or ICA--which devoted 80 per cent of its funds during the first several years of operation to such programs--has been a necessary stop-gap to meet recurrent crises, but that it has done little to solve the nation's basic problems or to impress upon it the genuineness of American good will. A parallel case could be made that the projects financed by Export-Import Bank loans, since they have been carefully thought through to meet bankers' specifications for self-liquidating projects, have been in general the soundest, the most efficient, and in the long run the most effective, despite the fact that the Indonesian Government, largely because of difficulties in meeting specifications, allowed $24 million out of the original $100 million, granted in 1950, to go undrawn upon until late 1958. A further case could be made that the year-by-year economic and technical assistance program, on a relatively much smaller scale and calling for relatively greater effort on the part of individual Americans and Indonesians alike, has special features to recommend it. While it falls far short of anticipated successes, it has necessitated the development of something of the spirit of co-operation and mutual understanding which, even more than material results, is the theoretical justification for much of the outlay.

The commodities, then, have been or are being delivered and consumed, and it is anybody's guess whether the Indonesian who benefits by them will recall ten years from now with either pleasure or gratitude that he received rice, wheat, cotton, and tobacco in 1959 through the courtesy of the United States Government and Bung Karno's regime. Most Indonesians have forgotten--if, indeed, they ever knew it--that they received the same commodities back in 1949 and earlier, through the courtesy of the United States Government and the Dutch colonial administration. Probably what is important, however, is not recall but survival.

The Export-Import Bank credits have now been either used or obligated, and sizeable additional credits have been granted or are being negotiated. Garuda Indonesian Airways, which has been and will be a primary beneficiary, maintains an impressive safety record but a still quite inadequate local flight schedule and an unbusinesslike way of losing money on prestige foreign flights and artificially low domestic fares. The $14 million Gresik Cement Plant near Surabaya is not an unqualified success. Since the plant was handed over to full Indonesian management this year, machinery has broken down, the accident rate has gone up, production has declined, and distribution has bogged down badly as a result of bureaucratic controls, transportation bottlenecks, and black marketeering. Nevertheless, it is a major step toward modern

Chart I

TOTAL ECONOMIC ASSISTANCE TO INDONESIA BY SOURCE & TYPE

1945-1959
(MILLIONS OF DOLLARS)
TOTAL AID $1,031.2

RECAPITULATION

U.S. AID	
GRANT	178.0
LOAN	210.6
SALES	96.7
	485.3 [x]

x) TOTAL POST-INDEPENDENCE (1950-1959) AID IS $ 836.15 MILL.

OTHER AID		
JAPAN:		
REPARATIONS	20.0	
DEBT CANCELATION	176.0	
		196.0
SOVIET-BLOC LOANS		204.0
U.N. GRANT	9.7	
COLOMBO PLAN	4.2	
		13.9
WESTERN EUROPEAN CREDIT		132.0
GRAND TOTAL		1,031.2

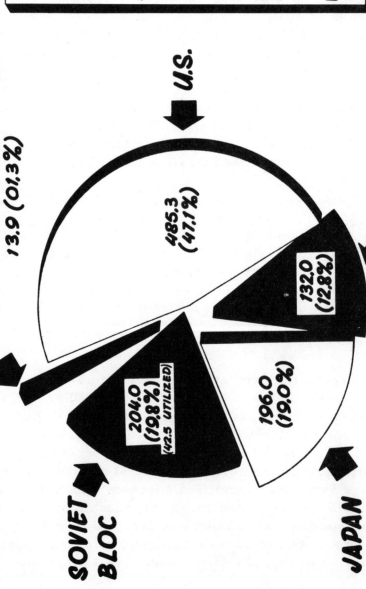

U.N. & COLOMBO PLAN
13.9 (01.3%)

U.S.

485.3
(47.1%)

SOVIET BLOC
204.0 (19.8%)
(42.5 UTILIZED)

196.0 (19.0%)

132.0 (12.8%)

WESTERN EUROPEAN CREDIT

JAPAN

COMMUNICATIONS MEDIA DIVISION
International Cooperation Administration
DJAKARTA INDONESIA

Note: There is a discrepancy of $60 million in United States aid funds between Charts I and II. Chart I was prepared early in 1959; the other after the close of the fiscal year.

Chart II

U.S. ECONOMIC AID TO INDONESIA

IN MILLIONS - U.S. $
TOTAL AID : $ 395.2 MILLION
1950 TO JUNE 30, 1959

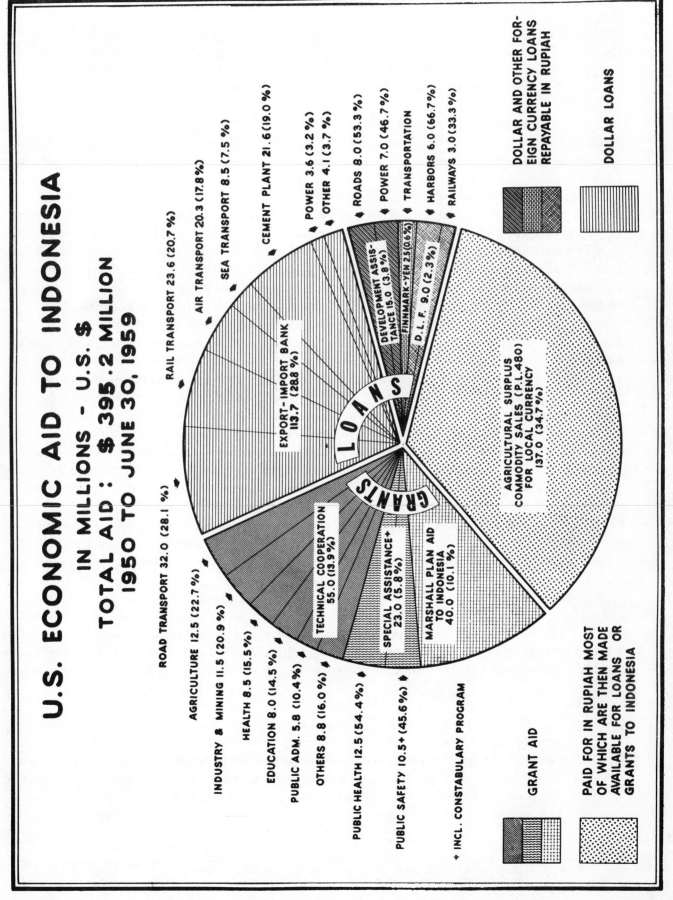

RAIL TRANSPORT 23.6 (20.7 %)

AIR TRANSPORT 20.3 (17.8%)

SEA TRANSPORT 8.5 (7.5 %)

CEMENT PLANT 21.6 (19.0%)

POWER 3.6 (3.2 %)

OTHER 4.1 (3.7 %)

ROADS 8.0 (53.3 %)

POWER 7.0 (46.7 %)

TRANSPORTATION

HARBORS 6.0 (66.7%)

RAILWAYS 3.0 (33.3 %)

DOLLAR AND OTHER FOR-
EIGN CURRENCY LOANS
REPAYABLE IN RUPIAH

DOLLAR LOANS

ROAD TRANSPORT 32.0 (28.1 %)

AGRICULTURE 12.5 (22.7 %)

INDUSTRY & MINING 11.5 (20.9 %)

HEALTH 8.5 (15.5 %)

EDUCATION 8.0 (14.5 %)

PUBLIC ADM. 5.8 (10.4 %)

OTHERS 8.8 (16.0 %)

PUBLIC HEALTH 12.5 (54.4 %)

PUBLIC SAFETY 10.5+ (45.6%)

+ INCL. CONSTABULARY PROGRAM

EXPORT-IMPORT BANK
113.7 (28.8 %)

DEVELOPMENT ASSIS-
TANCE 15.0 (3.8 %)

FINNMARK-YEN 2.5 (0.6%)

D.L.F. 9.0 (2.3 %)

LOANS

GRANTS

TECHNICAL COOPERATION
55.0 (13.9 %)

SPECIAL ASSISTANCE+
23.0 (5.8 %)

MARSHALL PLAN AID
TO INDONESIA
40.0 (10.1 %)

AGRICULTURAL SURPLUS
COMMODITY SALES (P.L.480)
FOR LOCAL CURRENCY
137.0 (34.7 %)

GRANT AID

PAID FOR IN RUPIAH MOST
OF WHICH ARE THEN MADE
AVAILABLE FOR LOANS OR
GRANTS TO INDONESIA

Indonesian industrial development, and its potential annual output of 250,000 tons of cement is enough to meet one half of Indonesia's requirements. The output potential can be increased to 375,000 tons annually when a new $6.9 million Export-Import loan results in repairs and enlargement of the plant.

ICA projects continue to proliferate, if not always to flourish, and it is in them that one can best see the day-to-day course of Indonesian-American co-operative effort. The 1950-59 economic and technical assistance program, like all such programs, has come in for unduly severe criticism on the part of only mildly interested or only moderately well-informed American and Indonesian observers; it has likewise come in for unduly inflated kudos on the part of program propagandists. For a variety of reasons, it presents an extraordinarily difficult problem in evaluation. In the first place, the program has been conducted on a scale which was scarcely calculated to solve Indonesia's critical problems, with Congressional appropriations varying from about $7 million to $15 million per year. The scale of the program has been determined, however, less by the American Government's willingness to spend than by the Indonesian Government's willingness to accept and to co-operate. In the second place, the program has consisted of highly miscellaneous and scattered projects. The diffusion of effort, however, has been the result less of ICA's desire to spread itself thinly over many aspects of the Indonesian economy than of the failure of the Indonesian Government ever to plan, or to permit to be planned, an over-all development program into which the ICA program could be integrated. Consequently, if anything at all was to be accomplished, opportunities have had to be seized upon wherever and whenever they offered. Finally, although there is by no means a very consistent record of clear successes in the various project fields--agriculture, health, education, administration, information, industry, fisheries, among others--there is now a considerable body of evidence that a good part of the investment is paying off both in Indonesian development and in Indonesian-American good will.

Some of the more significant projects are the following:

(1) University contracts calling for provision to Indonesian universities by American universities of professors, equipment, books, and other assistance, including further training of graduate students in the United States. For example:

(A) A five-year (1954-59) contract with the University of California providing five to ten American professors of medicine who have helped reorganize and revitalize the University of Indonesia's Medical Faculty at Djakarta so effectively that urgently needed graduates are now emerging at the rate of about 100 per year, a rate soon to be stepped up to 150.[2]

---

[2] See A Binational Project in Medical Education (WAH-19-'56), an AUFS publication.

(B) A contract with the University of Kentucky providing 17 American professors for the Technical Faculty of the University of Indonesia at Bandung which had been crippled by loss of its Dutch staff; a similar contract with the University of Kentucky for assistance to the Agricultural College at Bogor.

(C) A contract with UCLA providing 12 professors of engineering and science to Gadjah Mada University in Jogjakarta.

(2) Provision of funds, equipment, supplies, and personnel to assist in a massive new program to eliminate malaria as a major health problem in Indonesia.

(3) An ICA loan, made available April 30, 1957, to provide diesel-powered generators for small cities and towns throughout the archipelago; also loans for construction of an economically critical 270 miles of road in Sumatra, and for renovation of the South Sumatra railroad.

(4) Experimentation in corn and rice seeds, with the result that a new strain of corn has been introduced to double the former yield, and that new varieties of rice give from 15 to 35 per cent higher yield than the old; also experimentation in plant entomology, showing how the use of simple and inexpensive insecticides can increase rice crops by 50 per cent.

(5) Provision of equipment and technical assistance to Radio Indonesia, the Government Film Unit, and other branches of the Ministry of Information.

(6) Provision of power boats, engines, refrigeration, and other equipment for the antiquated Indonesian fishing industry.

(7) Study grants for 2,000 Indonesian students (by mid-September 1959) to continue their training in the United States in a wide variety of professional fields.

There can be no guarantee, of course, that Indonesian students returning from the United States are going to be more understanding of American policies and objectives; but the American visitor who moves about Indonesia even for a brief time is likely to encounter in altogether unexpected places the friendly interest and assistance of Indonesian grantees. There is no assurance, either, that Indonesian farmers and fishermen are going to adopt improved techniques, and, indeed, the corn, rice, and fish yields to date have not been increased to anything like the spectacular degree which is demonstrably possible. But Indonesia's food deficit is relatively small--as compared, say, with India's--and even moderate improvement can spell important national advance.

Few even of the most optimistic Americans would claim that ICA money and effort have been even 50 per cent as effective as both might well have been; but neither has the program been as ineffectual as might have been feared from the notable lack of enthusiasm which many key Indonesian officials display toward it. Bung Karno, for instance, seems scarcely aware that the effort is being made. Chief Minister Djuanda, who has been closely associated with the American aid program from the very moment of its inception, appeared to be just barely able to summon enough interest to write this very tepid and equivocal endorsement as an introduction to the latest ICA published report:[3] ". . .The program, limited if considered relative to the enormous and growing needs of Indonesia, has been steadily continued. It has contributed and will contribute not only to the economic development of Indonesia but also to the understanding of the people of Indonesia and the United States."

Chief Minister Djuanda's phrase, "limited if considered relative to the enormous and growing needs of Indonesia," introduces the basic anomaly of Indonesian official reaction to the program. Over a period of years, the Indonesian Government not only exhibited little interest in expanding the scope of the program but seemed at times to be making deliberate efforts to restrict it. The aid program, in Indonesia as elsewhere, generates so-called "counterpart funds," or local currency payments by the local government for supplies and equipment received, these funds to be used by mutual agreement for economic development projects which will supplement the basic program. In Indonesia, the counterpart funds generated between 1950 and mid-1959 came to the equivalent of about US$280 million. The rupiah equivalent, however, is calculated at the totally unrealistic official exchange rate, thus automatically reducing the actual counterpart account to something between 30 and 10 per cent of what might be expected. Only about 40 per cent of the counterpart funds has ever been released for use, and that only after inflation had reduced their value even further. On the other hand, for certain of the projects the Indonesian Government has put up local funds which--again calculated at the official exchange rate--more than match United States dollar funds. Still, the anomaly remains that with the need for economic development projects as critical as it has been, and with various projects being undertaken by the Indonesian Government by measures requiring deficit financing, the theoretically available counterpart funds have been allowed merely to accumulate in a blocked account--to minimize the danger of inflation, according to the official explanation. On the whole, in view of the desperate economic straits to which Indonesian Government deficit financing has led, it is perhaps just as well that the blame cannot be attributed to American Government insistence on release of counterpart funds.

Chief Minister Djuanda's reference to the "enormous and growing needs of Indonesia" is indicative of a new attitude toward aid which has been

---

[3] Indonesian-United States Cooperation ... Through June 30, 1958. (Vol. 1 of a series of reports to be published at intervals by the U.S. of A. Operations Mission to Indonesia with the co-operation of the Indonesian State Planning Bureau.)

growing up in Indonesia over the last several years, one which is leading perhaps, to a new crisis in Indonesian-American relations. For a period of years, when only Western aid, especially American, was readily available, the Indonesian Government looked with suspicion upon aid programs in general as potentially prejudicial to the politik bebas. Beginning about the time (1956) when Bung Karno negotiated a $100 million loan from the USSR--in a matter of minutes, it would appear, from his various references to the transaction-- the Indonesian Government began to awaken to the possibility of offsetting aid from one bloc with aid from the other, and then to the possibility of getting the two blocs to start bidding competitively to provide larger and larger amounts on easier and easier terms. The full awakening coincided, unfortunately, with the nearly disastrous 1958 period in American-Indonesian relations, when the United States Government was felt to be cooler by far toward Indonesia's needs and desires than was the USSR.

The sequence of events began actually in the summer of 1957. The Djakarta Government, faced with long-drawn-out guerrilla movements in many areas and threatening insurrection of whole provinces, sought to buy new and modern equipment for its armed forces. The United States Government, without ever stating a categorical refusal, made discouraging response to tentative Indonesian official and unofficial inquiries. The Djakarta Government looked elsewhere--to the Soviet bloc. In early 1958, when fighting broke out between the central Government and insurrectionist forces, a good many American observers, both official and unofficial, reported that the Indonesian Army had actually received arms shipments from the Communist bloc. There followed a spate of American criticisms of what appeared to be the Djakarta Government's pro-Communist tendencies and commitments. Simultaneously, Indonesian central Government officials declared that the insurrectionists had received sizeable shipments of arms and equipment from the Western bloc, whether with or without official cognizance or assistance. Djakarta's condemnation of American refusal to give aid to the central Government and of toleration, if not connivance, in the supply of aid to the insurrectionists, became much more vociferous and emotional than American criticism of Djakarta's presumed pro-Communist inclinations. Then, on May 18 the Djakarta forces shot down over Ambon a rebel bomber piloted by an American, one Allan L. Pope, who proved, according to well-documented Indonesian reports, to be a former military pilot. He was one of a group of American and Taiwanese mercenaries who enjoyed the pay of the rebels and various military privileges, it was alleged, in both the Philippines and Taiwan. Official and public sentiment against the United States ran high in Djakarta for a period of weeks. It began to die down only when the central Government achieved successes in putting down the regional insurrections, and the American Government gave assurances that it still supported the Sukarno regime and, what was more, supported it even more generously than before.

The American Government made a series of moves, of which the following were most noteworthy: (1) Announcement in early July of a US$8 million grant for building a highway in Sumatra; (2) Encouragement of the Indonesian Government in new applications for utilization of the remaining $24 million from the 1950 $100 million Export-Import Bank loan, and negotiation of new Eximbank loans to follow; (3) Announcement in late August of an American decision to supply the Indonesian Government with small arms and equipment; prompt delivery by Globemaster from Tokyo of the first installments; the subsequent announcement that the United States would supply sufficient material (value about $10 million) for 20 battalions (about 20,000 men, or 10 per cent of the Indonesian Army); (4) Announcement in May 1959 of a United States Government decision to sell Indonesia 50 military planes (price $23.5 million), described as "obsolete" World War II models, P-51 Mustang fighters and bombers; (5) Announcement in May 1959 of a United States Government agreement to supply Indonesia with an additional US$40.3 million worth of surplus cotton, rice, and tobacco; (6) Planning of an enlarged ICA program for the year 1960 and later. American assistance promised or delivered to Indonesia since the crisis of 1958 comes out, coincidentally, no doubt, at just about the same figure as the much-advertised USSR aid program.

The Indonesian Government today quite openly states its reliance upon foreign aid as the solution to its continuing economic and financial crisis, also its expectation that aid from the West will be counterbalanced by aid from the East, and that both will be readily forthcoming on request and without strings attached. In the last two years, Indonesian Government spokesmen point out, Indonesia has received about $450 to $500 million in new loans and grants, about half from the East and half from the West; and there is no reason to think the source of supply is drying up or that it will not be adequate for Indonesia's emergency needs. The Government, it must be said, has reason for its confidence. Offers of aid keep coming in, solicited and unsolicited, with China (just before the current crisis in Chinese-Indonesian relations) upping its offers by another $12 million; Hungary talking of more millions; and Yugoslavia and Czechoslovakia, among others, being eager to be counted in too. In terms of Indonesia's needs, perhaps the easiest indicator of any is that the national deficit ran to Rp. 8 billion last year and will run an estimated Rp. 18 billion this year, which at the present official exchange rate comes to about US$400 million. It would appear that the Indonesian Government needs either to effect economies or to improve its 1957-59 record of new loans and grants by about $200 million per year. Of course, there are Indonesian voices that call for caution: the loans, it is pointed out, must eventually be repaid and with interest. But the emergency is great and it is now, and delay can no doubt be negotiated in the date of repayment, or terms arranged, as with the United States, whereby repayment itself flows back into the Indonesian treasury.

The United States, whose greatest problem with the Indonesian Government with regard to aid programs at various points in the past has seemed to be indifference, is beginning to find that its greatest problem is importunity, accompanied by the open hint that if the United States and the Western nations do not provide strings-free aid, the USSR and the Communist nations will. American policy makers, therefore, already have a basic decision on their hands: whether to compete for the major projects, regardless of their economic and political soundness; whether to concede these projects to the Communist bloc; whether to compromise by competing at times, conceding at times, and proceeding in general on an <u>ad hoc</u> basis as before; whether to fall in with, or indeed to promote the proposals which have been made more and more commonly of late, that the major part of American aid should be channeled through a common international pool of development funds, internationally administered to avoid offense to the national sensitivities of the recipients, and overemphasis upon national objectives of the donors.

The choice is far from easy, and it is unlikely that any clear-cut decision will be made at all, American government agencies being sometimes as given to indecision as the Indonesian, and as dependent upon legislative action. But there will probably develop a new trend in American aid programs for Indonesia in which emphasis will be placed upon one or more of the above policy lines; and the trend will probably be determined by whatever attitude prevails among American officials and the American public regarding the extremely perplexing nation of Indonesia. The four commonest attitudes, each with a considerable element of validity, might be distinguished as the romantic, the idealistic, the pessimistic, and the pragmatic.

The romantic attitude toward Indonesia is one which is extremely easy to fall into, and in many respects comfortable to adhere to. It is, in brief, that the country is beautiful, rich, and alluring; that the people are the most gifted and personable of Southeast Asia; that current troubles are mere growing pains, greatly exaggerated in the reporting and likely very soon to disappear. In all this there is a large and appealing element of truth.

The idealistic attitude is that Indonesia, as the biggest and potentially the greatest nation of Southeast Asia, is going through a phase of national difficulty and evolution which is inevitable for any great nation; that this phase will lead, as did the American Revolution and the troubled decades that followed, to the emergence of a vital new people and country; that the new Indonesia will be dedicated to principles of liberalism which are not the same as those of the older nations, but principles of genuine and indigenous liberalism nevertheless--these still evolving principles being the best guarantee for the peaceful development of Southeast Asia. In this interpretation too, there is much that persuades and much that appeals.

The pessimistic attitude is that Indonesia, in the course of its first ten years of independence, has induced upon itself one of the most chronic and tragic cases of snafu which the modern world has seen, that its mere survival as a nation seems likely to depend not on deliberate Indonesian or foreign effort but on the intervention of Divine Providence. This is an attitude in which, I confess, I share, with the feeling also that since Indonesia's survival to date is due mainly to divine intervention, its future chances may be considerably better than any logical calculations would indicate.

The pragmatic attitude is that Indonesia, since it is the biggest, the richest, and potentially the greatest nation of Southeast Asia, cannot be permitted to hit the skids, and that if any such relatively modest sum in international fiscal terms as a few billion dollars will make the difference, then a few billion dollars must be forthcoming. The pragmatic attitude can perhaps be subdivided into the "soft pragmatic" and the "tough." The "soft pragmatic" is that by bailing Indonesia out, the United States can win Indonesia's abiding friendship. The "tough pragmatic" is that by bailing Indonesia out, the United States can enable Indonesia to go its own perhaps predetermined way, which may or may not be to American advantage; but that in either event, there is not a great deal we can do about it.

I would myself recommend an approach combining the pessimistic and the tough pragmatic. With regard to any upcoming decision regarding aid, I believe that the time has come to take cognizance of certain unhappy facts about aid programs for countries like Indonesia. First: everybody is offering aid these days. Aid programs are becoming an international mishmash and grab-bag. Aid programs ran into problems enough regarding efficient administration and sympathetic co-operation in the days when only the United States and other Western nations participated as donors. Under present conditions of competition for projects--any projects--these programs seem less likely than before to insure truly healthful development of Indonesia, or the achievement of any high-minded purpose on the part of the United States. Prospects for development of a truly comprehensive program designed to put Indonesia firmly on its feet, rather than merely to keep it from collapsing, seem increasingly dim. Second: nation-to-nation aid is always given with a political objective, if only the ultraplatitudinous "promotion of mutual friendship and understanding"; it is always accepted with political misgivings regarding "strings," visible or invisible, declared or denied, if only the ultraplatitudinous "bonds of mutual aspiration." Indonesians do not really believe in the possibility of a "no-strings" aid program, even when they are demanding it most vociferously; Americans, Russians, and others do not really believe in the feasibility or desirability of "no-strings" aid, even when they are proclaiming it most self-righteously. Such being the case, there seems to be one way to remove the stigma of hypocrisy which has to date tainted both the giving and the receiving of aid and has resulted in both wastefulness and suspicion; that is, to dispense aid on the basis of express commitment that it will be effectively utilized and eventually repaid. To implement such a proviso without giving rise to acrimony, aid should flow ideally not from nation to nation but through an impartial international agency which applies professional bankers' criteria and requires precise commitment and report.

The freshest breeze which could blow through the whole international aid community, now deaf to expressions of undying gratitude and eternal friendship between the uncommitted nations and those committed to either the anti-Communist or the Communist sides, might be an unhackneyed new expression of American intent and policy. Such a new policy line--subject, naturally, to adjustment in negotiation with other countries and in application over a period of months and years--might be stated approximately as follows:

The United States is willing to make aid available, not as a demonstration of gratuitous friendship and confidence, but as an outright gamble. The United States Government holds the view that unless rapid over-all development is achieved in nations like Indonesia, serious national and international disturbances are inevitable, and American interests, like those of Indonesia and all other nations, will suffer. The United States Government is eager, therefore, on a businesslike basis involving clear definition of projects, clear demonstration of their value, and clear commitment both to make use of other available resources and to repay aid funds, to provide American funds, equipment, supplies, and personnel. The United States can neither predict nor control the actual results of the development programs undertaken, but it is willing to proceed on the assumption that if they are calculated to serve Indonesia's best interests, they will serve American interests as well. It believes, however, that there must be proper safeguards against two serious hazards: one, that the United States in providing aid will interfere or seem to interfere in Indonesia's internal affairs; two, that Indonesia in accepting aid will fail or seem to fail to utilize it to optimum advantage. It proposes, therefore, the creation of yet one more international agency, one which will screen proposed aid projects, serve as intermediary in contract arrangements and administration, and provide regular progress reports on projects undertaken. The Indonesian Government will be free to request and to utilize supplies, equipment, and personnel of any nation or organization it choses, subject only to the approval of the screening commission. The United States Government will be free to accept or to decline any project proposed to it through the screening commission, whether the project expenses are to be borne by the United States, Indonesia, or another nation. The Indonesian Government will be expected to make use of aid funds for major economic development programs such as could not be undertaken solely with its own resources. The United States suggests that other nations offering aid to Indonesia enter into the arrangement for pooling of funds and for impartial international administration of them, as a measure to achieve the most efficient co-operative effort and the most effective subordination of political objectives.

The approach outlined above has the merit not so much of originality as of practicality, and of enabling the United States to take the initiative, rather than to be steered, toward a more truly international and co-operative effort. It has also the merit of forthrightness. International aid is and must be a gamble; impersonal, international stakes holders are preferable to national ones. Aid-receiving nations like Indonesia are far more likely to utilize aid effectively if they feel they are competing with one another for limited amounts on businesslike terms, rather than that aid-giving countries are competing to give unlimited amounts on practically no conditions at all. The policy also has the merit, if merit it can be conceded to be, of opportunism. It confronts the USSR and Communist China with an embarrassing decision to make, a decision in which the Western World stands to gain psychologically, regardless of whether the Communist bloc does or does not chose to co-operate. It serves, in short, to free the United States from the compulsion to press aid projects piecemeal upon suspicious recipients, and to practice what might be termed an American politik bebas in response to what has been to date the extremely baffling politik bebas of Indonesia.

[Charts on pages 4 and 5, courtesy Communications Media Division, International Cooperation Administration, Djakarta.]

SOUTHEAST ASIA SERIES
Vol. VII   No. 40
(Indonesia)

American Universities Field Staff

REPORTS SERVICE

BUNG KARNO'S INDONESIA

Part XXV: The Backward and the Forward Looks

by Willard A. Hanna

December 18, 1959

This publication is one of a continuing series on current developments in world affairs written by associates of the American Universities Field Staff. It is distributed by the AUFS as a useful addition to the American fund of information on foreign affairs.

AUFS Associates have been chosen for their skill in collecting, reporting, and evaluating data. Each has combined long personal observation and experience in his foreign area with advanced studies relating to it.

WILLARD A. HANNA, the author of this report, is based in Kuala Lumpur to write about Southeast Asian affairs. Before joining the AUFS in 1954, Dr. Hanna had spent a total of more than ten years in East and Southeast Asia as a teacher, administrator, and writer.

Publications under the imprint of the American Universities Field Staff are not selected to accord with an editorial policy and do not represent the views of its membership. Responsibility for accuracy of facts and for opinions expressed in the letters and reports rests solely with the individual writers.

When I began to accumulate and to analyze the material for a series of reports on Indonesia, of which this is the last, the general situation in Indonesia looked bleak and the prospects even bleaker. That was well over six months ago. I debated whether I should not take the advice of some of my friends and wait--for six months, say --in the hope that new government policies would produce beneficial effects. Today, the situation is grimmer than ever. Political tensions are now much more acute than before Bung Karno embarked upon his experiment in "guided democracy." The economic situation is now much more unfavorable than before he devised his drastic "economic and financial reforms," in line with his theory of "guided economy." Social unrest has mounted to truly dangerous proportions. The Government has failed to fulfill its promise to supply the people with adequate food and clothing at reasonable prices. Instead, it is concentrating its energies upon a campaign against Chinese middlemen, a move that is certain to result in further domestic disruption if not in international conflict. The nation has fallen into such depths of maladministration--and of either fatalistic or cynical acceptance of maladministration--that the labor required to regenerate it will have to be truly heroic.

Two questions are inescapable for anyone interested in Indonesia's regeneration: First, are

[WAH-36-'59]

there any Indonesian leaders heroic enough for the task? Second, is there anything the rest of the world can do that will really help? The usual, somewhat evasive answers to these questions are: First, the present Indonesian leaders, whatever their failings, are better than any known potential replacements. Second, large scale economic and technical assistance programs, whatever their shortcomings, afford the best demonstration of friendly foreign interest and the best chance for sound domestic development. In both these answers, I myself am disposed to concur, but with important reservations and qualifications.

The leaders to whom the Indonesian nation and the outside world may most hopefully look for heroism are not the few score at the top, most of whom have already discredited themselves, but a few hundred in the middle and lower official ranks, or in no official jobs at all. These lower echelon leaders are now frustrated and embittered. They have been blocked for years from developing their own or their nation's potential. However, there are still significant numbers of them--dedicated, capable, hard-working men and women--who are neither fanatical nationalists nor doctrinaire Marxists. They can still summon both the vigor and the courage for national reconstruction. They can, that is, provided a few of them can get into positions of responsibility or, alternatively, if a few of those persons already in positions of responsibility find it expedient to endorse not the reckless policies of ultranationalism but new policies of sober hard work. I do not profess to know precisely who the new top leaders or the reconstructable top leaders might be. Nevertheless, the human capacity for rising to an emergency being what it is, and innate Indonesian adaptability being what it is, I believe they may reasonably be expected to come forward.

There is no denying that the emergency is at hand. It could be made to lead to national rehabilitation rather than to national collapse, but only, I believe, if Indonesian leaders are determined this time to face squarely the real problems of national development; and if outsiders are determined to give assistance not on the basis of politics or panic or even humanitarianism, but rather on that of rational planning and sustained performance. These two conditions are interlocking, and it is precisely for that reason that outsiders could be of crucial importance.

International economic and technical assistance is indispensable to Indonesia's survival and regeneration as a unified, independent nation. Virtually unconditional "strings-free" assistance, however, is not the answer. It is this sort of assistance, to be sure, which Indonesia's present leaders demand, with the implied threat that their own collapse means chaos. Foreign nations now hesitate to deny it to them for fear of alienating them irrevocably. "Strings-free" assistance, however, can serve at best only to shore up the present shaky and incompetent Government, to prolong the present crisis, and to inhibit the development either of new leaders or of a new psychology of leadership. Only strings-attached aid, with responsibilities clearly spelled out for the recipient, the donor, and some kind of international supervisory commission, it seems to me, has much chance of accomplishing a truly useful purpose.

The problem, perhaps fortunately, is by no means unique to Indonesia. There exists, therefore, both the urgency and the rationale for yet one more international conference, one which might be devoted not to stereotyped discussions of political tensions, economic disequilibrium, and social welfare idealism, but to the blunt questions: how should aid be given, and how should it be received, and how should the performance of both donor and recipient be scrutinized. The subject came up briefly for unexpectedly outspoken consideration at the time of the recent Colombo Plan Conference in Jogjakarta. Bung Karno opened the conference by haranguing the donor nations on their "responsibility" to give strings-free aid, in expiation for the sins of colonialism. Some of the donor countries were moved to reply that another side of the question needed a bit of examination too. Indonesian delegates, among others, were impressed. Should the concept gain international respectability --that the giving and the receiving of aid entails responsible utilization of it and international accountability for it--then the Indonesian leaders, who are certainly among the shrewdest operators in Southeast Asia, might be stirred to the truly formidable effort required to put their nation in order. Until such a concept begins to prevail, Indonesia's leaders are most unlikely to manifest political sobriety, friendly foreign nations are most unlikely to gain or to display real confidence, and both are likely to become increasingly at odds with one another.

So, to the two crucial questions--are there capable Indonesian leaders, and are there ways in which other nations can really be of help--the answer, in my opinion is "Yes--but." Neither Indonesians nor foreigners will have much chance of success in Indonesia until both accept a supranational form of international supervision which neither is likely to welcome. To devise, gain acceptance of, and apply such discipline would involve the extreme hazard of Indonesia cracking up in the interim. To fail to do so seems to me to involve the virtual certainty that unless pure chance intervenes, Indonesia's present rulers, or successors of their type, will lead the nation into what Bung Karno himself, scanning the near horizon, sees and describes as "the abyss of [national] annihilation."

Willard G Hanna

THE PROPHECIES OF DJOJOBOJO

In years whose component digits can be reversed and inverted to read the same, declared the 12th-century Javanese Nostradamus, Djojobojo by name, momentous national events might be expected. The year 1961, naturally, is such a year. The fact that Djojobojo--if retroactively interpreted--correctly predicted the Dutch colonial period, the Japanese occupation, and the achievement of Indonesian independence, is given considerable emotional weight by those Indonesians who are at all inclined toward mysticism, as, indeed, are a very great many indeed. The countervailing facts that the years 1691 and 1881 produced no noteworthy events--although, to be sure, the volcano Krakatau did blow itself apart in 1883, perhaps just a bit off schedule--and that the Western numeration of the years could scarcely have been what Djojobojo had in mind, none of this diminishes a growing Indonesian prescience that the year 1961 may indeed prove crucial in modern Indonesian history.

If not 1961, then, even the less mystical are inclined to agree, by 1963 at latest Indonesia is destined for a new leader and a new regime. The year 1963, it is perhaps worth noting, carries a special connotation in the Western, if not the Eastern context. Years which are multiples of seven or nine are climacteric years, and the year 63 is the grand climacteric--a double East-West grand climacteric, indeed, when one considers that in 1963 President Sukarno himself will enter his sixty-third year.

Calculation of the odds for and against Indonesia's survival in 1961 and later as a single independent nation becomes a matter of sheer conjecture. It is important to give full weight to the forces of instability which have necessarily been emphasized in reports on the state of Indonesia during the last few extremely troubled years. It is equally important to review the factors of stability as well, of which, fortunately, there are some which are impressive.

The most impressive stabilizing force of all is that out of the population of 90 million, 75 million--the peasants and their families--still live extremely simple lives, relatively undismayed by political, economic, military, and social crisis. These 75 million continue, for the most part, to produce sufficient food to feed themselves; they have accumulated during years of relative plenty sufficient textiles to tide themselves over the immediate shortage; many of them are beginning actually to experience the benefits of a vastly expanded educational system and an improved health service; they do not absolutely demand many of the other amenities of life, except, for instance, bicycles, with which they are still fairly well stocked, and a few items like kerosene, salt, and tobacco which can still be obtained, despite recurrent shortages, although at an exorbitant markup in prices.

The 75 million may for a few more years yet, until the educated younger generation demands its rights, work patiently and on the whole happily at close to the subsistence level. They are unlikely to rebel so long as the government, in desperation, does not actually requisition their foodstuffs, or the guerrilla bands in audacious show of force do not further depredate their homes and fields. It is a moot point, however, whether the stability of the 75 million can counterbalance the instability of the remaining 15 million, the people of the cities and the larger towns. These 15 million are now critically subject both to the pressure of economic privation and the attraction of Communist promises. The majority of this 15 million, incidentally, lives on Java. Here, into 9% of the nation's land area, is crowded almost 60% of its population, consuming far more of the nation's food and wealth than it produces. Java, accordingly, may either give rise to the disorders that could easily spread and become nationwide; or it could itself be abandoned by the rest of the nation and left with the virtually impossible task of looking out for itself.

The second factor of stability might perhaps be termed the stability of Indonesian instability. Indonesian national crises, frequent and bitter as they are, never seem to go so deep or to last so long or to affect so many as is at first feared; one crisis gradually blends into another without much observable change. About the interminable Indonesian crisis, the more one observes and analyzes it, the more there seems to be an air of mirage. Certainly, things are rarely what they seem and even more rarely seem the same for any prolonged period.

It is well to remind oneself, therefore, that at the time of the 1958 crisis there was very plausible reason to believe that the rebel insurrectionary forces would either topple or capture the central Government, and in either event force major reforms. The reforms seemed likely to include curtailment of Communist activities, rationalization of the bureaucracy, abandonment of the ruinous economic policies of control, restraint, and exploitation of Indonesians by Indonesians, and muzzling of the Bung Karno-type of demagoguery. The 1958 rebellions failed, and the reforms fizzled out. The 1960 counterpart of the 1958 insurrections--the program of the Democratic League--is designed to achieve much the same set of reforms. The Democratic League may fail as suddenly as did the insurrections, especially since it has neither the military, nor the territorial, nor the financial support which the rebels enjoyed. Indonesia, meanwhile, may go rocking along, somehow miraculously avoiding the final crack-up which virtually every foreign observer has been expecting for years. It is a logically defensible extension of this line of reasoning, of course, to assert that in effect the crack-up has already occurred, and the Indonesia is in no sense a unified nation save that it still exhibits an ultranationalistic determination to be one.

The greatest basis for hope that Indonesia may survive as a single nation and emerge presently without final recourse to totalitarian or Communist methods, as a stable and powerful one, is the mere fact that of all nations in Southeast Asia Indonesia is the one which seems destined by geography, history, and resources, both natural and human, to become in every sense of the term a great power. A great many individual Indonesians display qualities of ability and dedication which may one day prevail over immense obstacles. Nevertheless, confidence in the destiny of the Indonesian nation and of the Indonesian people one day soon to be great rests not upon arguments of fact but of faith and of fate. It requires deliberate disregard of Western standards of judgment on the basis of scientific evaluation; it implies immersion in a sort of Indonesian mystique that in the long run all will work out for the best, although no one sees when or how.

The greatest difficulty which a Westerner experiences these days in adopting or adhering to any such concept, even one refortified by the argument that every other great nation, the United States included, has passed through its prolonged period of initial troubles, is the fact that many of the leading Indonesians themselves are now finding it difficult to maintain their accustomed buoyancy about their nation's prospects. The defeat, frustration, and despair which one encounters among the great majority of those thinking Indonesians who are not officially committed to USDEK is a new and unsettling phenomenon. It constitutes, in fact, the most dismaying experience of any foreigner who visits Indonesia in 1960, expecting to find the old Indonesian gaiety undimmed even by recent adversity. "Things have never been worse," one of Indonesia's most distinguished national leaders told me, with his accustomed smile. Then the smile faded as he added, "But they will be."

The Bung Karno regime in Indonesia, in other words, is even less reassuring in 1960 than in 1959. The prospects that the next regime may be less, not more, benign are highly disconcerting to anyone, like myself, who believes that the Indonesian people deserve and the Indonesian leaders are capable of better, infinitely better. Still, to paraphrase Bung Karno, who arrived in New York a few years ago jauntily declaring: "The United States is a state of mind," one may very plausibly maintain that the Republic of Indonesia is in fact a state of emotion. Emotional recoil from the shambles to which the present regime has reduced the nation should not lead one to forget that Indonesia's problems--problems not on the order of India's, or even Japan's--after all, are solvable. Most of them would yield rather quickly to programs formulated on the basis of political and economic rationality.

Rationality has not yet run out among Indonesian leaders. The supply,

however, is ominously low and replenishment is the more difficult the longer
the Bung Karno regime survives. Contemporary Djojobojos, while they predict major change for 1961, or at latest 1962 or 1963, exhibit as much caution
as did their 12th-century predecessor, in risking the unequivocal prediction
that in the Indonesia of tomorrow, change will signify improvement. So, I
deeply regret to report, after a visit in mid-1960, just as after a visit in mid-
1959, do I.

W. A. H.

November 28, 1960